A Special Issue of
Self and Identity

The Implicit Self

T0316058

Edited by

Laurie A. Rudman
Rutgers University, Piscataway, NJ, USA

and

Steven J. Spencer
University of Waterloo, Waterloo, Ontario, Canada

 **Psychology Press**
Taylor & Francis Group

LONDON AND NEW YORK

Published 2007 by Psychology Press
27 Church Road, Hove, East Sussex BN3 2FA

Simultaneously published in the USA and Canada
by Psychology Press
711 Third Avenue New York, NY 10017

First issued in paperback 2015

*Psychology Press is an imprint of the Taylor & Francis Group,
an informa business*

British Library Cataloguing in Publication Data
A catalogue record for this book is available from the British Library

ISBN 13: 978-1-138-87772-6 (pbk)
ISBN 13: 978-1-84169-826-7 (hbk)
ISSN: 1529–8868

Cover design by Jim Wilkie, Emsworth, Hampshire, UK.
Typeset in the UK by KnowledgeWorks Global Ltd, Southampton.

Self and Identity*

Volume 6   Issue 2/3   April–September

CONTENTS

97 The Implicit Self
Laurie A. Rudman and Steven J. Spencer

101 The Exploration of Implicit Aspects of Self-esteem in Vulnerability–Stress Models of Depression
Jennifer A. Steinberg, Andrew Karpinski and Lauren B. Alloy

118 Implicit Self and Affect Regulation: Effects of Action Orientation and Subliminal Self Priming in an Affective Priming Task
Sander L. Koole and Linda H. M. Coenen

137 Perfectionism and Explicit Self-esteem: The Moderating Role of Implicit Self-esteem
Virgil Zeigler-Hill and Carol Terry

154 When "They" Becomes "We": Multiple Contrasting Identities in Mixed Status Groups
Amy K. Sanchez, Cristina Zogmaister and Luciano Arcuri

173 The Malleability of Men's Gender Self-concept
Cade McCall and Nilanjana Dasgupta

189 Autonomy and Control Motivation and Self-esteem
Holley S. Hodgins, Ariel B. Brown and Barbara Carver

209 When Apologies Fail: The Moderating Effect of Implicit and Explicit Self-esteem on Apology and Forgiveness
Judy Eaton, C. Ward Struthers, Anat Shomrony and Alexander G. Santelli

223 The Mask of Zeal: Low Implicit Self-esteem, Threat, and Defensive Extremism
Ian McGregor and Christian H. Jordan

238 Children and Social Groups: A Developmental Analysis of Implicit Consistency in Hispanic Americans
Yarrow Dunham, Andrew Scott Baron and Mahzarin R. Banaji

256 College Education and Motherhood as Components of Self-concept: Discrepancies between Implicit and Explicit Assessments
Thierry Devos, Priscila Diaz, Erin Viera and Roger Dunn

278 Subject Index

---

*This book is also a special issue of the journal *Self and Identity*, and forms issues 2 and 3 of Volume 6 (2007). The page numbers are taken from the journal and so begin with p. 97.

Self and Identity, 6: 97–100, 2007
http://www.psypress.com/sai
ISSN: 1529-8868 print/1529-8876 online
DOI: 10.1080/15298860601128271

The Implicit Self

LAURIE A. RUDMAN

Rutgers University, Piscataway, New Jersey, USA

STEVEN J. SPENCER

University of Waterloo, Waterloo, Ontario, Canada

William James (1890/1983) famously described the experience of the self as a stream of consciousness. There is little doubt that understanding the conscious experience of the self is important, but in seeking to gain a deeper understanding of the self, researchers are beginning to explore streams of thought that are outside of our conscious experience, or implicit views of the self. This volume contains research that is on the cutting edge of this trend.

Investigating implicit views of the self have required reaching beyond explicit measures, which are plagued not only by impression management and self-deception biases (Paulhus, 1986), but also by respondents' limited access to self-related knowledge (Greenwald & Banaji, 1995; Nisbett & Wilson, 1977). If people cannot accurately introspect about themselves, then even under the best of circumstances, self-reports can only tell us what people believe to be true. Recent advances in indirect assessment techniques, including the response latency paradigm, obviate many problems that compromise explicit measures because they provide information that people may not be willing or able to report. As a result, there is a growing literature on the *implicit self*—aspects of the self that are represented in memory via routinized associations (e.g., between self and evaluation, attributes, or social identities) that may not be readily available to introspection. Among the many reasons to use implicit measures to investigate the self is the fact that they advance social psychological theory by revealing phenomena that would otherwise be obfuscated. This property of implicit self-assessment is what inspired the present special issue of *Self and Identity*.

The guiding themes of this special issue are represented by the principal questions being asked by contemporary researchers on both sides of the Atlantic. These include: How does the implicit self regulate emotion and defend against ego-threats? When and how does it adapt to changes in social identity and social comparison? What are the consequences of discrepancies between explicit and implicit self-evaluations? When and how do implicit self-identities develop? How do implicit self-concept, self-esteem, and identity relate? What are the consequences of the

Correspondence should be addressed to: Laurie A. Rudman, Department of Psychology, Tillett Hall, Rutgers, The State University of New Jersey, 53 Avenue E, Piscataway, NJ 08854–8040, USA. E-mail: rudman@rci.rutgers.edu implicit self for intergroup relations? The ten articles selected for this double issue report on state-of-the-art research that advances both theory and methodology regarding these issues. They also extend the applications of the implicit self in important ways.

We have divided the special issue into three sections. The first section highlights exciting applications of the implicit self for understanding psychological dysfunction. Steinberg, Karpinski, and Alloy begin by reporting on their longitudinal study of risk factors for depressive symptoms. Their findings are among the first to demonstrate that low implicit self-esteem combined with a negative explanatory style puts people particularly at risk for depression following negative life events. They also show that implicit (but not explicit) self-esteem measures support vulnerability – stress models of depression. Next, Koole and Coenen present findings suggesting that the implicit self plays a significant role in automatic emotion regulation. For action-oriented people, subliminally priming the implicit self helps to down-regulate negative affect, whereas for state-oriented people, activating the implicit self incurs the persistence of negative affect. These results support a model of intuitive affect regulation, and further our understanding of what kinds of people are best able to defend against negative affect. Then, Zeigler-Hill and Terry report that people with low explicit but high implicit self-esteem are at risk for both maladaptive and adaptive perfectionism. Their results extend the "glimmer of hope" hypothesis (Spencer, Jordan, Logel, & Zanna, 2005), by which high implicit self-esteem is thought to protect people with low self-worth by providing a source of optimism, but they also suggest that the combination can lead to unrealistic expectations for the self. Finally, Sanchez, Zogmaister, and Arcuri's research on Southern Italians living in Northern Italy has implications for minority members' coping strategies. Their findings suggest that one way to cope with being a low status group member is to implicitly identify with the higher status group and that this strategy is particularly likely for those who do not have a shared superordinate identity with the higher status group. In this way, low status group members can gain some of the prestige of the higher status out-group without forfeiting identification with their in-group.

The second section emphasizes the effects of threat on the implicit self. The first two papers extend our understanding of the malleability of self-associations in the context of various ego-threats. McCall and Dasgupta report that men assigned to a subordinate role tend to compensate for this threat by increasing their implicit (but not explicit) associations between self and leadership. Consistent with self-determination theory, Hodgins, Brown, and Carver report that subtly priming control motives (i.e., the sense that one's actions are dictated by others) decreases implicit self-esteem, whereas priming autonomy motives (i.e., the sense that one's actions are self-determined) increases implicit self-esteem. Explicit self-esteem did not show comparable effects. They also find that men are more likely than women to possess fragile or defensive self-esteem, defined as the combination of high explicit/ low implicit self-esteem. The next two papers further explore reactions to threat for people with fragile or defensive self-esteem. Eaton, Struthers, Shomrony, and Santelli report that fragile self-esteem predicts low forgiveness and greater interest in retaliation in response to apologies for a transgression. A likely mechanism for this pattern is that apologies lend confidence to the inference that one has been harmed, and people with defensive self-esteem react negatively to this certainty. McGregor and Jordan extend their work on defensive zeal by showing that people with fragile self-esteem respond to an intellectual threat by endorsing extreme opinions toward capital punishment, the US invasion of Iraq, and suicide bombing. They also endorse unrealistically high consensus estimates for their extreme opinions. Because McGregor and Jordan's results are the first to demonstrate that extremism is a spurious consequence of defensive zeal, they provide an important addition to the growing literature on this topic.

The third section consists of two papers that explore the interrelations among implicit self-related constructs. They are also similar in their investigation of Hispanic Americans—to date, an under-investigated group in the implicit social cognition literature. Dunham, Barrow, and Banaji assessed implicit self-esteem, self-concept, and group identity in Hispanic American children and adults. Past research suggests that implicit self-associations are balanced via cognitive consistency principles (Greenwald et al., 2002) in a pattern that can be characterized as "If I am X and I am good, then X is good" where X equals any social identity. Interestingly, Dunham and his colleagues report that only young children show this pattern, suggesting that implicit consistency in Hispanic Americans may decline with age. They also found greater automatic in-group bias when the contrasting target group was low in social status (African Americans) compared to when it was high (White Americans). These results are among the first to examine implicit associations in very young children, made possible by the authors' creative adaptation of the Implicit Association Test. In the final paper, Devos, Diaz, Viera, and Dunn measured self-identity in Latina and White American female students and found that implicitly, participants more strongly identified with motherhood than education, whereas explicitly, they more strongly identified with education. Moreover, participants showed balanced implicit cognitions (e.g., if they associated self with motherhood and they had high self-esteem, motherhood was evaluated favorably), in support of the unified theory (Greenwald et al., 2002).

Taken together, the papers presented in this special issue demonstrate the importance of using implicit self-assessment to advance social psychological theory. Among the conceptual frameworks tested are vulnerability – stress models of depression, personality systems interactions theory, the extended self model, self-determination theory, and the unified theory. In each case, the theory would not be supported if researchers were constrained to self-reports. In addition, the authors in this special issue have extended the applications of the implicit self to domains that have been under investigated. These include the clinical consequences of the implicit self, the developmental trajectory of implicit associations, and the impact of being a minority member on implicit self-constructs. Finally, the authors used empirical approaches that are methodologically sophisticated and richly variegated. Among the methods employed are the Implicit Association Test, the name letter effect, the Go/No Go Association Task, and subliminal priming. To paraphrase Thurstone (1928), the implicit self can be measured. As a consequence, we hope this special issue will inspire future investigations of this intriguing and important domain of inquiry.

References

Greenwald, A. G., & Banaji, M. R. (1995). Implicit social cognition: Attitudes, self-esteem, and stereotypes. *Psychological Review, 102*, 4 – 27.

Greenwald, A. G., Banaji, M. R., Rudman, L. A., Farnham, S. D., Nosek, B. A., & Mellott, D. S. (2002). A unified theory of implicit attitudes, stereotypes, self-esteem, and self-concept. *Psychological Review, 109*, 3 – 25.

James, W. (1983). *The principles of psychology*. Cambridge, MA: Harvard University Press. (First published 1890).

Nisbett, R. E., & Wilson, T. D. (1977). Telling more than we can know: Verbal reports on mental processes. *Psychological Review, 84*, 231–259.

Paulhus, D. L. (1986). Self-deception and impression management in test responses. In A. Angleitner & J. S. Wiggins (Eds.), *Personality assessment via questionnaire* (pp. 143–165). New York: Springer-Verlag.

Spencer, S. J., Jordan, C. H., Logel, C. E. R., & Zanna, M. P. (2005). Nagging doubts and a glimmer of hope: The role of implicit self-esteem in self-image maintenance. In A. Tesser, J. V. Wood, & D. A. Stapel (Eds.), *On building, defending and regulating the self: A psychological perspective* (pp. 153–170). New York: Psychology Press.

Thurstone, L. L. (1928). Attitudes can be measured. *American Journal of Sociology, 33*, 529–554.

Self and Identity, 6: 101 – 117, 2007
http://www.psypress.com/sai
ISSN: 1529-8868 print/1529-8876 online
DOI. 10.1080/15298860601118884

The Exploration of Implicit Aspects of Self-esteem in Vulnerability – Stress Models of Depression

JENNIFER A. STEINBERG
ANDREW KARPINSKI
LAUREN B. ALLOY

Temple University, Philadelphia, Pennsylvania, USA

Research investigating vulnerable self-esteem as a risk factor for depression has largely relied on self-report measures, which are susceptible to self-presentational biases and neglect individuals' automatic, nonconscious self-attitudes. Accordingly, the current study incorporated implicit self-esteem techniques, along with traditional self-report measures, into a longitudinal investigation of depressive vulnerability. Findings revealed that in contrast to the Rosenberg Self-Esteem Scale and the Initials-Preference Task, the self – other Implicit Association Test was the only self-esteem measure to yield the hypothesized three-way interaction with cognitive risk and negative events in predicting depressive symptoms over time. Specifically, for individuals at high cognitive risk for depression, the effects of life stress on depressive symptoms were especially pernicious for those demonstrating lower self – other Implicit Association Test scores.

Various theoretical models of depression highlight vulnerable self-esteem as a key factor in the onset, maintenance, and recurrence of this disorder (see Roberts & Monroe, 1992, for review). Vulnerable self-esteem is typically viewed as a latent diathesis that leads to depression when activated by negative events. Extensive research has demonstrated cross-sectional associations between self-esteem and depression, indicating that individuals with higher levels of subclinical depressive symptoms or with current episodes of clinical depression report lower levels of self-esteem than those who are nondepressed (see Bernet, Ingram, & Johnson, 1993, for a review). However, there has been weak and inconsistent evidence regarding level of self-esteem as a *predictor* of depressive episodes and symptoms (see Coyne & Gotlib, 1983; Haaga, Dyck, & Ernst, 1991, for reviews). Furthermore, studies have failed to find consistent evidence that self-esteem level and stressful life events interact to predict future depression (see Roberts & Monroe, 1999, for a review). As a result of these findings, some have argued that low self-esteem is a symptom of depression, as opposed to a stable vulnerability factor (Abramson, Metalsky, & Alloy, 1989; Butler, Hokanson, & Flynn, 1994). Yet, others (e.g., Kernis et al., 1998) have argued that self-esteem is a complex, multi-dimensional construct and have examined other facets as potential risk factors for depression. For example, self-esteem lability, or the degree to which self-esteem fluctuates over time, has been found to reliably

Correspondence should be addressed to: Jennifer A. Steinberg, Zucker Hillside Hospital, Division of Child and Adolescent Psychiatry, Ambulatory Care Pavilion—Lower Level, 75 – 59 263rd Street, Glen Oaks, NY 11004, USA. E-mail: jstein05@temple.edu predict episodes of depression both alone and in interaction with life stress (Kernis et al., 1998; see Roberts & Monroe, 1999, for a review).

Another, as yet unexplored, aspect of self-esteem that may confer vulnerability to depression is implicit self-esteem. Since Greenwald and Banaji's (1995) seminal paper, researchers increasingly have acknowledged the existence of attitudes that operate outside of conscious awareness and control, and an important application of this work has involved attitudes toward the self or self-esteem. Until recently, the implicit operation of self-attitudes was largely neglected due to the reliance on self-report measures, such as the Rosenberg Self-Esteem Scale (RSES; Rosenberg, 1965) in research. This reliance undoubtedly is rooted in several strengths of explicit self-esteem measures; in general, these measures tend to have excellent psychometric properties, including internal consistency and test – retest reliability (e.g., Rosenberg, 1979), and tend to be very practical, inexpensive, and easy to administer to large groups. Despite their strengths, direct measures of self-esteem also have a number of limitations. First, they are susceptible to self-presentational biases, as evidenced by their positive correlations with impression management and self-deception tendencies (Lindeman & Verkasalo, 1995). Second, given that direct measures strictly assess explicit, consciously held beliefs, they neglect the automatic, implicit self-attitudes that reside outside of conscious awareness. This omission is particularly problematic for research on the etiology of depression, as many of the self-schemata and dysfunctional attitudes thought to play a vital role in the development of depression are conceptualized as operating in an implicit fashion (Beck, 1967, 1987; Clark, Beck, & Alford, 1999; De Houwer, 2002). Researchers have recognized these limitations and developed alternatives to self-report measures. These alternative measures are designed to assess implicit self-esteem, or aspects of self-esteem that operate outside of conscious awareness and control (Greenwald & Banaji, 1995). When individuals complete measures of implicit self-esteem, they are either unable to control their responses to the task or, unlike traditional self-report, they are unaware that their self-esteem is being measured.

The most widely used measure of implicit self-esteem is the self – other Implicit Association Test (self – other IAT; Greenwald & Farnham, 2000). The self – other IAT is a five-stage, computerized categorization task, which directly assesses the relative strength of automatic positive and negative associations with self and with others. Although the self – other IAT has not demonstrated cross-sectional associations with depression in preliminary investigations, $r(66) = .09$, ns (Steinberg & Karpinski, 2003), other findings suggest that it may be of use in studies of depressive vulnerability. First, the self-associations assessed by the self – other IAT are sensitive to formerly depressed individuals' susceptibility to negative self-relevant thoughts in the context of sad moods. For example, in Gemar, Segal, Sagrati, and Kennedy's (2001) study, formerly-depressed and never-depressed patients completed a self – other IAT before and after a negative mood induction. Whereas the self – other IAT scores of never-depressed participants did not change as a function of the mood induction, formerly-depressed patients evidenced greater negativity in their self-associations following the sad-mood induction. Second, the self – other IAT has demonstrated sensitivity to the dysfunctional attitudes and reduced tendency for self-favoring common among socially anxious individuals (de Jong, 2002; de Jong, Pasman, Kindt, & van den Hout, 2001). In fact, de Jong et al. (2001) speculated that, "there is no a priori reason to suspect that the IAT could not be applied to the whole range of psychopathological phenomena in which dysfunctional beliefs are thought to play an important role" (p. 110). Given the high rates of comorbidity between anxiety and depression (e.g., Watson & Kendall, 1989) and the central role of dysfunctional beliefs in cognitive theories of depression (e.g., Abramson et al., 1989; Beck, 1967, 1987), an investigation of self–other IAT scores as predictors of depression is warranted.

Another widely used measure of implicit self-esteem is the Initials-Preference Task (IPT), which indirectly measures self-positivity by capitalizing on individual differences in the tendency to evaluate stimuli associated with the self more favorably than stimuli not associated with the self (see Greenwald & Banaji, 1995). On this measure, individuals rate their preferences for the 26 letters of the alphabet. From these ratings, an IPT effect is derived, which reflects individuals' preferences for their own initials as opposed to other letters of the alphabet (Hoorens & Nuttin, 1993; Kitayama & Karasawa, 1997).

Research suggests that individuals' preferences for their initials do, in fact, have important implications. In their 2000 study, Bosson, Swann, and Pennebaker found that name letter preferences influenced interpersonal factors, including interpretation of ambiguous social communication and preferences for positive versus negative feedback. Other research has shown that these preferences may also impact major life decisions. For example, Pelham and colleagues used archival data to demonstrate that the positive associations individuals have with their name letters impact the careers they choose and where they choose to live (Pelham, Mirenberg, & Jones, 2002), as well as the people they marry (Jones, Pelham, Carvallo, & Mirenberg, 2004). Although the implications of name letter preferences for interpersonal dynamics and important life decisions have been demonstrated, the emotional and behavioral consequences of these preferences is an area ripe for research. In a pilot study, Steinberg and Karpinski (2003) found that the IPT was sensitive to self-esteem differences between subclinically depressed and nondepressed individuals, and a logical extension of this work is to examine whether name letter preferences can predict future depression.

The current study expanded upon previous research by incorporating the self–other IAT and the IPT, along with traditional explicit self-report measures of self-esteem and cognitive style, into a longitudinal investigation of depressive vulnerability. Many prominent cognitive theorists (e.g., Abramson et al., 1989; Beck, 1967, 1987) posit vulnerability–stress models, in which negative cognitive styles increase one's risk for depression following stressful life events. In Beck's theory (1967, 1987), for example, cognitively vulnerable individuals are thought to possess negative schemata concerning such themes as worthlessness, loss, and failure which, when activated by the occurrence of negative events, lead to depression through their influence on the processing of negative self-referent information. In the hopelessness theory (Abramson et al., 1989), individuals who tend to attribute negative events to stable and global causes, assume that aversive consequences will follow, and interpret the event's occurrence as meaning that they are flawed, are hypothesized to be at increased risk for depression due to their tendency to generate negative inferences regarding the causes, consequences, and implications of negative events. Findings from the Cognitive Vulnerability to Depression (CVD; Alloy & Abramson, 1999) Project, which followed individuals chosen to be at high or low cognitive risk for depression based on the presence versus absence of the cognitive styles delineated as vulnerabilities in Beck's theory and hopelessness theory, supported both models. Namely, when compared to their low-risk counterparts, high-risk participants demonstrated a greater likelihood of having a first onset and recurrences of Diagnostic and Statistical Manual of Mental Disorders (DSM-IV;

American Psychiatric Association, 1994) and Research Diagnostic Criteria (RDC; Spitzer, Endicott, & Robins, 1978) major depressive disorder, RDC minor depressive disorder, and hopelessness depression during the 2.5-year follow-up period (Alloy et al., 2006). Supporting the specificity of these cognitive styles to depression versus other forms of psychopathology, with the exception of prospective risk group differences for anxiety comorbid with depression, there were no lifetime history or prospective risk group differences in anxiety or other Axis I disorders (Alloy et al., 2000, 2006). Furthermore, a separate study found that negative cognitive styles interacted with stressful life events to predict increases in clinician-rated depressive symptomatology among participants with RDC lifetime diagnoses of unipolar depression (Reilly-Harrington, Alloy, Fresco, & Whitehouse, 1999).

Predictions. Similar to negative cognitive styles, we hypothesized that low levels of implicit self-esteem, as assessed by the self – other IAT and the IPT, would signify increased vulnerability to depression. There are two possible ways in which implicit self-esteem may predict depression. First, there may be a *direct effect* of implicit self-esteem. Second, implicit self-esteem may *interact* with negative events to predict depression. We examined both possibilities in the current longitudinal study of depressive symptoms by administering the self – other IAT, the IPT, the RSES, and a measure of life stress to individuals identified as low or high cognitive risk for depression (based on Beck's theory and hopelessness theory). We hypothesized that individuals with lower levels of implicit self-esteem would be at heightened risk for depressive symptoms due to their tendency for automatic negative evaluations of the self and self-associated stimuli (direct effect), as well as their increased susceptibility to the depressogenic impact of life stress (interaction effect). We further predicted that these effects would be particularly pronounced among cognitively high-risk individuals whose negative inferential styles and self-schemata are associated with increased processing of negative self-referent information (Alloy, Abramson, Murray, Whitehouse, & Hogan, 1997), as well as depressogenic attributions and inferences following negative events.

Method

Participants and Procedure

Undergraduates enrolled in introduction to psychology were screened for inclusion in the proposed study. A modified Dysfunctional Attitudes Scale (DAS; Weissman & Beck, 1978), the Cognitive Style Questionnaire (CSQ; Alloy et al., 2000), and the Beck Depression Inventory-II (BDI-II; Beck, Steer, & Brown, 1996) were administered as part of the screening packet. The DAS and the CSQ were used to assess the cognitive vulnerabilities featured in Beck's theory and the hopelessness theory, respectively. Similar to the procedures used in the CVD Project (Alloy et al., 2000), high-risk participants were those scoring in the top third (most negative) of the screening sample on both the DAS and the negative composite (stability + globality + consequences + self dimensions) of the CSQ. Low-risk participants included those scoring in the bottom quartile (most positive) of the screening sample on both measures. From the pool of potential high- and low-risk participants, those with more than mild to moderate depressive symptoms (BDI-II > 15) were excluded. Given that the proposed study sought to examine the role of self-esteem in the prediction of depression, a relatively nondepressed initial sample was ideal.[1] The final study sample consisted of 181 participants, but 2 failed to return for the second session. The overall sample included 98 high-risk participants, 110 females, and 61 non-Caucasians.

During Session 1, participants were administered the self – other IAT (Greenwald & Farnham, 2000), the IPT (Nuttin, 1985, 1987), the RSES (Rosenberg, 1965) and a baseline measure of depressive symptoms (BDI-II). In Session 2, participants completed a follow-up measure of depression (BDI-II) and a Life Events Scale (LES; Alloy & Clements, 1992; Needles & Abramson, 1990). Participants completed the two sessions approximately four months apart (mean duration = 123.66 days).

Measures

Cognitive styles. As discussed above, the DAS (Weissman & Beck, 1978) and the CSQ (Alloy et al., 2000) were used to assess participants' cognitive vulnerability to depression, as specified by Beck's theory (1967, 1987) and the hopelessness theory (Abramson et al., 1989), respectively. The DAS (Weissman & Beck, 1978) is a 40-item self-report inventory that assesses maladaptive attitudes, such as perfectionistic performance standards, sensitivity to social criticisms, expectations of control, and rigid ideas about the world. Participants' response options range on a 7-point Likert-type scale, from "*totally agree*" to "*totally disagree*". As in the CVD Project, 24 items were added to the original 40 to assess dysfunctional attitudes in both achievement and interpersonal domains. The expanded DAS has exhibited excellent internal consistency ($\alpha = .90$; Alloy et al., 2000, $\alpha = .93$; current study), good retest reliability over 1 year ($r = .78$, $p < .0001$; Alloy et al., 2000), and predictive validity for depressive episodes (Alloy et al., 2006).

The CSQ is a self-report measure used to assess individuals' tendency to make internal, stable, and global attributions and to infer negative consequences and negative characteristics about themselves following the occurrence of a negative life event. A composite score was created for inferences (mean ratings for the stability, globality, consequences, and self-implication dimensions) generated in response to hypothetical negative events. The CSQ composite for negative events has demonstrated good internal consistency ($\alpha = .88$; Alloy et al., 2000, $\alpha = .97$; current study), retest reliability over 1 year ($r = .80$, $p < .0001$; Alloy et al., 2000), and predictive validity for episodes of depression (Alloy, Reilly-Harrington, Fresco, Whitehouse, & Zechmeister, 1999; Alloy et al., 2006).

In the CVD project, using data from the Temple site only ($n = 2405$), the CSQ composite for negative events and the DAS were moderately correlated ($r = .44$), and similar findings were reported by Haeffel and colleagues (2005; $r = .47$). Given that neither cognitive style measure has been found to be a perfect predictor of future depression, choosing on the basis of being high or low on both increases the chances of finding truly vulnerable and nonvulnerable participants (Alloy et al., 2000, 2006).

Self – other IAT (Greenwald & Farnham, 2000). The self – other IAT procedure followed the standard paradigm outlined by Greenwald and colleagues (see Greenwald & Farnham, 2000; Greenwald, McGhee, & Schwartz, 1998) with minor modifications. The evaluative dimension was labeled *pleasant* and *unpleasant* and the attitude object dimension was labeled *self* and *other*. Five target words were used for each of the evaluative dimensions (pleasant: *smart, bright, success, splendid, valued*; unpleasant: *stupid, ugly, failure, awful, useless*). Five target words were also selected to be associated with each of the attitude objects (self: *participant's first name, participant's last name, me, I, myself*; other: *him, her, their, them, they*).

Participants completed five stages of the task and responded to blocks of 30 trials for the single-dimension blocks, and blocks of 60 trials for the critical combined blocks. Stages one (pleasant vs. unpleasant), two (self vs. other), and four (other vs. self) were practice stages to familiarize participants with the categorizations. In stage three, the categorizations from stages one and two were combined (pleasant + self vs. unpleasant + other), and in stage five, the categorizations from stages one and four were combined (pleasant + other vs. unpleasant + self). Error feedback was not provided.

Self–other IAT scores were computed using the newer D-score algorithm (Greenwald, Nosek, & Banaji, 2003), with higher scores indicating a positive bias for the *self* as compared to *others*. To compute a reliability coefficient, IAT scores calculated with the first 30 trials from each of the critical stages were correlated with IAT scores calculated with the second 30 trials from each of the critical stages ($\alpha = .72$). Participants who had error rates greater than 20% or whose mean latencies were greater than 2000 ms were excluded from analyses ($n = 4$). The mean error rate for the remaining participants ($n = 177$) was .05.

IPT (Nuttin, 1985, 1987). On the IPT, participants indicated their liking for each letter of the alphabet using a 6-point scale, ranging from *"extremely ugly"* to *"extremely beautiful"*. To calculate IPT scores, letter ratings were converted into z-scores and the average was taken of participants' first and last initials. Internal consistency of the IPT was computed by correlating participants' ratings of their first and last initials, $r = .28$. Although some studies have found the internal consistency of the IPT to be adequate (Bosson et al., 2000; Koole, Dijksterhuis, & van Knippenberg, 2001), other studies have reported similar, low internal consistencies (Karpinski, Steinberg, Versek, & Alloy, in press; Bosson, Brown, Zeigler-Hill, & Swann, 2003). Although the reason for these discrepancies is unclear, the IPT's weak internal consistency is not necessarily surprising, given the multitude of factors other than self-esteem that influence participants' ratings of their initials.

RSES (Rosenberg, 1965). The RSES is a 10-item measure that assesses global feelings of self-worth and is the most commonly used self-report measure of self-esteem. All responses were made on a scale ranging from 1 (*strongly disagree*) to 4 (*strongly agree*), and $\alpha = .89$.

BDI–II (Beck et al., 1996). The 21-item BDI-II was used to measure depressive symptomatology. On the BDI-II, participants rated the occurrence of each symptom during the "past two weeks, including today" using a 4-point scale, and $\alpha = .87$.

Life Events Scale (LES; Alloy & Clements, 1992; Needles & Abramson, 1990). The LES includes 177 major and minor episodic events, as well as more chronic situations in a wide range of domains pertinent to college students. On the LES, participants reported the occurrence and frequency of positive and negative events that took place during the four months between Sessions 1 and 2. To reduce subject burden, the LES included "skip-out" sections that enabled the participant to skip parts that were not applicable to him or her. In addition, there was a "write-in" section in which the participant indicated the occurrence of positive and negative events that were not covered on the LES.

LES events scores have demonstrated excellent reliability and validity (Alloy & Clements, 1992; Alloy et al., 1999; Needles & Abramson, 1990), and have been shown to interact with cognitive styles to predict the onset and remission of depressive symptoms (Alloy & Clements, 1992; Alloy et al., 1999; Needles & Abramson, 1990). Findings have revealed that major events, which involve more severe threats to relationships, economic stability, or health, more consistently predict depressive onset than minor stressors (Brown & Harris, 1989; Monroe & Hadjiyannakis, 2002; Monroe & McQuaid, 1994). Accordingly, event scores were calculated by summing the total number of discrete "major" events endorsed. Major events were defined as those having a significant impact on a person (e.g., not being accepted into graduate school, break-up of parents' marriage, boyfriend/girlfriend being unfaithful), and the a priori categorizations developed by Alloy and Abramson (1999) were used.

Results

Descriptive statistics. A series of analyses was conducted to determine whether any of the study variables were significantly related to participant characteristics, such as ethnicity, gender, and socioeconomic status. With regard to ethnicity, given extremely unequal cell sizes with some cells as small as 5 participants, categories were collapsed to form Caucasian ($n = 120$) and non-Caucasian ($n = 61$) groups for comparison purposes. Time 2 BDI-II scores did not vary according to participants' ethnicity. However, there were ethnic differences on self-esteem measures, with non-Caucasian participants evidencing higher levels of self-esteem on the IPT, $t(178) = -2.43$, $p = .02$, $d = -0.36$, the self–other IAT, $t(175) = -2.06$, $p = .04$, $d = -0.31$, and the RSES, $t(179) = -2.45$, $p = .02$, $d = -0.37$. Non-Caucasian participants also reported a greater number of negative events, $t(177) = -3.26$, $p < .01$, $d = -0.49$, and were less likely than their Caucasian counterparts to be classified as high risk based on their DAS and CSQ scores, $\chi^2(1, n = 181) = 4.92$, $p = .027$. With regard to gender, males and females did not differ on measures of self-esteem, life events, risk status, or depression ($ps > .10$). Finally, age and SES variables, including parental education and parental income, were unrelated to BDI-II scores. Age and SES variables were also generally unrelated to the self-esteem measures, with the exception of a negative correlation between IPT scores and age, $r(178) = -.18$, $p = .02$, indicating lower levels of name initials preferences with increasing age. In line with Miller and Chapman's (2001) argument, none of these demographic variables were included as covariates in subsequent analyses because they were not related to the dependent variable (Time 2 BDI-II scores).

The means and standard deviations of the study variables are presented in Table 1. As Table 1 shows, low-risk participants were less depressed than their high-risk counterparts at both Time 1 and Time 2. When compared to high-risk participants, low-risk individuals had higher levels of self-esteem on both implicit and explicit measures, although findings for the IPT failed to reach significance.

Finally, risk group differences did not emerge for total number of negative events, suggesting similar levels of stress for the low- and high-risk groups.

Correlation analyses. As shown in Table 2, the intercorrelations among measures of self-esteem, negative events, and depression were examined for low-risk and high-risk participants. Supporting previous findings, implicit measures did not correlate with each other ($rs < .08$). Although the RSES was unrelated to measures of implicit self-esteem among low-risk participants, significant positive associations emerged among high-risk individuals. The RSES demonstrated the expected negative correlation with the BDI-II among low- and high-risk participants. Whereas implicit self-esteem was not significantly related to depression among low-risk participants, among the high-risk group a significant negative correlation was observed between the self–other IAT and Time 1 BDI-II scores,

TABLE 1 Means and Standard Deviations for Study Variables

	Low risk ($n = 83$)		High risk ($n = 98$)		
	Mean	*SD*	*Mean*	*SD*	Test for difference
Time 1 Measures					
BDI	4.71	4.63	10.96	6.04	$t(179) = -7.70, p < .01$
RSES	6.41	0.58	5.08	0.90	$t(179) = 11.55, p < .01$
IPT	1.45	1.32	1.15	1.50	$t(178) = 1.44, p = .15$
Self–other IAT	0.67	0.28	0.56	0.31	$t(175) = 2.41, p = .02$
Time 2 Measures					
BDI	4.34	3.73	8.16	6.22	$t(177) = -4.89, p < .01$
Events	2.19	2.18	2.53	2.35	$t(177) = -0.99, p = .32$

Note: BDI = Beck Depression Inventory-II. RSES = Rosenberg Self-esteem Scale. IPT = Initials-preference Task. Self–other IAT = Self–other Implicit Association Test. Events = Total number of negative events.

TABLE 2 Correlations Among Measures of Self-Esteem, Negative Events, and Depressive Symptoms

	1	2	3	4	5	6
1. RSES	–	.28**	.21*	.01	−.41***	−.24*
2. IPT	.03	–	−.02	.19	−.07	.08
3. Self–other IAT	.14	.07	–	−.09	−.23*	−.10
4. Events	.06	.08	.19	–	.27**	.38***
5. BDI—Time 1	−.52***	.004	.16	.25*	–	.56***
6. BDI—Time 2	−.27*	.05	.12	.42***	.62***	–

Note: Correlation coefficients for high- and low-risk participants are reported above and below the diagonal, respectively. RSES = Rosenberg Self-esteem Scale. IPT = Initials-preference Task. Self–other IAT = Self–other Implicit Association Test. Events = Total number of negative events. BDI = Beck Depression Inventory-II. *$p < .05$; **$p < .01$; ***$p < .0001$.

$r(93) = -.23$, $p = .03$. None of the implicit measures of self-esteem correlated with Time 2 BDI-II scores for either low- or high- risk participants ($|rs| < .13$), providing little evidence for a direct link between implicit self-esteem and future depression. Negative events were positively associated with depression, but were not significantly associated with either explicit or implicit self-esteem ($rs < .20$).

Analysis plan. To examine the vulnerability–stress hypothesis, separate linear regression analyses were conducted for each of the self-esteem measures. Using participants' Time 2 BDI-II scores as the criterion variable, the following predictors were entered simultaneously: (1) Time 1 BDI-II scores (covariate); (2) main effects of Risk, Self-esteem, and Events; (3) all possible two-way interactions; and (4) the Risk × Self-esteem × Events three-way interaction. Significant interactions were decomposed with simple slope analyses to determine the relationship between negative events and depression within the low- and high-risk groups. In all of these analyses, Time 1 BDI-II scores were a strong, significant predictor of Time 2 BDI-II scores, $\beta s > .55$, $ps < .01$.

Self–other IAT and depression. Although a marginal Events effect emerged, it was qualified by a marginal three-way interaction between Risk, self–other IAT, and Events, $t(167) = -1.77$, $p = .079$, $\beta = -.17$, $\Delta R^2 = .01$ (see Table 3). Follow-up analyses examined the self–other IAT × Events interaction separately among low- and high-risk participants (see Figure 1).

For high-risk participants, the predicted self–other IAT × Events interaction emerged, $t(89) = -2.04$, $p = .04$, $\beta = -.17$, $\Delta R^2 = .03$. As shown in Figure 1, although depression levels did not vary as a function of stress among high-risk individuals with high implicit self-esteem, for those with low implicit self-esteem, increased stress was associated with higher levels of depression. For low-risk participants, only a main effect of events was observed, $t(77) = 3.12$, $p = .003$, $\beta = .28$, $\Delta R^2 = .08$, indicating that a greater number of negative events was associated with

TABLE 3 Predicting Time 2 Depressive Symptoms

	Model 1: Self–other IAT		Model 2: IPT		Model 3: RSES	
	β	p	β	p	β	p
BDI—Time 1	.57	<.01	.56	<.01	.55	<.01
Risk	.03	.61	.06	.36	.15	.11
Events	.18	.06	.19	.03	.01	.98
Self-esteem	−.03	.76	.02	.81	.23	.21
Risk × Events	.001	.99	.07	.45	.21	.19
Risk × Self-esteem	.04	.68	.05	.58	−.18	.19
Events × Self-esteem	.03	.78	−.01	.95	.19	.30
Risk × Events × Self-esteem	−.17	.08	−.06	.50	−.13	.40

Note: Time 2 BDI-II scores are the dependent measure in each model. Each model uses a different measure of self-esteem as a predictor. Self–other IAT = Self–other Implicit Association Test. IPT = Initials-preference Task. RSES = Rosenberg Self-esteem Scale. BDI = Beck Depression Inventory-II. Risk = Cognitive risk status. Events = Total number of negative events.

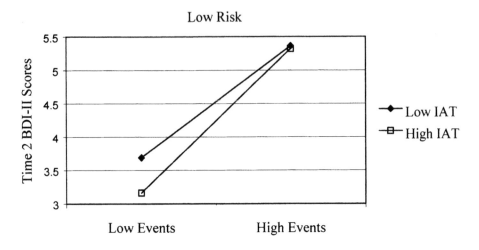

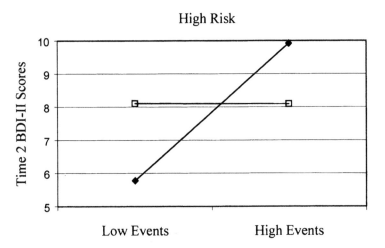

FIGURE 1   Time 2 depressive symptoms as a function of self–other IAT scores and negative events.

higher depression levels, irrespective of implicit self-esteem level. However, it should be noted that BDI-II scores were very low in the low-risk group, even among participants with many negative life events.

The IPT and depression.   This analysis revealed only a significant main effect for negative life events, $t(169) = 2.20$, $p = .029$, $\beta = .19$, $\Delta R^2 = .06$, indicating a positive association between life stress and Time 2 depression. This main effect was not modified by any higher order interactions, $ps > .45$.

RSES and depression.   For this analysis, there were not any significant main effects ($ps > .11$), nor were there any significant two- or three-way interactions, $ps > .18$.

Implicit × explicit self-esteem.   For completeness, analyses were conducted to examine whether implicit and explicit self-esteem interact to predict depression, either alone or in interaction with negative life events or risk status. Using participants' Time 2 BDI-II scores as the criterion variable, separate linear regression analyses were conducted for the self–other IAT and the IPT, with the following variables entered simultaneously: Time 1 BDI-II scores (covariate), implicit self-esteem, explicit self-esteem, negative life events, risk status, and all two-, three-, and four-way interactions. None of the interaction terms were significant for analyses involving the self–other IAT ($ps > .48$) or the IPT ($ps > .17$). Thus, there was no evidence that implicit and explicit self-esteem interacted to predict Time 2 depression, or that explicit self-esteem moderated the interaction between implicit self-esteem, negative events, and risk status.

Discussion

In the field of self-esteem research, there has been an over reliance on explicit measurement, which neglects nonconscious aspects of the self-concept. This omission is particularly problematic for research on vulnerability to depression, as many prominent theories argue that the dysfunctional self-attitudes underlying depression operate in an implicit fashion (Beck, 1967, 1987; Clark et al., 1999; De Houwer, 2002). Over the past decade, measures of implicit self-esteem have emerged that aim to circumvent social desirability biases and to capture aspects of self-esteem that reside outside of conscious awareness and control. In the current study, we incorporated the self–other IAT and the IPT, which have demonstrated the strongest empirical support among implicit self-esteem measures, into a longitudinal investigation of risk for depressive symptoms. By so doing, we examined the extent to which measures of implicit self-esteem may enhance our ability to predict depression. The current findings suggest that the incorporation of implicit measurement into research on vulnerability to depression may be a fruitful endeavor.

Preliminary analyses examined correlations among measures of self-esteem and depression. As in previous research, the RSES was negatively correlated with BDI-II scores (at Time 1 and Time 2). However, with the exception of the self–other IAT, which was negatively correlated with BDI-II scores at Time 1 (only among high-risk participants), measures of implicit self-esteem were unrelated to Time 1 and Time 2 depression scores. Thus, the current study revealed rather weak findings regarding the direct relationship between implicit self-esteem and depressive symptoms.

However, the focal hypothesis of the current study involved the vulnerability–stress model of depressive etiology. That is, moving beyond investigating the direct relationship between self-esteem and depression, we sought to examine the way in which one's implicit and explicit self-attitudes interact with life stress and cognitive style to predict depressive symptoms. In this way, we examined the degree to which incorporating implicit self-esteem measurement enhanced the ability to predict depression.

Perhaps the most interesting finding to emerge was that, in contrast to the RSES and the IPT, the self–other IAT was the only self-esteem measure that yielded the hypothesized three-way interaction with cognitive risk and negative events. An investigation of the interaction revealed that, in contrast to the low-risk group in which a two-way interaction failed to emerge, among high-risk participants, the positive association between negative events and depression was modified by a higher order interaction with self–other IAT scores. For high-risk participants who had high self–other IAT scores, stressful life events were unrelated to depression.

However, for high-risk participants with low self – other IAT scores, negative events were associated with higher levels of Time 2 depressive symptoms.

Thus, for high-risk individuals with high self – other IAT scores, the presence of automatic positive self-associations may buffer the depressogenic impact of severe life stress. By contrast, for those with low self – other IAT scores, the negative effects of stress may be exacerbated. This pattern of findings makes intuitive sense. That is, among individuals who make stable and global attributions for negative events, catastrophize about the events' consequences, and interpret the events' occurrence as meaning that they are flawed in some way, the effects of life stress on depressive symptoms are especially pernicious for those who also have automatic negative self-associations.

For high-risk individuals who experienced few negative life events, an unexpected and somewhat puzzling pattern emerged. Specifically, among high-risk participants with fewer negative life events, those with lower self – other IAT scores were less depressed than those with higher self – other IAT scores. One possible explanation for this pattern is that these individuals experienced many negative self-relevant events in the past (and thus have low IAT self-esteem scores), but few negative events over the four-month prospective period of the study. Relatively speaking, the recent past may have been less negative and less stressful than the more distant past, resulting in a decrease in depression. This explanation is clearly speculative without a Time 1 measure of events, and future studies should incorporate multiple stress assessments to examine the moderating impact of negative events on the relationship between self-esteem and depression over time.

In short, the findings suggest that unlike the IPT, the self – other IAT may capture an underlying risk factor for depression, particularly among those with negative cognitive styles. The stronger support for the self – other IAT appears to result from both theoretical and methodological factors. First, many prominent cognitive theorists (e.g., Beck, 1967, 1987; Clark et al., 1999) posit that evaluative self-associations of which the individual is unaware contribute to depressive vulnerability. In contrast to the IPT, which provides an indirect measure of self-positivity by quantifying name letter preferences, the self – other IAT provides a more direct measurement of these automatic associations that are thought to lead to depression. Second, within the social psychology literature, self-discrepancy theory (e.g., Higgins, 1987; Higgins, Klein, & Strauman, 1985) has demonstrated that differences between one's actual self and ideal self may lead to depression. Given that the ideal self is multiply determined and impacted by one's perceptions of others, this theory implies that in order to predict depression, implicit measures should assess associations that a person has with self *and* with others. Thus, although the self – other IAT has been criticized for providing a joint measure of self versus other esteem that may derive from comparison to an "other" that is very negative (Karpinski, 2004), the relative nature of its measurement may prove a strength in studies of depressive vulnerability. For example, the stronger predictive power of the self – other IAT may reflect the fact that having very positive associations with other compared to self makes one particularly vulnerable to depression in response to negative life events. Finally, whereas the self – other IAT demonstrated adequate reliability, the IPT demonstrated poor internal consistency. The IPT's poor internal consistency suggests, as one would expect, that factors other than individuals' implicit self-attitudes impact their name letter ratings. Thus, when compared to the IPT, the self – other IAT has stronger theoretical support as a predictor of depression and greater reliability, which contributed to its superior performance in the present study.

Despite its contributions to understanding the role of implicit self-esteem in depressive vulnerability, the current study has several limitations. First, although findings for the self–other IAT supported the hypothesized pattern and have important implications for predicting depression, the effect was small, accounting for only 1% of variance in Time 2 depression scores. Thus, independent replication is needed to make sure that the present findings are reliable. Second, depression was assessed using self-report questionnaire as opposed to diagnostic interview. Although self-presentation concerns (e.g., Lindeman & Verkasalo, 1995) may limit the accuracy of participants' self-reported depressive symptoms, previous studies reveal moderate-to-strong convergent validity between the BDI-II and clinical ratings of nonpsychiatric participants (*rs* ranging from .55 to .73; Beck, Steer, & Garbin, 1988). Nevertheless, a logical extension of the current research is to examine the relationship between implicit self-esteem and depressive disorder using structured diagnostic interview techniques. Third, the study's sample involved nondepressed undergraduate participants who, based on their cognitive styles, were identified as either high- or low-risk for depression. Although this design enabled a prospective examination of depressive vulnerability and maximized effect sizes by comparing groups with extreme scores on cognitive vulnerability measures (Alloy & Abramson, 1999), the generalizability of the findings to other populations remains an open question. Fourth, although the study's design enabled a demonstration of the temporal precedence of low self-esteem as a precursor to depressive symptoms, it cannot establish a causal role for this variable. Future research should examine whether addressing low self-esteem in the context of preventive measures impacts the likelihood of future depression. Finally, given that life events were assessed via self-report, there is a risk of reporting biases (e.g., high-risk participants or those with low self-esteem may be more likely to report negative events). However, a recent study based on CVD Project life events data (Safford, Alloy, Abramson, & Crossfield, in press) found that high-risk participants did not exhibit reporting biases and in the current study, neither self-esteem nor risk status was related to the number of negative events reported.

The current study provides preliminary evidence regarding the utility of implicit self-esteem measures for the study of vulnerability to depression. In line with prominent cognitive theories of depression (e.g., Beck, 1967, 1987; Clark et al., 1999), our findings suggest that evaluative self-associations of which the individual is unaware could play a causal role in depression. This finding, intuitive to many cognitive and psychoanalytic clinicians, has potential implications for both the detection and treatment of depression. With regard to early detection and prevention, the self–other IAT may provide a window into the automatic negative self-attitudes that individuals may be unable or unwilling to report. When used in conjunction with traditional self-report questionnaires and diagnostic interviews, the self–other IAT may help to provide a more comprehensive, multi-faceted picture of self-esteem that recognizes both implicit and explicit processes. This measurement technique may also serve psychologists well as they assess the efficacy of their treatments for depression (see de Jong et al., 2001). In addition to examining changes in self-reported self-worth, which has inherent demand characteristics, clinicians may examine the extent to which automatic self-associations change in response to treatment. Such an empirical application seems particularly well-suited to cognitive therapy for depression, which emphasizes the role of identifying, evaluating, and modifying automatic self-related thoughts in promoting symptom relief (Beck, 1995).

In line with previous research, our findings show that the self – other IAT and the IPT do not appear to capture overlapping aspects of the implicit self-esteem construct. This does not, however, signify that implicit measures are not valid or potentially useful. In fact, in the current study, the self – other IAT emerged as a stronger predictor of depressive symptoms in the context of life stress than the RSES. It is through the increasing recognition of the multi-faceted nature of self-esteem (e.g., Kernis et al., 1998) that researchers can move beyond dichotomous thinking regarding the utility of these measures to examine the specific situations or conditions under which the measures are useful. Stronger theories regarding implicit and explicit self-esteem and their measurement are needed so that researchers can make empirically informed decisions regarding how and when to use these techniques.

Note

1. In order to obtain a sufficient sample of high-risk participants that were relatively nondepressed at Time 1, a more inclusive sample was recruited (those scoring in the top third on both the DAS and the CSQ), as compared to the original CVD project, which included the top quartile on both measures.

References

Abramson, L. Y., Metalsky, G. I., & Alloy, L. B. (1989). Hopelessness depression: A theory-based subtype of depression. *Psychological Review, 96*, 358 – 372.

Alloy, L. B., & Abramson, L. Y. (1999). The Temple – Wisconsin Cognitive Vulnerability to Depression Project: Conceptual background, design, and methods. *Journal of Cognitive Psychotherapy, 13*, 227 – 262.

Alloy, L. B., Abramson, L. Y., Hogan, M. E., Whitehouse, W. G., Rose, D. T., Robinson, M. S., et al. (2000). The Temple – Wisconsin Cognitive Vulnerability to Depression Project: Lifetime history of Axis I psychopathology in individuals at high and low cognitive risk for depression. *Journal of Abnormal Psychology, 109*, 403 – 418.

Alloy, L. B., Abramson, L. Y., Murray, L. A., Whitehouse, W. G., & Hogan, M. E. (1997). Self-referent information processing in individuals at high and low cognitive risk for depression. *Cognition and Emotion, 11*, 539 – 568.

Alloy, L. B., Abramson, L. Y., Whitehouse, W. G., Hogan, M. E., Panzarella, C., & Rose, D. T. (2006). Prospective incidence of first onsets and recurrences of depression in individuals at high and low cognitive risk for depression. *Journal of Abnormal Psychology, 109*, 403 – 418.

Alloy, L. B., & Clements, C. (1992). Illusion of control: Invulnerability to negative affect and depressive symptoms after laboratory and natural stressors. *Journal of Abnormal Psychology, 101*, 234 – 245.

Alloy, L. B., Reilly-Harrington, N., Fresco, D. M., Whitehouse, W. G., & Zechmeister, J. S. (1999). Cognitive styles and life events in subsyndromal unipolar and bipolar disorders: Stability and prospective prediction of depressive and hypomanic mood swings. *Journal of Cognitive Psychotherapy: An International Quarterly, 13*, 21 – 40.

American Psychiatric Association. (1994). *Diagnostic and statistical manual of mental disorders* (4th ed.). Washington, DC: Author.

Beck, A. T. (1967). *Depression: Clinical, experimental, and theoretical aspects.* New York: Harper & Row.

Beck, A. T. (1987). Cognitive models of depression. *Journal of Cognitive Psychotherapy, 1*, 5 – 37.

Beck, A. T., Steer, R. A., & Brown, G. K. (1996). *Manual for the Beck Depression Inventory-II.* San Antonio, TX: Psychological Corporation.

Beck, A. T., Steer, R. A., & Garbin, M. G. (1988). Psychometric properties of the Beck Depression Inventory: Twenty-five years of evaluation. *Clinical Psychology Review, 8,* 77 – 100.

Beck, J. S. (1995). *Cognitive therapy: Basics and beyond.* New York: Guilford Press.

Bernet, C. Z., Ingram, R. E., & Johnson, B. R. (1993). Self-esteem. In C. G. Costello (Ed.), *Symptoms of depression* (pp. 141 – 159). New York: Wiley.

Bosson, J. K., Brown, R. P., Zeigler-Hill, V., & Swann, W. B. (2003). Self-enhancement tendencies among people with high explicit self-esteem: The moderating role of implicit self-esteem. *Self and Identity, 2,* 169 – 187.

Bosson, J. K., Swann, W. B., & Pennebaker, J. W. (2000). Stalking the perfect measure of implicit self-esteem: The blind men and the elephant revisited? *Journal of Personality and Social Psychology, 79,* 631 – 643.

Brown, G. W., & Harris, T. O. (Eds.). (1989). *Life events and illness.* New York: Guilford Press.

Butler, A. C., Hokanson, J. E., & Flynn, H. A. (1994). A comparison of self-esteem lability and low trait self-esteem as vulnerability factors for depression. *Journal of Personality and Social Psychology, 66,* 166 – 177.

Clark, D. A., Beck, A. T., & Alford, B. A. (1999). *Scientific foundations of cognitive theory and therapy of depression.* New York: Wiley.

Coyne, J. C., & Gotlib, I. H. (1983). The role of cognition in depression: A critical appraisal. *Psychological Bulletin, 94,* 472 – 505.

De Houwer, J. (2002). The Implicit Association Test as a tool for studying dysfunctional associations in psychopathology: Strengths and limitations. *Journal of Behavior Therapy, 33,* 115 – 133.

de Jong, P. J. (2002). Implicit self-esteem and social anxiety: Differential self-favouring effects in high and low anxious individuals. *Behaviour Research and Therapy, 40,* 501 – 508.

de Jong, P. J., Pasman, W., Kindt, M., & van den Hout, M. A. (2001). A reaction time paradigm to assess (implicit) complaint-specific dysfunctional beliefs. *Behaviour Research and Therapy, 39,* 101 – 113.

Gemar, M. C., Segal, Z. V., Sagrati, S., & Kennedy, S. J. (2001). Mood-induced changes on the Implicit Association Test in recovered depressed patients. *Journal of Abnormal Psychology, 110,* 282 – 289.

Greenwald, A. G., & Banaji, M. R. (1995). Implicit social cognition: Attitudes, self-esteem, and stereotypes. *Psychological Review, 102,* 4 – 27.

Greenwald, A. G., & Farnham, S. D. (2000). Using the Implicit Association Test to measure self-esteem and self-concept. *Journal of Personality and Social Psychology, 79,* 1022 – 1038.

Greenwald, A. G., McGhee, D. E., & Schwartz, J. L. K. (1998). Measuring individual differences in implicit cognition: The Implicit Association Test. *Journal of Personality and Social Psychology, 74,* 1464 – 1480.

Greenwald, A. G., Nosek, B. A., & Banaji, M. R. (2003). Understanding and using the Implicit Association Test: I. An improved scoring algorithm. *Journal of Personality and Social Psychology, 85,* 197 – 216.

Haaga, D. A., Dyck, M. J., & Ernst, D. (1991). Empirical status of cognitive theory of depression. *Psychological Bulletin, 110,* 215 – 236.

Haeffel, G. J., Abramson, L. Y., Voelz, Z. R., Metalsky, G. I., Halberstadt, L., Dykman, B. M., et al. (2005). Negative cognitive styles, dysfunctional attitudes, and the remitted depression paradigm: A search for the elusive cognitive vulnerability to depression factor among remitted depressives. *Emotion, 5,* 343 – 348.

Higgins, E. T. (1987). Self-discrepancy: A theory relating self and affect. *Psychological Review, 94,* 319 – 340.

Higgins, E. T., Klein, R., & Strauman, T. (1985). Self-concept discrepancy theory: A psychological model for distinguishing among different aspects of depression and anxiety. *Social Cognition, 3*, 51–76.

Hoorens, V., & Nuttin, J. M. (1993). Overevaluation of own attributes: Mere ownership or subjective frequency? *Social Cognition, 11*, 177–200.

Jones, J. T., Pelham, B. W., Carvallo, M., & Mirenberg, M. C. (2004). How do I love thee? Let me count the Js: Implicit egotism and interpersonal attraction. *Journal of Personality and Social Psychology, 87*, 665–683.

Karpinski, A. (2004). Measuring self-esteem using the Implicit Association Test: The role of the other. *Personality and Social Psychology Bulletin, 30*, 22–34.

Karpinski, A., Steinberg, J. A., Versek, B., & Alloy, L. B. (2005). The Breadth-based Adjective Rating Task (BART) as an indirect measure of self-esteem. *Social Cognition*.

Kernis, M. H., Whisenhunt, C. R., Waschull, S. B., Greenier, K. D., Berry, A. J., Herlocker, C. E., et al. (1998). Multiple facets of self-esteem and their relations to depressive symptoms. *Personality and Social Psychology Bulletin, 24*, 657–668.

Kitayama, S., & Karasawa, M. (1997). Implicit self-esteem in Japan: Name letters and birthday numbers. *Personality and Social Psychology Bulletin, 23*, 736–742.

Koole, S. L., Dijksterhuis, A., & van Knippenberg, A. (2001). What's in a name: Implicit self-esteem and the automatic self. *Journal of Personality and Social Psychology, 80*, 669–685.

Lindeman, M., & Verkasalo, M. (1995). Personality, situation, and positive–negative asymmetry in socially desirable responding. *European Journal of Personality, 9*, 125–134.

Miller, G. A., & Chapman, J. P. (2001). Misunderstanding analysis of covariance. *Journal of Abnormal Psychology, 110*, 40–48.

Monroe, S. M., & Hadjiyannakis, K. (2002). The social environment and depression: Focusing on severe life stress. In I. H. Gotlib & C. L. Hammen (Eds.), *Handbook of depression* (pp. 314–340). New York: Guilford Press.

Monroe, S. M., & McQuaid, J. R. (1994). Measuring life stress and assessing its impact on mental health. In W. R. Avison & I. H. Gotlib (Eds.), *Stress and mental health: Contemporary issues and prospects for the future* (pp. 43–73). New York: Plenum Press.

Needles, D. J., & Abramson, L. Y. (1990). Positive life events, attributional style, and hopefulness: Testing a model of recovery from depression. *Journal of Abnormal Psychology, 99*, 156–165.

Nuttin, J. M., Jr. (1985). Narcissism beyond gestalt awareness: The name letter effect. *European Journal of Social Psychology, 15*, 353–361.

Nuttin, J. M., Jr. (1987). Affective consequences of mere ownership: The name letter effect in twelve European languages. *European Journal of Social Psychology, 17*, 381–402.

Pelham, B. W., Mirenberg, M. C., & Jones, J. T. (2002). Why Susie sells seashells by the seashore: Implicit egotism and major life decisions. *Journal of Personality and Social Psychology, 82*, 469–487.

Reilly-Harrington, N., Alloy, L. B., Fresco, D. M., & Whitehouse, W. G. (1999). Cognitive styles and life events interact to predict bipolar and unipolar symptomatology. *Journal of Abnormal Psychology, 108*, 567–578.

Roberts, J. E., & Monroe, S. M. (1992). Vulnerable self-esteem and depressive symptoms: Prospective findings comparing three alternative conceptualizations. *Journal of Personality and Social Psychology, 62*, 804–812.

Roberts, J. E., & Monroe, S. M. (1999). Vulnerable self-esteem and social processes in depression: Toward an interpersonal model of self-esteem regulation. In T. Joiner & J. C. Coyne (Eds.), *The interactional nature of depression* (pp. 149–187). Washington, DC: American Psychological Association.

Rosenberg, M. (1965). *Society and the adolescent self-image*. Princeton, NJ: Princeton University Press.

Rosenberg, M. (1979). *Conceiving the self*. New York: Basic Books.

Safford, S. M., Alloy, L. B., Abramson, L. Y., & Crossfield, A. G. (in press). Negative cognitive style as a predictor of negative life events in depression-prone individuals: A test of the stress-generation hypothesis. *Journal of Affective Disorders.*

Spitzer, R., Endicott, J., & Robins, E. (1978). Research diagnostic criteria: Rationale and reliability. *Archives of General Psychiatry, 35*, 773–782.

Steinberg, J. A., & Karpinski, A. (2003). *The relationship between measures of implicit self-esteem and depression.* Unpublished raw data, Temple University, Philadelphia, PA, USA.

Watson, D., & Kendall, P. C. (1989). Understanding anxiety and depression: Their relation to negative and positive affective states. In P. C. Kendall & D. Watson (Eds.), *Anxiety and depression: Distinctive and overlapping features* (pp. 3–26). San Diego, CA: Academic Press.

Weissman, A., & Beck, A. T. (1978). *Development and validation of the Dysfunctional Attitudes Scale: A preliminary investigation.* Paper presented at the meeting of the American Educational Research Association, Toronto, Canada.

Self and Identity, 6: 118–136, 2007
http://www.psypress.com/sai
ISSN: 1529-8868 print/1529-8876 online
DOI: 10.1080/15298860601118835

Psychology Press
Taylor & Francis Group

Implicit Self and Affect Regulation: Effects of Action Orientation and Subliminal Self Priming in an Affective Priming Task

SANDER L. KOOLE
LINDA H. M. COENEN

Vrije Universiteit Amsterdam, Amsterdam, The Netherlands

Two studies examined the impact of subliminal self-activation on affect regulation among action- versus state-oriented individuals. Action orientation is a regulatory mode characterized by decisiveness and initiative, whereas state orientation is a regulatory mode characterized by indecisiveness and hesitation. According to the model of intuitive affect regulation (Koole & Kuhl, in press), action-oriented individuals have stronger associations between the implicit self and affect regulation systems than state-oriented individuals. This prediction was tested in an affective priming task (Fazio, Sanbonmatsu, Powell, & Kardes, 1986). As expected, subliminal self primes triggered down-regulation of negative affect among action-oriented participants. By contrast, subliminal self primes triggered persistence of negative affect among state-oriented participants. Supraliminal self primes had no parallel effects. The implicit self may thus play a key role in affect regulation and volitional action control.

The self plays a vital role in people's emotional lives. Such common emotions as guilt, shame, and nostalgia only arise in relation to the self (Sedikides, Wildschut, & Baden, 2004; Tangney & Dearing, 2002). Likewise, people's sense of self-esteem shapes their emotional reactions to success and failure (Brown & Dutton, 1995). Finally, affirming the self protects people against negative ruminations and stress (Cresswell et al., 2005; Koole, Smeets, van Knippenberg, & Dijksterhuis, 1999), whereas focusing on the self's shortcomings renders people vulnerable to anxiety and depression (Higgins, 1987; Pyszczynski & Greenberg, 1987).

To date, research on the interface between self and emotion has relied almost exclusively on conscious, explicit measures. Recent work, however, suggests that self and emotion are to a large extent mediated by unconscious, implicit processes (Conner & Barrett, 2005; Greenwald & Banaji, 1995; Hetts, Sakuma, & Pelham, 1999; Spencer, Jordan, Logel, & Zanna, 2005; Koole & DeHart, in press; Tesser & Martin, 1996; Zajonc, 1998). The question thus arises whether self and emotion also

This research was supported by an Innovation Grant from the Netherlands Organization for Scientific Research (NWO) to SK.

Correspondence should be addressed to: Sander L. Koole, Department of Social Psychology, Vrije Universiteit Amsterdam, van der Boechorststraat 1, NL-1081 BT Amsterdam, The Netherlands. E-mail: SL.Koole@psy.vu.nl interface on implicit levels. In the present research, we provide some initial answers to this question. More specifically, we suggest that the implicit self has important affect regulation functions. Efficient affect regulation supports volitional action control (Koole & Kuhl, in press). It therefore stands to reason that the affect regulation functions of the implicit self may be more developed among action-oriented individuals, who are characterized by decisiveness and initiative, than among state-oriented individuals, who are characterized by indecisiveness and hesitation. In the following, we explain the theoretical rationale for linking the implicit self to affect regulation among action- versus state-oriented individuals. Furthermore, we present two empirical studies that tested our theoretical analysis.

Implicit Self: Research Findings and Models

Consciousness has traditionally been considered a core characteristic of selfhood (Baumeister, 1998; Kihlstrom & Klein, 1994). Nevertheless, there is growing evidence for the importance of implicit processes within the self. The earliest and most extensive evidence relates to implicit positivity towards self (Koole & DeHart, in press; Pelham, Carvallo, & Jones, 2005; Spencer et al., 2005). As it turns out, people evaluate self-associated stimuli more positively than self-dissociated stimuli, even when people are unaware of any association between the self and the stimuli at hand. This tendency towards "implicit self-esteem" (Greenwald & Banaji, 1995) is pervasive across many different domains and even influences major life decisions (Pelham et al., 2005).

The implicit self includes not just global evaluations of the self (i.e., implicit self-esteem), but also contains more differentiated self-knowledge. For instance, implicit self-evaluations in one motive domain (e.g., autonomy) do not necessarily transfer to implicit self-evaluations in other motive domains (e.g., relatedness or competence; Koole, 2004). Likewise, subliminal presentation of other persons can instigate social comparison processes on both evaluative (good – bad) and descriptive (e.g., intelligent – stupid) dimensions (Stapel & Blanton, 2005). Finally, representations of collective identities (such as gender or sports-team membership) can vary independently of implicit representations of individual identity (Hetts et al., 1999; Rudman & Goodwin, 2004; Sherman & Kim, 2005).

In view of the broad range of implicit self phenomena, it seems quite challenging to explain which cognitive representations might underlie the implicit self. The most popular type of current theoretical models hold that the implicit self is based on associations (Dijksterhuis, 2004; Gawronski, Bodenhausen, & Becker, in press; Greenwald et al., 2002). According to associative models, implicit self processes are based on automatic associations between self-representations and other representations. These automatic associations are formed by frequently pairing the self with other representations (Dijksterhuis, 2004). Once established, automatic associations can be activated by relevant cues (which trigger the relevant associations). Associative processes are generally assumed to be primitive (i.e., computationally simple) and relatively insensitive to attempts at strategic control. Associative models thus imply that the implicit self will support mainly relatively rigid forms of action control, such as habitual behavior.

Although associations are likely to be important in the implicit self, the implicit self may involve more than merely associations. For instance, some studies have found that subliminal self primes can lead people to break with habitual patterns of thought (i.e., social stereotyping; Macrae, Bodenhausen, & Milne, 1998). Other work has found that implicit self-representations vary as a function of self-defense motives. When the self is threatened, for instance, individuals with high self-esteem (Jones, Pelham, Mirenberg, & Hetts, 2002) and action-oriented individuals (Koole, 2004) display increases in implicit self-esteem relative to no-threat conditions. Similar defensive increases in implicit self-esteem are not observed among individuals with low self-esteem or low action orientation. Finally, recent studies have found that measured or manipulated implicit self-esteem predicts lowered negative affect (Conner & Barrett, 2005; Dijksterhuis, 2004), suggesting that the implicit self plays in important role in affect regulation. In sum, there is converging evidence that the implicit self is involved in strategic forms of self-regulation. This link between the implicit self and self-regulation would not be a priori predicted by associative models.

The Implicit Self and Intuitive Affect Regulation

The involvement of the implicit self in strategic self-regulation suggests that the implicit self may be mediated—at least in part—by more complex cognitive processes. In line with this, *personality systems interactions (PSI) theory* has proposed that complex cognitive integration processes play an important role in the implicit self (Kuhl, 2000; Kuhl & Koole, 2004). According to PSI theory, the implicit self is grounded in parallel-distributed processing that integrates inputs from many different subsystems. Parallel-distributed processing can handle vast amounts of complex information at much higher speeds than serial processing (Rumelhart, McClelland, & the PDP Research Group, 1986). Implicit self-representations therefore have the computational capacity to integrate the totality of the person's needs, motives, and autobiographical experiences in flexible and context-sensitive ways.

From the perspective of PSI theory, the implicit self is—at least in principle— ideally suited for supporting affect regulation. First, the implicit self is capable of fast and efficient information processing (much faster than the conscious processing). This is most convenient, because people's affective reactions often unfold very rapidly (Berridge & Winkielman, 2003; Zajonc, 1998). Second, the implicit self has access to the totality of the person's goals, motives, and needs that are relevant to the given situation. The implicit self can thus regulate the person's affective states in a manner that is sensitive to the person's broader goals, motives, needs, and contextual demands. Affect regulation that is controlled by the implicit self is flexible, due to the large processing capacity of the implicit self, and efficient, due to the rapid processing abilities of the implicit self. We refer to affect regulation that is controlled by the implicit self as *intuitive affect regulation* (Koole & Jostmann, 2004; Koole & Kuhl, in press).

Intuitive affect regulation is a complex process. Consequently, people have to learn how to use the implicit self to engage in intuitive affect regulation (Koole & Kuhl, in press; Kuhl, 2000). A schematic model of this learning process is displayed in Figure 1. Intuitive affect regulation skills are assumed to depend on associations between the implicit self and emotion systems. When the implicit self has formed strong associations with emotion systems (see the left half of Figure 1), the implicit self will be better able to control the person's affective states. When the implicit self has formed weak associations with emotion systems (see the right half of Figure 1), the implicit self will be less able to control the person's affective states. The skill model further assumes that the formation of associations between the implicit self and emotion systems depends on the social environment (Kuhl, 2000). When the

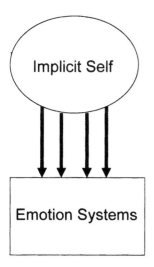

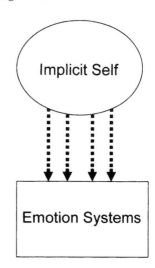

(A) Strong intuitive affect regulation skills   (B) Weak intuitive affect regulation skills

FIGURE 1 Model of intuitive affect regulation.

social environment supports the person's autonomy in dealing with aversive situations, the implicit self will be able to develop strong connections with the affect systems. By contrast, when the social environment is hostile, indifferent, or controlling, the implicit self becomes inhibited and thereby less able to connect with emotion systems.

Although intuitive affect regulation skills are by definition inaccessible to introspection, people may observe the consequences of these skills (or lack thereof) in their behavior. Individuals with strong intuitive affect regulation skills will be able to maintain positive affect even in the face of obstacles and frustrations. Strong intuitive affect regulation skills thus allow individuals to pursue their goals in an unhesitating manner, even under stressful circumstances. Consequently, strong intuitive affect regulation skills may go hand in hand with action orientation. Action orientation is a *meta-static* (change-promoting) regulatory mode that is characterized by decisiveness and initiative (Kuhl, 1984, 1994). By contrast, individuals with weak intuitive affect regulation skills will be vulnerable to intrusions by aversive affective states, especially under stressful circumstances. Weak intuitive affect regulation skills should therefore be associated with state orientation. State orientation is a *cata-static* (change-preventing) regulatory mode that is characterized by indecisiveness and hesitation.

Kuhl (1981, 1994) developed a scale for assessing individual differences in action versus state orientation. Research on action versus state orientation fits well with the model of intuitive affect regulation. First, autonomy-supportive parenting styles are associated with enhanced action orientation in children (see Koole, Kuhl, Jostmann, & Finkenauer, 2006, for a review). The developmental precursors of action orientation thus correspond with the conditions that theoretically should foster intuitive affect regulation skills. Second, action-oriented individuals are more efficient affect regulators than state-oriented individuals, as evidenced in self-reports (e.g., Baumann, Kaschel, & Kuhl, 2005; Brunstein & Olbrich, 1985), physiological functioning (Heckhausen & Strang, 1988), and implicit measures (Jostmann, Koole, van der Wulp, & Fockenberg, 2005; Koole & Fockenberg, 2006; Koole & Jostmann, 2004). Finally, there is initial evidence that action-oriented individuals use the implicit self to regulate affect (Koole & Jostmann, 2004). Among action-oriented individuals, increases in affect regulation (i.e., faster recognitions of happy faces among angry crowds) were found to be mediated by increases in self-activation (as measured by a response-latency task). State-oriented individuals showed no such mediation. The latter findings bolster the notion that the affect regulation functions of the implicit self are especially developed among action-oriented individuals.

The Present Research and Hypotheses

In the present research, we further addressed the role of the implicit self in affect regulation among action- versus state-oriented individuals. Previous research on this topic was correlational and measured the implicit self in a self-evaluation task that called participants' attention to the self (Koole & Jostmann, 2004). The present research extended this work by examining the causal impact of the implicit self on affect regulation. Moreover, the present research used a subliminal procedure to activate the implicit self, thereby ruling out any influence of conscious self-reflection.

To activate the implicit self, we used a subliminal priming technique (e.g., Macrae et al., 1998). If the implicit self is indeed strongly associated with affect systems among action-oriented individuals, then priming the implicit self should trigger intuitive affect regulation among action-oriented individuals. Because state-oriented individuals are assumed to have weak associations between the implicit self and affect systems, priming the implicit self should not trigger intuitive affect regulation among state-oriented individuals.

To measure affect regulation, we used an affective priming task (Fazio et al., 1986), a widely researched paradigm that measures rapid affective processing (see Fazio, 2001; Klauer & Musch, 2003, for reviews). In the affective priming task, participants are presented with a number of positively and negatively valenced words (e.g., *hate, love*) and are asked to classify these target words as positive or negative as quickly as possible. Briefly before each target word (usually around 300 ms), a positive or negative prime word is flashed. Although the affective priming task has traditionally been used to measure automatic activation of affective responses, the task can also be used to investigate intuitive affect-regulation processes. In particular, past research has shown that intuitive affect regulation promotes faster evaluations of positive targets and slower evaluations of negative targets (Koole & Fockenberg, 2006). Evaluation latencies following negative affective primes therefore served as our index of intuitive affect regulation in the present research.

The implicit self primes were embedded in the affective priming task. As can be seen in Figure 2A, we set the time between the affective prime and target presentation at 300 ms, a stimulus onset asynchrony (SOA) that is commonly used to investigate automatic affective priming (e.g., Fazio et al., 1986). Moreover, intuitive affect regulation processes are most effective in the affective priming task with an SOA of around 300 ms (Koole & Fockenberg, 2006). As can be seen in Figure 2B, we added two brief stimulus presentations before the presentation of the fixation point. The first stimulus was presented as a forward mask, whereas the second stimulus contained the self prime manipulation. Pilot tests had shown that this intermediate prime was not consciously perceptible. The contents of the subliminal primes were experimentally varied, such that they were either or not self-related.

(A) Standard affective priming task

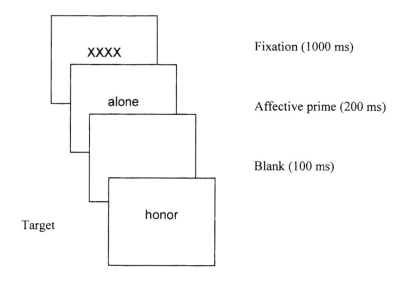

(B) Modified affective priming task

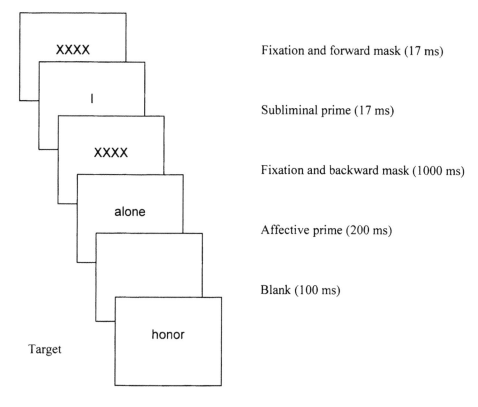

FIGURE 2 Standard (A) and modified (B) versions of the affective priming task.

We assumed that subliminally priming self-related words would activate the implicit self. Among action-oriented participants, the subliminal self primes were therefore expected to trigger intuitive affect regulation, as indicated by faster evaluations of positive targets and slower evaluations of negative targets in response to negative affective primes. No increase in intuitive affect regulation due to subliminal self priming was predicted for state-oriented participants. Study 1 provided an initial test of these predictions. Study 2 sought to replicate Study 1 and examined whether similar effects could be obtained with supraliminal self primes.

Study 1

Method

Participants and Design

Fifty paid volunteers from the Vrije Universiteit Amsterdam (22 women and 28 men,[1] average age 21) participated in the study. The design was 2 (Orientation: action vs. state; between participants) × 2 (Self Prime: yes vs. no; within participants) × 2 (Affective Prime: positive vs. negative; within participants) × 2 (Target Valence: positive vs. negative; within participants) mixed factorial. The main dependent variable consisted of response latencies in the affective priming task.

Procedure and Materials

Upon arrival in the laboratory, participants were led to individual cubicles, each containing a computer. The experimenter explained that the instructions of the present research would be administered via a computer-program and left. Participants started the program by pressing a button on the keyboard. Participants were first informed that the investigation would consist of a number of unrelated studies, which were supposedly administered together for efficiency reasons. Participants first completed a set of personality questionnaires that included an assessment of individual differences in action versus state orientation and some other personality traits. Participants subsequently performed an affective priming task. Finally, participants supplied some biographical information, and were thanked, debriefed, and paid.

Assessment of action versus state orientation. Individual differences in action versus state orientation were assessed by the demand-related[2] subscale (AOD) of the Action Control Scale (ACS90). The ACS90 has been developed and extensively validated by Kuhl and associates (Kuhl, 1994; see Diefendorff, Hall, Lord, & Strean, 2000; Koole & Kuhl, in press; Kuhl & Beckmann, 1994, for reviews). Effects of the ACS90, have been found across a wide range of different measures and domains, including intention memory, physiological arousal, medicine intake, therapeutic outcomes, athletic performance, and work psychology. Moreover, the effects of the ACS90 are not due to self-efficacy (Diefendorff, 2004), implicit or explicit achievement motivation (Heckhausen & Strang, 1988; Jostmann & Koole, 2006), neuroticism (Baumann & Kuhl, 2002), self-esteem (Koole, 2004), conscious emotion regulation strategies (Koole & Jostmann, 2004), or any of the "Big Five" personality dimensions (Diefendorff et al., 2000).

The AOD scale has 12 items (Cronbach's alpha = .74). An illustrative item is: "When I know I must finish something soon: A. I have to push myself to get started.

B. I find it easy to get it over and done with". In this example, the action-oriented option is B (in the actual scale, the order of action- versus state-oriented choices was counter-balanced; for the other AOD items, see Diefendorff et al., 2000). Action-oriented choices were coded as "1", whereas state-oriented choices were coded as "0" and summed for the entire subscale. Participants who made 7 or more action-oriented choices were assigned to the action-oriented group ($N = 21$); participants who made 6 or fewer action-oriented choices were assigned to the state-oriented group ($N = 29$).[3]

Other individual differences. Our personality assessment also included the Threat-related subscale of the ACS90 (AOT; Cronbach's alpha = .78) and measures of extraversion and neuroticism. The latter two measures were based on Hofstee, De Raad, and Goldberg (1992). For the extraversion scale (Cronbach's alpha = .79), there were three adjectives indicating high extraversion (*outgoing, spontaneous,* and *open*) and six adjectives indicating low extraversion (*closed, introverted, surly, reserved, inscrutable,* and *inaccessible*). For the neuroticism scale (Cronbach's alpha = .81), there were three adjectives indicating low neuroticism (*sober-minded, imperturbable, and cool*) and six adjectives indicating high neuroticism (*panicky, emotional, overly sensitive, nervy, sentimental,* and *hypersensitive*).

Affective priming task. The affective priming task was modeled after Fazio et al. (1986) and Koole and Fockenberg (2006). The task was described as a study on the evaluation of words. During each trial, a row of four Xs would appear in the center of the computer screen. After this, a prime word was flashed on the computer screen for 17 ms. During one half of the trials, the prime word was self-related ("ik", which means "I" in Dutch). During the remaining trials, the prime word was neutral ("de" which means "the" in Dutch). The subliminal prime was immediately overwritten by a second row of four Xs that remained on screen for 1000 ms. The rows of Xs served as a fixation point and as forward and backward masks of the intervening priming word. Next, an affective prime word appeared on the computer screen for 200 ms. Participants were told to ignore these briefly appearing words, as they were merely meant to serve as distracters. After the affective prime word disappeared, the computer screen went blank for 100 ms before the appearance of the target word. Thus, the SOA was 300 ms.

As soon as the target word appeared, participants were to indicate the valence of the sentence as quickly and accurately as possible. Participants were to press the "a" button (placed to the extreme left of the keyboard) when the target word was negative or the "6" button (placed on the number pad to the extreme right of the keyboard) when the target word was positive. The target word disappeared from the screen after participants responded. At that point, the computer screen went blank for one second before the onset of the next trial. The affective priming task began with 4 warm-up trials, followed by 24 experimental trials. The trials were presented in a different random order for each participant.

The stimuli for the affective priming task were pilot-tested in previous research (Koole & Fockenberg, 2006). The negative primes were: *alleen* (alone), *kwaad* (angry), *straf* (punishment), *streng* (authoritarian), *dwang* (force), and *schelden* (to scold). The positive primes were: *eer* (honor), *liefde* (love), *aandacht* (attention), *aardig* (kind), *beloning* (reward), and *vrienden* (friends). The negative targets were: *haat* (hate), *schuldig* (guilty), *schaamte* (shame), *ruzie* (quarrel), *slaan* (to hit), and *verlaten* (abandoned). The positive targets were: *trots* (proud), *vrede* (peace), *samen* (together), *vertrouwen* (trust), *geven* (to give), and *gezellig* (cozy). Notably, the stimuli were all related to social rewards or punishments, in line with our theoretical assumption that intuitive affect regulation is socially conditioned (Koole & Kuhl, in press). All affective primes and targets appeared twice, once with a subliminal self prime and once with a subliminal neutral prime. The trials of the affective priming task were presented in a different random order for each participant.

Results

Before the main analysis, we removed wrong responses (4.2% of all responses) from the dataset. To reduce the role of outliers, we replaced responses >1500 ms by 1500 ms (4.0% of all responses) and responses <300 ms by 300 ms (0.09% of all responses). Notably, we obtained equivalent results when we deleted outliers from the dataset or log-transformed the evaluation latencies.

We subjected average evaluation latencies to a 2 (orientation) × 2 (self prime) × 2 (affective prime) × 2 (target valence) analysis of variance (ANOVA). Relevant means are displayed in Table 1. The analysis yielded a marginal effect of target valence, which indicated that positive targets were evaluated more quickly than negative targets, $F(1, 48) = 3.43$, $p = .070$ ($M = 766$ vs. $M = 790$). The analysis further revealed a marginal interaction between orientation, self prime, and target valence, $F(1, 48) = 3.35$, $p = .073$, and a significant interaction between orientation, affective prime, and target valence, $F(1, 48) = 6.19$, $p < .02$. Most importantly, there was a significant interaction between orientation, self prime, affective prime, and target valence, $F(1, 48) = 5.51$, $p < .03$. To interpret this four-way interaction, we analyzed the results by self prime condition.

In the self-priming conditions, a 2 (orientation) × 2 (affective prime) × 2 (target valence) ANOVA yielded an interaction between orientation and target valence, $F(1, 48) = 4.47$, $p = .073$, and the predicted three-way interaction between orientation, affective prime, and target valence, $F(1, 48) = 12.58$, $p < .002$. To further understand this effect, we analyzed the results separately for positive and negative primes. Following positive primes, there were no significant effects, $Fs < 1$. Following negative primes, there was a significant interaction between orientation and target valence, $F(1, 48) = 30.44$, $p < .001$. The latter effect implied that action- versus state-oriented participants responded differently to negative primes. Following negative

TABLE 1 Average Evaluation Latencies in Milliseconds as a Function of Orientation, Subliminal Self Prime, Affective Prime, and Target Valence (Study 1)

	Affective prime valence			
	Positive target valence		Negative target valence	
	Positive	Negative	Positive	Negative
Subliminal self prime				
Action orientation	762 (163)	730 (163)	693 (116)	802 (151)
State orientation	779 (294)	799 (243)	853 (241)	768 (198)
Subliminal non-self prime				
Action orientation	749 (159)	763 (155)	739 (155)	765 (129)
State orientation	792 (284)	862 (262)	840 (254)	805 (209)

primes, state-oriented participants were significantly slower to evaluate positive rather than negative targets, $F(1, 20) = 10.77$, $p < .005$ ($M = 853$ vs. $M = 768$). Action-oriented participants displayed the opposite pattern. Following negative primes, action-oriented participants were significantly faster to evaluate positive rather than negative targets, $F(1, 28) = 21.86$, $p < .001$ ($M = 693$ vs. $M = 802$).

In the non-self-priming conditions, a 2 (orientation) × 2 (affective prime) × 2 (target valence) ANOVA only yielded a marginal effect of target valence, $F(1, 48) = 3.70$, $p = .060$. Positive targets were evaluated more quickly than negative targets ($M = 768$ vs. $M = 802$). No other effects were significant, $ps < 1$.

Supplementary analyses.   AOD was significantly positively correlated with AOT, $r(50) = .46$, and significantly negatively correlated with neuroticism, $r(50) = -.47$ (both $ps < .002$). AOD was not significantly correlated with extraversion, $r(50) = .16$, $p = .267$. When we repeated our analyses with AOT instead of AOD, we found a four-way interaction between orientation, self prime, affective prime, and target valence that paralleled the pattern obtained for AOD, $p < .05$. The AOT scale may have had a parallel effect because of its strong correlation with the AOD scale. However, because we only predicted effects of AOD, it remained to seen whether this effect could be replicated. Neither extraversion nor neuroticism yielded equivalent effects as AOD.

Discussion

As expected, subliminally priming the self differentially influenced action- versus state-oriented individuals in their responses to negative affective primes. When action-oriented participants were subliminally primed with the self, they responded to negative primes with slower evaluations of negative rather than positive targets. This pattern is consistent with an attentional switch away from negative affect and towards positive affect. Subliminal self primes thus triggered intuitive affect regulation among action-oriented participants.

Subliminal self priming led to the opposite pattern among state-oriented participants. Indeed, when subliminally primed with the self, state-oriented participants responded to negative primes with faster evaluations of negative rather than positive targets. This pattern is consistent with persistence of negative affect. Although we did not anticipate this effect, Koole and Kuhl (2003) reasoned on theoretical grounds that activating the implicit self in a negative context increases the likelihood that the self makes contact with painful experiences (see also Kaschel & Kuhl, 2003; Rosahl, Tennigkeit, Kuhl, & Haschke, 1993). Because state-oriented individuals do not have well-developed affect regulation skills, implicit self-activation might render them more vulnerable in the confrontation with negative affect. However, the effects of subliminal self priming among state-oriented individuals were unexpected. It was therefore important to establish if we could replicate these effects in Study 2.

Notably, Study 1 failed to find an overall affective priming effect. It is conceivable that the subliminal self primes somehow inhibited the emergence of an overall affective priming effect. It should be noted, however, that lack of an overall affective priming effect does not invalidate the finding of intuitive affect regulation in Study 1. Indeed, three recent experiments found intuitive affect regulation in an affective-priming task regardless of whether an overall affective priming was present, absent, or even reversed (Koole & Fockenberg, 2006). These findings suggest that intuitive affect regulation and overall affective priming effects are driven by distinct mechanisms. Intuitive affect regulation is presumably driven by dynamic self-regulation processes (Koole & Kuhl, in press), whereas overall affective priming effects probably result from response competition (Klauer & Musch, 2003).

Study 2

In Study 2, we sought to replicate the main findings of Study 1. Moreover, we added a condition with supraliminal self primes to the experimental design, to see if these would induce analogous effects as the subliminal priming manipulation. The model of intuitive affect regulation assumes that implicit self-representations are more strongly associated with emotion systems than explicit self-representations (Koole & Kuhl, in press; Kuhl, 2000). We thus expected that subliminal self primes would elicit stronger effects on intuitive affect regulation than supraliminal self primes.

Method

Participants and Design

Seventy-four paid volunteers from the Vrije Universiteit Amsterdam (38 women and 36 men, average age 21) participated in the study. The design was 2 (Orientation: action vs. state; between participants) × 2 (Self Prime Duration: 17 ms vs. 300 ms; between participants) × 2 (Self Prime: yes vs. no; within participants) × 2 (Affective Prime: positive vs. negative; within participants) × 2 (Target Valence: positive vs. negative; within participants) mixed factorial. The main dependent variable consisted of response latencies in the affective priming task.

Procedure and Materials

The assessment of AOD (Cronbach's alpha = .73) and AOT (Cronbach's alpha = .79), procedure and materials were largely the same as in Study 1. On the basis of their AOD scores, 40 participants were classified as action-oriented and 34 participants as state-oriented.

Study 2 differed from Study 1 in three respects. First, we added an experimental group for which the self primes were presented for 300 ms rather than 17 ms. Second, instead of measuring extraversion and neuroticism, we administered the Rosenberg Self-Esteem Scale (Cronbach's alpha = .84). Third, after the personality assessment, we measured participants' moods using the abbreviated Profile of Mood Scales (POMS; Shacham, 1983). The 32 POMS items were coded such that higher scores indicated more negative mood and averaged into a single index (Cronbach's alpha = .93).

Results

Before the main analysis, we removed wrong responses (8.0% of all responses) from the data set. We also replaced responses > 1500 ms with 1500 ms (6.3% of all responses) and responses < 300 ms with 300 ms (0.04% of all responses). The results were highly similar when we deleted these outliers or log-transformed the response latencies.

We subjected average evaluation latencies to a 2 (orientation) × 2 (self prime duration) × 2 (self prime) × 2 (affective prime) × 2 (target valence) ANOVA. This analysis revealed the predicted five-way interaction between orientation, self prime duration, self prime, affective, $F(1, 70) = 4.33$, $p < .05$. To unpack this interaction effect, we analyzed our results separately by self prime duration.

Subliminal self prime conditions. In the subliminal self prime conditions, we conducted a 2 (orientation) × 2 (self prime) × 2 (affective prime) × 2 (target valence) ANOVA. This analysis yielded an interaction between orientation and target valence, $F(1, 38) = 8.30$, $p < .007$, and the predicted interaction between orientation, self prime, affective prime, and target valence, $F(1, 38) = 7.80$, $p < .009$. Relevant means to this interaction are displayed in Table 2. We further analyzed this effect by self prime.

In the subliminal self-priming conditions, a 2 (orientation) × 2 (affective prime) × 2 (target valence) ANOVA yielded the predicted interaction between orientation, affective prime, and target valence, $F(1, 38) = 7.85$, $p < .009$. To further understand this effect, we analyzed the results separately by affective prime. Following positive primes, there were no significant effects, $ps > .21$. Following negative primes, there was a significant interaction between orientation and target valence, $F(1, 38) = 7.95$, $p < .009$. This interaction implied that action- versus state-oriented individuals responded differently to negative primes. Following negative primes, state-oriented participants were non-significantly slower to evaluate positive rather than negative targets, $F(1, 17) = 2.38$, $p = .141$ ($M = 846$ vs. $M = 784$). Action-oriented participants displayed the opposite pattern. Following negative primes, action-oriented participants were significantly faster to evaluate positive rather than negative targets, $F(1, 21) = 7.19$, $p = .014$ ($M = 740$ vs. $M = 805$).

In the subliminal non-self-priming conditions, a 2 (orientation) × 2 (affective prime) × 2 (target valence) ANOVA yielded a significant interaction between orientation, prime valence, and target valence, $F(1, 38) = 8.02$, $p < .008$. To further understand this effect, we analyzed the results separately by affective prime. Following negative primes, there were no significant effects, $ps > .27$. Following positive primes, there was a significant interaction between orientation and target valence, $F(1, 38) = 9.15$, $p < .004$. This interaction implied that action- versus state-oriented individuals responded differently to positive primes. Following positive primes, state-oriented participants were significantly slower to evaluate positive rather than negative targets, $F(1, 17) = 7.64$, $p < .02$ ($M = 857$ vs. $M = 763$). Action-oriented participants displayed the opposite pattern. Following positive primes,

TABLE 2 Average Evaluation Latencies in Milliseconds as a Function of Orientation, Subliminal Self Prime, Affective Prime, and Target Valence (Study 2)

	Affective prime valence			
	Positive target valence		Negative target valence	
	Positive	Negative	Positive	Negative
Subliminal self prime				
Action orientation	830 (178)	795 (227)	740 (127)	805 (184)
State orientation	799 (246)	833 (289)	846 (350)	784 (225)
Subliminal non-self prime				
Action orientation	754 (173)	812 (205)	793 (189)	797 (176)
State orientation	857 (300)	763 (258)	855 (274)	792 (252)

action-oriented participants were non-significantly faster to evaluate positive rather than negative targets, $F(1, 20) = 2.57$, $p = .124$ ($M = 755$ vs. $M = 812$). Because the latter effects did not emerge in Study 1, caution is warranted in interpreting the findings in the subliminal non-self-priming conditions.

Supraliminal self-prime conditions. In the supraliminal self prime conditions, we conducted a 2 (orientation) × 2 (self prime) × 2 (affective prime) × 2 (target valence) ANOVA. There was a main effect of target valence, $F(1, 32) = 4.15$, $p = .050$, which indicated that positive targets were evaluated more quickly than negative targets ($M = 773$ vs. $M = 803$). There was also a main effect of affective prime, $F(1, 32) = 6.30$, $p < .02$, which indicated that evaluations were quicker after positive than after negative primes ($M = 766$ vs. $M = 809$). There was a significant interaction between affective prime and target valence, $F(1, 32) = 8.19$, $p < .008$. In line with the affective priming effect, evaluations were quicker when they were preceded by congruent rather than incongruent affective primes ($M = 772$ vs. $M = 803$). Finally, there was an interaction between self prime and affective prime, $F(1, 32) = 5.20$, $p < .03$. Positive primes led to quicker evaluations than negative primes when the affective primes were preceded by self primes, $F(1, 33) = 9.33$, $p < .005$ ($M = 755$ vs. $M = 824$), but not when affective primes were preceded by non-self primes, $F(1, 33) = <1$.

Supplementary analyses. AOD was not reliably correlated with AOT, self-esteem, or negative mood, $ps > .12$. AOT was negatively correlated with negative mood, $r(74) = -.33$, $p < .005$. The effects of AOT, self-esteem, or negative mood did not parallel the effects of AOD.

Discussion

As in Study 1, the results of Study 2 showed that subliminal self primes led to intuitive affect regulation among action-oriented participants and persistence of negative affect among state-oriented participants. Study 2 further demonstrated that supraliminal self primes did not induce the same effects as subliminal self primes. Thus, differential affect regulation processes among action-oriented versus state-oriented participants were specifically triggered by subliminal self-activation. Finally, a general affective priming effect emerged when the affective priming task included supraliminal self primes, but not when the task included subliminal self primes. This set of findings is important, because it indicates that the affective priming stimuli in the present research were sufficiently strong to elicit affective priming (cf. Koole & Fockenberg, 2006). The subliminal self primes in Studies 1 and 2 may have disrupted the emergence of an overall affective priming effect, perhaps by inducing general increases in self-regulation (Macrae et al., 1998). This possibility may be tested in future research.

General Discussion

In the present research, we examined the role of the implicit self in affect regulation among action- versus state-oriented individuals. In two studies, we measured action versus state orientation and manipulated subliminal exposure to self primes in an affective priming task (Fazio et al., 1986). Intuitive affect regulation was indexed by faster evaluations of positive targets and slower evaluations of negative targets in response to negative affective primes (Koole & Fockenberg, 2006). Persistence of negative affect was indexed by slower evaluations of positive targets and faster evaluations of negative targets in response to negative affective primes. The results showed that subliminal self primes led to intuitive affect regulation among action-oriented individuals and persistence of negative affect among state-oriented individuals (Studies 1 and 2). Supraliminal self primes had no differential effects on action- versus state-oriented individuals (Study 2).

The present research provides further support for the model of intuitive affect regulation (Koole & Kuhl, in press). Previous research found correlational evidence that implicit self-representations mediate the unfolding of intuitive affect regulation processes among action-oriented individuals (Koole & Jostmann, 2004). The present research goes beyond this earlier work by demonstrating the causal role of the implicit self in triggering intuitive affect regulation among action-oriented individuals. Moreover, previous research used a response-latency measure of self-activation that did not completely rule out a potential influence of conscious self-reflection. By using a subliminal priming technique to manipulate activation of the implicit self, the present research demonstrates more conclusively that intuitive affect regulation among action-oriented individuals is under the control of the implicit self.

The implicit self triggered very different processes among state-oriented individuals, who displayed persistence of negative affect after subliminal self priming. This pattern of effects might seem counterintuitive. Nevertheless, these effects fit with previous observations. State-oriented individuals normally do not activate the implicit self when they are coping with negative affect (Koole & Jostmann, 2004). As the present findings indicate, state-oriented individuals may have good reasons to eschew this strategy. Activating the implicit self in a negative context may initially increase the likelihood that the self makes contact with negative experiences (Kaschel & Kuhl, 2003; Koole & Kuhl, 2003; see Koole & Fockenberg, 2006; Rosahl et al., 1993, for evidence). Down-regulation of this negative affect occurs in a subsequent stage, but only when the implicit self has strong connections with the person's emotion systems. Without strong intuitive affect regulation skills, activating the implicit self in a negative context may therefore increase persistence of negative affect. Using the implicit self in coping with negative affect thus appears to be a risky strategy for state-oriented individuals.

On the basis of the present research, one might wonder if the implicit self invariably undermines affect regulation among state-oriented individuals. Fortunately, a more optimistic conclusion is possible. It should be noted that the present research manipulated the implicit self on a trial-by-trial basis. The effects of the implicit self were thus measured on a *phasic* timescale (i.e., within a few seconds or less). The phasic timescale fits well with the self-regulatory style of action-oriented individuals, which is characterized by very rapid and dynamic processing (Koole & Kuhl, in press). However, the phasic timescale does not fit very well with the self-regulatory style of state-oriented individuals, which is characterized by relatively slow and static processing. It is therefore conceivable that state-oriented individuals may benefit from the implicit self on a slower timescale.

We recently examined the consequences of subliminal self-activation on a tonic timescale (i.e., over several minutes; Koole & Heslenfeld, 2006). In this study, a group of action- versus state-oriented participants performed a similar affective priming task to that in the present research. This time, however, participants repeated the task 10 consecutive times. The results during the first blocks replicated the present research: subliminal self-activation activated intuitive affect regulation among action-oriented individuals and persistence of negative affect among state-oriented participants. After the third block, however, the pattern shifted: subliminal self-activation no longer influenced action-oriented participants but exerted a significant influence on state-oriented participants, who displayed increased activation of positive affect in response to subliminal self-activation. These initial findings suggest that more extended activation of the implicit self may have more beneficial consequences among state-oriented individuals.

The differential effects of short versus long activation of the implicit self can be explained in terms of the model of intuitive affect regulation (Koole & Kuhl, in press; see Figure 1). Presumably, action-oriented individuals have strong associations between the implicit self and emotion systems. Consequently, action-oriented individuals need only minimal amounts of activation to mobilize the affect regulation resources of the implicit self. By contrast, state-oriented individuals are presumed to have weak associations between the implicit self and emotion systems. State-oriented individuals will therefore need greater amounts of activation to mobilize the affect regulation resources of the implicit self. In practice, these rather subtle processing differences imply that state-oriented individuals require more extended support from their social environment (e.g., their significant others) than action-oriented individuals. Past work has indeed found that external motivational support is more beneficial to state-oriented individuals than to action-oriented individuals (see Koole, Kuhl, Jostmann, & Vohs, 2005).

In more general terms, the present findings have important implications for the theoretical understanding of the implicit self. As discussed earlier, most theories to date suggested that the implicit self is entirely based on simple associations (e.g., Greenwald et al., 2002). Nevertheless, the present findings are difficult to explain in terms of simple associative processing. Priming the implicit self led action-oriented individuals to respond with faster evaluations of positive targets and slower evaluations of negative targets after negative affective primes. In associative terms, this would imply that action-oriented individuals have automatic associations between positive and negative affect. The latter seems theoretically implausible, and is at odds with findings in Study 2 showing that, in the absence of subliminal self primes, action-oriented individuals displayed automatic priming of negative affect. The present findings are therefore consistent with models that attribute more complex, integrative functions to the implicit self (Koole & DeHart, in press; Kuhl, 2000).

The present research further supports the notion that the self has important affect regulation functions. This notion has been put forward by various theorists of the self (e.g., Brown & Dutton, 1995; Conner & Barrett, 2005; Higgins, 1987; Tesser, 2000). A prominent theory in this regard is Tesser's (2000) confluence model, which holds that various self-esteem maintenance mechanisms help individuals to maintain an affective balance. Like the model of intuitive affect regulation, the confluence model assumes that the self can facilitate affect regulation, and that this process often occurs on implicit levels. However, intuitive affect regulation is assumed to support efficient self-regulation (or action control) rather than self-esteem maintenance. Consistent with this, action orientation has been linked to more efficient self-regulation, especially under stressful conditions (Jostmann & Koole, 2006, in press). By contrast, self-esteem maintenance has been found to interfere with self-regulation under stressful conditions (Baumeister, Heatherton, & Tice, 1993). Thus, although intuitive affect regulation bears some surface similarity with self-esteem maintenance, the two processes are likely to be driven by distinct underlying mechanisms.

The present research is not without limitations. First, our operationalization of action versus state orientation was correlational rather than experimental. Action orientation can be increased through therapy (Schulte, Hartung, & Wilke, 1997) or directed exercise (Stiensmeier-Pelster & Schürmann, 1994). It would thus be important to establish whether situationally induced action orientation yields similar effects as chronic action orientation. Second, the present research used only one type of self prime (the word "I" in Dutch). Future work should address the impact of other self-related stimuli on affect regulation. For example, personal names or name letters might be strong primes of the implicit self (Koole & Pelham, 2003). Finally, the present research relied exclusively on the affective priming task to assess affect regulation. Future work should include different implicit and explicit measures to document the influence of the implicit self on affect regulation.

Concluding Remarks

Psychologists have long known that the self is closely tied up with people's emotions. The present research adds to this that the self can even regulate people's emotional reactions on implicit levels. Activating the implicit self was found to promote efficient affect regulation among action-oriented individuals and persistence of negative affect among state-oriented individuals. The implicit self may thus play an important role in people's emotional lives.

Notes

1. In Studies 1 and 2, we found no effects of gender. Consequently, this factor was dropped from the analyses.
2. Kuhl (1994) introduced the labels "failure-related" and "decision-related" action orientation to what we refer to as "threat-related" and "demand-related" action orientation, respectively. The new labels map directly on to relevant constructs within PSI theory (e.g., Kuhl, 2000).
3. Equivalent results were obtained when AOD scores were used as continuous variables in regression analyses that paralleled the ANOVAs reported in the main body of this article. Because a regression approach made it impossible to inspect the absolute means in Studies 2 and 3, we report the ANOVA results in the main body of this article.

References

Baumann, N., Kaschel, R., & Kuhl, J. (2005). Striving for unwanted goals: Stress-dependent discrepancies between explicit and implicit achievement motives reduce subjective well-being and increase psychosomatic symptoms. *Journal of Personality and Social Psychology, 89*, 781–799.

Baumann, N., & Kuhl, J. (2002). Intuition, affect and personality: Unconscious coherence judgments and self-regulation of negative affect. *Journal of Personality and Social Psychology, 83*, 1213–1223.

Baumeister, R. F. (1998). The self. In D. Gilbert, S. T. Fiske, & G. Lindzey (Eds.), *Handbook of social psychology* (4th ed., Vol. 1, pp. 680–740). New York: McGraw-Hill.

Baumeister, R. F., Heatherton, T. F., & Tice, D. M. (1993). When ego threats lead to self-regulation failure: Negative consequences of high self-esteem. *Journal of Personality and Social Psychology, 64*, 141–156.

Berridge, K. C., & Winkielman, P. (2003). What is an unconscious emotion: The case for unconscious "liking". *Cognition and Emotion, 17*, 181–211.

Brown, J. D., & Dutton, K. A. (1995). The thrill of victory, the complexity of defeat: Self-esteem and people's emotional reactions to success and failure. *Journal of Personality and Social Psychology, 68,* 712–722.

Brunstein, J. C., & Olbrich, E. (1985). Personal helplessness and action control: Analysis of achievement-related cognitions, self-assessments, and performance. *Journal of Personality and Social Psychology, 48,* 1540–1551.

Conner, T., & Barrett, L. F. (2005). Implicit self-attitudes predict spontaneous affect in daily life. *Emotion, 5,* 476–488.

Creswell, J. D., Welch, W., Taylor, S. E., Sherman, D. K., Gruenewald, T., & Mann, T. (2005). Affirmation of personal values buffers neuroendocrine and psychological stress responses. *Psychological Science, 16,* 846–851.

Diefendorff, J. M. (2004). Examination of the roles of action-state orientation and goal orientation in the goal-setting and performance process. *Human Performance, 17,* 375–395.

Diefendorff, J. M., Hall, R. J., Lord, R. G., & Strean, M. L. (2000). Action-state orientation: Construct validity of a revised measure and its relationship to work-related variables. *Journal of Applied Psychology, 85,* 250–263.

Dijksterhuis, A. (2004). I like myself but I don't know why: Enhancing implicit self-esteem by subliminal evaluative conditioning. *Journal of Personality and Social Psychology, 86,* 345–355.

Fazio, R. H. (2001). On the automatic activation of associated evaluations: An overview. *Cognition and Emotion, 15,* 115–141.

Fazio, R. H., Sanbonmatsu, D. M., Powell, M. C., & Kardes, F. R. (1986). On the automatic evaluation of attitudes. *Journal of Personality and Social Psychology, 50,* 229–238.

Gawronski, B., Bodenhausen, G. V., & Becker, A. P. (in press). I like it, because I like myself: Associative self-anchoring and post-decisional change of implicit evaluations. *Journal of Experimental Social Psychology.*

Greenwald, A. G., & Banaji, M. R. (1995). Implicit social cognition: Attitudes, self-esteem, and stereotypes. *Psychological Review, 102,* 4–27.

Greenwald, A. G., Banaji, M. R., Rudman, L. A., Farnham, S. D., Nosek, B. A., & Mellott, D. S. (2002). A unified theory of attitudes, stereotypes, and self-concept. *Psychological Review, 109,* 3–25.

Heckhausen, H., & Strang, H. (1988). Efficiency under record performance demands: Exertion control—an individual difference variable? *Journal of Personality and Social Psychology, 55,* 489–498.

Hetts, J. J., Sakuma, M., & Pelham, B. W. (1999). Two roads to positive regard: Implicit and explicit self-evaluation and culture. *Journal of Experimental Social Psychology, 35,* 512–559.

Higgins, E. T. (1987). Self-discrepancy: A theory relating self and affect. *Psychological Review, 94,* 319–340.

Hofstee, W. K. B., De Raad, B., & Goldberg, L. R. (1992). Integration of the Big Five and Circumplex approaches to trait structure. *Journal of Personality and Social Psychology, 63,* 146–163.

Jones, J. T., Pelham, B. W., Mirenberg, M. C., & Hetts, J. J. (2002). Name letter preferences are not merely mere exposure: Implicit egotism as self-regulation. *Journal of Experimental Social Psychology, 38,* 170–177.

Jostmann, N. B., & Koole, S. L. (2006). *On the regulation of cognitive control: The moderating role of action versus state orientation.* Manuscript submitted for publication.

Jostmann, N. B., & Koole, S. L. (2006). On the waxing and waning of working memory: Action orientation moderates the impact of demanding relationship primes on working memory capacity. *Personality and Social Psychology Bulletin, 32,* 1716–1728.

Jostmann, N. B., Koole, S. L., Van der Wulp, N., & Fockenberg, D. (2005). Subliminal affect regulation: The moderating role of action versus state orientation. *European Psychologist, 10,* 209–217.

Kaschel, R., & Kuhl, J. (2003). Motivational counseling in an extended functional context: Personality systems interaction theory and assessment. In M. Cox & E. Klinger (Eds.), *Motivating people for change: A handbook of motivational counseling.* Chichester, UK: Wiley.

Kihlstrom, J. F., & Klein, S. B. (1994). The self as a knowledge structure. In R. S. Wyer, Jr. & T. K. Srull (Eds.), *Handbook of social cognition* (Vol. 1, pp. 153–208). Hillsdale, NJ: Lawrence Erlbaum Associates, Inc.

Klauer, K. C., & Musch, J. (2003). Affective priming: Findings and theories. In J. Musch & K. C. Klauer (Eds.), *The psychology of evaluation: Affective processes in cognition and emotion* (pp. 7–49). Mahwah, NJ: Lawrence Erlbaum Associates, Inc.

Koole, S. L. (2004). Volitional shielding of the self: Effects of action orientation and external demands on implicit self-evaluation. *Social Cognition, 22,* 117–146.

Koole, S. L., & DeHart, T. (in press). Self-affection without self-reflection: Origins, models, and consequences of implicit self-esteem. In C. Sedikides & S. Spencer (Eds.), *The self in social psychology.* New York: Psychology Press.

Koole, S. L., & Fockenberg, D. A. (2006). *Dynamic regulation of affective priming: The moderating role of action versus state orientation.* Manuscript submitted for publication.

Koole, S. L., & Heslenfeld, D. (2006). Unpublished data, Vrije Universiteit Amsterdam.

Koole, S. L., & Jostmann, N. (2004). Getting a grip on your feelings: Effects of action orientation and external demands on intuitive affect regulation. *Journal of Personality and Social Psychology, 87,* 974–990.

Koole, S. L., & Kuhl, J. (2003). In search of the real self: A functional perspective on optimal self-esteem and authenticity. *Psychological Inquiry, 14,* 43–48.

Koole, S. L., & Kuhl, J. (in press). Dealing with unwanted feelings: The role of affect regulation in volitional action control. In J. Shah & W. Gardner (Eds.), *Handbook of motivation science.* New York: Guilford.

Koole, S. L., Kuhl, J., Jostmann, N. B., & Finkenauer, C. (2006). Self-regulation in interpersonal relationships: The case of action versus state orientation. In K. D. Vohs & E. Finkel (Eds.), *Self and relationships: Connecting intrapersonal and interpersonal processes* (pp. 360–385). New York: Guilford.

Koole, S. L., Kuhl, J., Jostmann, N., & Vohs, K. D. (2005). On the hidden benefits of state orientation: Can people prosper without efficient affect regulation skills? In A. Tesser, J. Wood, & D. A. Stapel (Eds.), *On building, defending, and regulating the self: A psychological perspective* (pp. 217–243). London, UK: Taylor & Francis.

Koole, S. L., & Pelham, B. W. (2003). On the nature of implicit self-esteem: The case of the name letter effect. In S. Spencer, S. Fein, & M. P. Zanna (Eds.), *Motivated social perception: The Ontario symposium* (Vol. 9, pp. 93–116). Hillsdale, NJ: Lawrence Erlbaum Associates, Inc.

Koole, S. L., Smeets, K., van Knippenberg, A., & Dijksterhuis, A. (1999). The cessation of rumination through self-affirmation. *Journal of Personality and Social Psychology, 77,* 111–125.

Kuhl, J. (1981). Motivational and functional helplessness: The moderating effect of state versus action orientation. *Journal of Personality and Social Psychology, 40,* 155–170.

Kuhl, J. (1984). Volitional aspects of achievement motivation and learned helplessness: Toward a comprehensive theory of action-control. In B. A. Maher (Ed.), *Progress in experimental personality research* (Vol. 13, pp. 99–171). New York: Academic Press.

Kuhl, J. (1994). Action versus state orientation: Psychometric properties of the Action Control Scale (ACS-90). In J. Kuhl & J. Beckmann (Eds.), *Volition and personality: Action versus state orientation* (pp. 47–59). Göttingen, Germany: Hogrefe & Huber.

Kuhl, J. (2000). A functional-design approach to motivation and self-regulation: The dynamics of personality systems interactions. In M. Boekaerts, P. R. Pintrich, & M. Zeidner (Eds.), *Handbook of self-regulation* (pp. 111–169). San Diego, CA: Academic Press.

Kuhl, J., & Beckmann, J. (1994). *Volition and personality: Action versus state orientation.* Göttingen, Germany: Hogrefe & Huber.

Kuhl, J., & Koole, S. L. (2004). Workings of the will: A functional approach. In J. Greenberg, S. L. Koole, & T. Pyszczynski (Eds.), *Handbook of experimental existential psychology* (pp. 411–430). New York: Guilford.

Macrae, C. N., Bodenhausen, G. V., & Milne, A. B. (1998). Saying no to unwanted thoughts: Self-focus and the regulation of mental life. *Journal of Personality and Social Psychology, 74*, 578–589.

Pelham, B. W., Carvallo, M., & Jones, J. T. (2005). Implicit egotism. *Current Directions in Psychological Science, 14*, 106–110.

Pyszczynski, T., & Greenberg, J. (1987). Self-regulatory perseveration and the depressive self-focusing style: A self-awareness theory of reactive depression. *Psychological Bulletin, 102*, 122–138.

Rosahl, S. K., Tennigkeit, M., Kuhl, J., & Haschke, R. (1993). Handlungskontrolle und langsame Hirnpotentiale: Untersuchungen zum Einfluss subjektiv kritischer Wörter (Erste Ergebnisse) [Action control and slow brain potentials: Investigations on the influence of subjectively critical words. Preliminary findings]. *Zeitschrift für Medizinische Psychologie, 2*, 1–8.

Rudman, L. A., & Goodwin, S. A. (2004). Gender differences in automatic in-group bias: Why do women like women more than men like men? *Journal of Personality and Social Psychology, 87*, 494–509.

Rumelhart, D. E., McClelland, J. L., & The PDP Research Group (Eds.). (1986). *Parallel distributed processing* (Vol. 1). Cambridge, MA: MIT Press.

Schulte, D., Hartung, J., & Wilke, F. (1997). Handlungskontrolle der Angstbewältigung: Was macht Reizkonfrontationsverfahren so effektiv? [Action control in coping with anxiety: What makes exposure so effective?]. *Zeitschrift für Klinische Psychologie, 26*, 118–128.

Sedikides, C., Wildschut, T., & Baden, D. (2004). Nostalgia: Conceptual issues and existential functions. In J. Greenberg, S. L. Koole, & T. Pyszczynski (Eds.), *Handbook of experimental existential psychology* (pp. 200–214). New York: Guilford.

Shacham, S. (1983). A shortened version of the Profile of Mood States. *Journal of Personality Assessment, 47*, 305–306.

Sherman, D. K., & Kim, H. S. (2005). Is there an "I" in "team"? The role of the self in group-serving judgments. *Journal of Personality and Social Psychology, 88*, 108–120.

Spencer, S. J., Jordan, C. H., Logel, C. E., & Zanna, M. P. (2005). Nagging doubts and a glimmer of hope: The role of implicit self-esteem in self-image maintenance. In A. Tesser, J. Wood, & D. A. Stapel (Eds.), *On building, defending and regulating the self: A psychological perspective.* New York: Psychology Press.

Stapel, D. A., & Blanton, H. (2004). From seeing to being: Subliminal social comparisons affect implicit and explicit self-evaluations. *Journal of Personality and Social Psychology, 87*, 468–481.

Stiensmeier-Pelster, J., & Schürmann, M. (1994). Antecedents and consequences of action versus state orientation: Theoretical and empirical remarks. In J. Kuhl & J. Beckmann (Eds.), *Volition and personality: Action versus state orientation* (pp. 329–340). Göttingen, Germany: Hogrefe & Huber.

Tesser, A. (2000). On the confluence of self-esteem maintenance mechanisms. *Personality and Social Psychology Review, 4*, 290–299.

Tesser, A., & Martin, L. L. (1996). The psychology of evaluation. In E. T. Higgins & A. W. Kruglanski (Eds.), *Social psychology: Handbook of basic principles* (pp. 400–432). London: Guilford.

Zajonc, R. B. (1998). Emotions. In D. Gilbert, S. T. Fiske, & G. Lindzey (Eds.), *Handbook of social psychology* (4th ed., Vol. 1, pp. 591–632). New York: McGraw-Hill.

Self and Identity, 6: 137–153, 2007
http://www.psypress.com/sai
ISSN: 1529-8868 print/1529-8876 online
DOI: 10.1080/15298860601118850

Ψ Psychology Press
Taylor & Francis Group

Perfectionism and Explicit Self-esteem: The Moderating Role of Implicit Self-esteem

VIRGIL ZEIGLER-HILL

University of Southern Mississippi, Hattiesburg, Mississippi, USA

CAROL TERRY

University of Oklahoma, Norman, Oklahoma, USA

It has recently been proposed that individuals with discrepant low self-esteem (i.e., low explicit self-esteem but high implicit self-esteem) may be characterized as possessing a glimmer of hope (Spencer, Jordan, Logel, & Zanna, 2005). That is, these individuals may exhibit more optimism and less self-protection than is typically seen among individuals with low self-esteem. Consistent with the glimmer of hope hypothesis, we proposed that individuals with discrepant low self-esteem would report relatively high levels of perfectionism. The results of the present study support this prediction: Among individuals with low explicit self-esteem, those with high implicit self-esteem reported higher levels of maladaptive and adaptive perfectionism. Overall, the results suggest that the inclusion of implicit self-esteem enhances our understanding of the relationship between perfectionism and explicit self-esteem.

Previous research has found high self-esteem to be associated with markers of psychological adjustment such as happiness and satisfaction with life (e.g., Diener, 1984; Robins, Hendin, & Trzesniewski, 2001; Tennen & Affleck, 1993; see Baumeister, Campbell, Krueger, & Vohs, 2003, for a review); however, there is also a *dark side* to high self-esteem. That is, high self-esteem has been linked to a variety of potentially negative outcomes including aggression (Baumeister, Bushman, & Campbell, 2000; Baumeister, Smart, & Boden, 1996; Papps & O'Carroll, 1998), prejudice (Crocker, Thompson, McGraw, & Ingerman, 1987; Fein & Spencer, 1997; Verkuyten, 1996; Verkuyten & Masson, 1995), and the employment of self-protective or self-enhancing strategies (Baumeister, Heatherton, & Tice, 1993; Baumeister, Tice, & Hutton, 1989; Blaine & Crocker, 1993; Fitch, 1970; Miller & Ross, 1975; Tice, 1991). Thus, research suggests that high self-esteem is not always everything it is cracked up to be. In an attempt to better understand the paradox of high self-esteem, two forms of high self-esteem have been proposed: secure high self-esteem and fragile high self-esteem. Individuals with secure high self-esteem are characterized by positive attitudes toward the self that are realistic, well-anchored,

We would like to thank Ryan P. Brown for his comments on an earlier draft of this manuscript.

Correspondence should be addressed to: Virgil Zeigler-Hill at the Department of Psychology, University of Southern Mississippi, 118 College Drive #5025, Hattiesburg, MS 39406, USA. E-mail: virgil@usm.edu and resistant to threat (see Kernis, 2003, for a review). In contrast, individuals with fragile high self-esteem are characterized by feelings of self-worth that are vulnerable to challenge, need almost constant validation, and require some degree of self-deception. At present, there are three primary models for distinguishing between secure and fragile self-esteem: contingent self-esteem (Crocker & Wolfe, 2001; Deci & Ryan, 1995), unstable self-esteem (Kernis, Grannemann, & Barclay, 1989), and discrepant implicit and explicit self-esteem (Bosson, Brown, Zeigler-Hill, & Swann, 2003; Jordan, Spencer, Zanna, Hoshino-Browne, & Correll, 2003b; see Kernis & Paradise, 2002, for a review of these models of fragile high self-esteem). The present study will focus on discrepant self-esteem and examine its implications for the characteristic of perfectionism.

Explicit self-esteem is often defined as conscious feelings of self-liking, self-worth, and acceptance (e.g., Brown, 1993; Kernis, 2003). In contrast, implicit self-esteem is believed to consist of nonconscious, automatic, and over learned self-evaluations (Greenwald & Banaji, 1995; Pelham & Hetts, 1999). Dual-process models—which propose that there are two modes of information-processing—provide a means for considering both implicit and explicit self-esteem (e.g., Epstein, 1994; Epstein & Morling, 1995; Smith & DeCoster, 2001; Strack & Deutsch, 2004; Wilson, Lindsey, & Schooler, 2000). In general, dual-process models propose that humans have a cognitive system that is (potentially) rational, deliberative, and conscious, as well as an experiential system that is affective, automatic, and nonconscious. It is believed that explicit self-esteem is derived primarily from the cognitive system as the result of self-relevant feedback and experiences. In contrast, implicit self-esteem may originate in the experiential system as the result of the automatic and holistic processing of affective experiences (Epstein & Morling, 1995).

The most common method for assessing explicit self-esteem is the administration of a self-report questionnaire such as the Rosenberg Self-Esteem Scale (Rosenberg, 1965). In contrast, measures of implicit self-esteem cannot merely rely on simple self-reports because the attitudes of interest are believed to lie outside of conscious awareness. The measures of implicit self-esteem that have been developed during the past decade have used a variety of methods to capture this elusive construct (see Fazio & Olson, 2003, for a review of implicit measures). Three of the most promising of these measures assess implicit self-esteem by determining the ease with which individuals are able to pair pleasant words with the self (i.e., Implicit Association Test; Greenwald & Farnham, 2000), how quickly positive words come to mind following exposure to a self-relevant prime (i.e., Implicit Self-Evaluation Survey; Pelham & Hetts, 1999), and the degree to which an individual favors stimuli associated with the self such as the letters in one's own name (i.e., initials-preference task; Nuttin, 1987).

Consistent with the notion that implicit and explicit self-esteem are derived from independent sources, measures of implicit self-esteem are, at best, only weakly correlated with measures of explicit self-esteem under normal conditions (e.g., Bosson, Swann, & Pennebaker, 2000; Farnham, Greenwald, & Banaji, 1999; Greenwald & Farnham, 2000; Hetts, Sakuma, & Pelham, 1999; Jordan et al., 2003b; Koole, Dijksterhuis, & van Knippenberg, 2001; Pelham & Hetts, 1999; Pelham et al., 2005; Zeigler-Hill, 2006). However, it should be noted that there are conditions under which the relationship between implicit self-esteem and explicit self-esteem becomes stronger. For example, Pelham and his colleagues (2005) found that the association between implicit and explicit self-esteem is stronger among women than it is among men. The authors proposed this gender difference may be due to the tendency for women to focus more attention on their intuitive or affective experiences than is typically found among men. In an extension of this work, Jordan, Whitfield, and Zeigler-Hill (2006) directly examined whether individual differences in information-processing style were associated with the strength of the relationship between implicit and explicit self-esteem. As expected, a stronger correlation emerged for implicit self-esteem and explicit self-esteem among those individuals who focused more attention upon their affective and intuitive responses to stimuli and situations than for individuals who did not rely as heavily upon this type of information. In addition to these information-processing effects, other studies have found stronger correlations between implicit self-esteem and explicit self-esteem when individuals have been exposed to self-concept threats (Hetts et al., 1999; Jones, Pelham, Mirenberg, & Hetts, 2002) or experienced high cognitive load (Koole et al., 2001).

Discrepant Self-esteem

Due to differences in the types of information processed by the implicit and explicit systems—as well as differences in the methods by which this information is processed—it is possible for discrepancies to form between implicit and explicit self-esteem. The discrepancy between implicit self-esteem and explicit self-esteem is particularly interesting because the resulting attitudinal ambivalence about the self may motivate behaviors intended to resolve the inconsistency between one's conscious and nonconscious feelings of self-worth (Newby-Clark, McGregor, & Zanna, 2002; Spencer et al., 2005). The discrepancies that develop between implicit self-esteem and explicit self-esteem may take either of two forms: discrepant high self-esteem or discrepant low self-esteem. Individuals with discrepant high self-esteem possess high explicit self-esteem but low implicit self-esteem. This is the form of discrepant self-esteem that has been the primary focus of research in this area (e.g., Bosson et al., 2003; Jordan et al., 2003b; Zeigler-Hill, 2006). Individuals with discrepant high self-esteem are believed to consciously possess positive feelings about the self that are fragile because of the underlying insecurities and self-doubts associated with their low implicit self-esteem. This view of discrepant high self-esteem (i.e., overt grandiosity concealing unacknowledged negative feelings about the self) is consistent with classic views concerning narcissism (Kernberg, 1970; Kohut, 1971). In fact, the relationship between discrepant high self-esteem and narcissism has been supported by the results of recent studies using different measures of implicit self-esteem (Jordan et al., 2003b, Study 1; Zeigler-Hill, 2006). Other findings also support the idea that the positive self-views of individuals with discrepant high self-esteem are vulnerable to challenge. For example, individuals with discrepant high self-esteem experience self-esteem that is unstable over time (Zeigler-Hill, 2006), display increased self-enhancement tendencies (Bosson et al., 2003), are more defensive (Jordan et al., 2003b, Studies 2 & 3), react to uncertainty-threats with strong compensatory conviction (McGregor & Marigold, 2003, Study 3), respond to failure with exaggerated consensus estimates for personal beliefs (McGregor, Nail, Marigold, & Kang, 2005, Study 1), and will engage in racial/ethnic discrimination against others in order to maintain their threatened self-image (Jordan, Spencer, & Zanna, 2005).

Although previous research has focused primarily on discrepant *high* self-esteem, researchers are also beginning to take an interest in discrepant *low* self-esteem (i.e., low explicit self-esteem but high implicit self-esteem). One way of thinking about individuals with discrepant low self-esteem is that the high implicit self-esteem of these individuals may provide them with a *glimmer of hope* that may result in more optimism and less self-protection than is typically seen among individuals with low explicit self-esteem (Spencer et al., 2005). The glimmer of hope hypothesis is based on the idea that implicit self-esteem serves as a preconscious attitude toward the self that may enter into consciousness under certain conditions (Jordan et al., 2003b; Jordan, Logel, Spencer, Zanna, & Whitfield, in press; Spencer et al., 2005). For individuals with discrepant low self-esteem, it is believed that their high implicit self-esteem may seep into consciousness at certain times and lead these individuals to develop more optimistic attitudes about their performance relative to other individuals with low levels of explicit self-esteem.

Spencer et al. (2005) described three studies that are consistent with the glimmer of hope hypothesis. The first study involved participants taking a difficult intellectual test and receiving negative feedback about their performance (Jordan, Spencer, & Zanna, 2003a). Participants were then given the option of taking a similar test in order to improve their initial performance or taking a test in a completely different domain. Interestingly, explicit self-esteem had no effect on whether participants chose to persevere or not. Only implicit self-esteem was associated with the perseverance of participants. That is, high implicit self-esteem may have helped individuals with high explicit self-esteem as well as those with low explicit self-esteem believe they could improve on the initial task (i.e., implicit self-esteem may have offered them hope that they could improve their performance).

The second study that supports the glimmer of hope hypothesis was conducted by Bosson and her colleagues (2003, Study 1). Participants in this study completed measures of implicit and explicit self-esteem, followed by Weinstein's (1980) measure of unrealistic optimism. In addition, participants were also asked to rate the accuracy of a series of personality profiles that ranged from highly flattering (". . . this person thinks extremely highly of him/herself, and possesses a very positive attitude toward him/herself") to highly unflattering (". . . this person has a fairly negative attitude toward him/herself a lot of the time"). Participants with discrepant low self-esteem reported higher levels of unrealistic optimism than individuals with congruent low self-esteem. The level of unrealistic optimism reported by individuals with discrepant low self-esteem was similar to that reported by individuals with congruent high self-esteem (i.e., high explicit self-esteem and high implicit self-esteem) but not as high as that reported by individuals with discrepant high self-esteem. Similar results were also obtained for the perceived accuracy of the highly flattering personality profile. These results may be taken as evidence for the glimmer of hope hypothesis because individuals with discrepant low self-esteem report relatively high levels of optimism and view flattering personality descriptions as being relatively accurate. Similarly, the third study that was consistent with the glimmer of hope hypothesis found that among individuals with low explicit self-esteem, those with relatively high levels of implicit self-esteem were less likely to engage in self-handicapping (Spalding & Hardin, 1999).

The predictions for the present study are consistent with the glimmer of hope hypothesis. That is, we believe that the high implicit self-esteem of individuals with discrepant low self-esteem may result in these individuals possessing more hope with regard to their abilities and future performance than is typical for individuals with low explicit self-esteem. This high level of hopefulness may result in individuals with discrepant low self-esteem adopting more rigorous standards for their own performance—and judging their performance more harshly when they fail to meet these standards—than individuals with congruent low self-esteem. We predict that the discrepancy between low explicit self-esteem and high implicit self-esteem will be associated with the adoption of perfectionistic standards.

Perfectionism

In recent years, perfectionism has garnered increased attention. A good deal of this recent attention has focused on the psychological functioning of perfectionists. This literature has found perfectionism to be associated with a variety of negative outcomes including depression (Blatt, Quinlan, Pilkonis, & Shea, 1995), suicide (Blatt, 1995), eating disorders (Brouwers & Wiggum, 1993; Tyrka, Waldron, Graber, & Brooks-Gunn, 2002), and obsessive-compulsive disorders (Frost, Steketee, Cohn, & Griess, 1994). These findings are consistent with the early theoretical framework concerning perfectionism that viewed perfectionists as individuals who would frequently experience distress as a result of their inability to meet their extremely high standards (e.g., Horney, 1950). More specifically, perfectionists were believed to experience low self-esteem as they compulsively attempted to achieve the lofty goals they established for themselves. However, more recent conceptualizations of perfectionism suggest that perfectionism is not a unidimensional construct. Rather, perfectionistic subtypes may exist (e.g., Hamachek, 1978).

Although several multidimensional models of perfectionism have been generated (e.g., Frost, Marten, Lahart, & Rosenblate, 1990; Hewitt & Flett, 1991), investigators have begun combining these multiple dimensions into two primary dimensions believed to measure *adaptive* (or normal) and *maladaptive* (or neurotic) forms of perfectionism (e.g., Hewitt & Flett, 1991). Adaptive perfectionism describes characteristics that are viewed as socially desirable and appear to be associated with healthy psychological functioning. For example, adaptive perfectionism has been found to be associated with problem-focused coping (Dunkley & Blankstein, 2000) and positive affect (Frost, Heimberg, Holt, Mattia, & Neubauer, 1993). It is important to note that for adaptive perfectionists the high personal standards and painstaking efforts that characterize these individuals are mostly associated with feelings of personal satisfaction and achievement as well as an ensuing sense of self-esteem.

In contrast, perfectionism can also describe the tendency to set extremely—or impossibly—high personal standards, accompanied by an intense need to avoid failure. The darker side of the construct becomes evident in attitudes and behaviors that are clearly maladaptive such as constant and harsh self-scrutiny, difficulty deriving satisfaction from performance (even when successful), and constant concerns about the evaluations of others (Davis, 1997; Dunkley, Zuroff, & Blankstein, 2003). Maladaptive perfectionists believe that even the most minor of mistakes are indicative of failure and, just as importantly, that any sign of failure will lead others to lose respect for them and ultimately reject them (Frost et al., 1993). Maladaptive perfectionism has been found to be associated with dysphoric mood (e.g., Grzegorek, Slaney, Franze, & Rice, 2004), emotional reactivity (Dunkley et al., 2003), anxiety (Suddarth & Slaney, 2001), and over-reliance on social comparison (Slaney, Rice, & Ashby, 2002).

Overview of the Present Study

The present study examined whether individuals with discrepant low self-esteem report high levels of maladaptive and adaptive perfectionism. Previous research has found explicit self-esteem to be negatively correlated with maladaptive perfectionism and positively correlated with adaptive perfectionism (e.g., Ashby & Rice, 2002). However, recent advances in self-esteem research suggest that such studies may have provided an incomplete picture of the relationship between perfectionism and self-esteem. A more complete examination of this relationship may require the inclusion of implicit self-esteem. Thus, the present study extended previous research by examining whether implicit self-esteem moderates the relationship between explicit self-esteem and perfectionism. More specifically, it was predicted that individuals with discrepant low self-esteem would report higher levels of maladaptive perfectionism. The rationale for this prediction is that high implicit self-esteem may motivate individuals with low explicit self-esteem to resolve their inconsistent feelings of self-worth by attempting to raise their level of explicit self-esteem through the adoption of perfectionistic standards. Although predictions are less clear for adaptive perfectionism, it is possible that the glimmer of hope believed to characterize those with discrepant low self-esteem may allow these individuals to experience some of the benefits associated with adaptive perfectionism (e.g., satisfaction with accomplishments).

Method

Participants and Procedure

Participants were 575 undergraduates enrolled in psychology courses who participated in return for partial fulfillment of a research participation requirement. Participants completed measures of explicit self-esteem, implicit self-esteem, perfectionism, and additional measures that are not relevant to the current investigation. Of the 575 participants who began the study, 12 participants were excluded due to failure to provide complete information. Analyses were conducted using the 563 remaining participants (226 men and 337 women). The average age of these participants was 19.37 years ($SD = 3.13$). The racial/ethnic composition was 78% White, 7% Black, 5% Asian, 3% Native American, 1% Hispanic, and 6% Other.

Measures

Explicit self-esteem. Participants completed the Rosenberg Self-Esteem Scale (Rosenberg, 1965), a well-validated measure of global self-regard (Blaskovich & Tomaka, 1991; Demo, 1985). Test–retest correlations greater than .80 have previously been reported (Rosenberg, 1965; Silber & Tippett, 1965). Participants were instructed to complete the scale according to how they typically or generally feel about themselves. Responses were made on scales ranging from 1 (*strongly disagree*) to 4 (*strongly agree*). For the present sample, the internal consistency of this measure was high, $\alpha = .86$.

Implicit self-esteem. The measure of implicit self-esteem employed in the present study was the preference for one's own initials. This measure is based on research concerning the name letter effect (Greenwald & Banaji, 1995; Kitayama & Karasawa, 1997; Nuttin, 1985, 1987). Research on the name letter effect has shown that individuals tend to like the letters that appear in their own name more than other individuals like these same letters. However, the extent to which this is true varies widely across individuals, providing an index of implicit self-esteem. Participants were asked to evaluate each letter of the alphabet using response scales ranging from 1 (*I dislike this letter very much*) to 7 (*I like this letter very much*). Initials-preference scores were calculated by establishing the normative rating of each letter for participants whose names did not contain that letter. Then, the participant's preferences for their initials were computed by subtracting the normative evaluation of these letters from the participant's evaluation of his or her initials. Finally, the participant's preferences for his or her first and last initials were summed (see Koole et al., 2001, for further details on the computation of initials-preference scores). Initials-preference scores reflect the degree to which participants evaluate their initials more positively than other participants evaluate these same letters, and a stronger preference for one's own initials is believed to be indicative of a high level of implicit self-esteem. Previous research has demonstrated the reliability and validity of initials-preference scores (Bosson et al., 2000; Jones et al., 2002; Koole et al., 2001; Koole & Pelham, 2003; Koole, Smeets, van Knippenberg, & Dijksterhuis, 1999; Shimizu & Pelham, 2004). The correlation between participants' preferences for their first and last initials served as an index of internal consistency for this measure, $r = .51$, $p < .001$. The initials-preferences task was employed in the present study because it is the only measure of implicit self-esteem with acceptable psychometric properties (e.g., Bosson et al., 2000) that can be easily administered in a large group setting.

Perfectionism. The measure of perfectionism employed in the present study was the Multidimensional Perfectionism Scale (MPS; Frost et al., 1990). The MPS contains 35 items for which responses were made on scales ranging from 1 (*strongly disagree*) to 5 (*strongly agree*). Initially, Frost and his colleagues found that the MPS was composed of six subscales: Concern Over Mistakes (e.g., "People will probably think less of me if I make a mistake"), Personal Standards (e.g., "I set higher goals than most people"), Parental Criticism (e.g., "I never felt like I could meet my parents' standards"), Parental Expectations (e.g., "My parents have expected excellence from me"), Doubts About Actions (e.g., "Even when I do something very carefully, I often feel that it is not quite right"), and Organization (e.g., "Neatness is very important to me"). More recently, however, a number of independent programs of research using various measures of perfectionism have tended to support a two-dimensional factor structure consisting of adaptive perfectionism and maladaptive perfectionism (e.g., Frost et al., 1993). For the MPS, the Personal Standards and Organization subscales map onto the dimension of adaptive perfectionism, whereas the remaining four subscales (i.e., Concern Over Mistakes, Parental Criticism, Parental Expectations, and Doubts About Actions) comprise the dimension of maladaptive perfectionism (Rice, Ashby, & Slaney, 1998). For the present sample, the internal consistencies of the adaptive and maladaptive perfectionism scales were .88 and .91, respectively.

Results

Descriptive Statistics

Table 1 presents the means, standard deviations, and intercorrelations for all of the measures in the present study. Although a significant correlation emerged between

TABLE 1 Intercorrelations and Descriptive Statistics for Measures of Explicit Self-Esteem, Implicit Self-Esteem, Adaptive Perfectionism, and Maladaptive Perfectionism

	1	2	3	4
1. Explicit self-esteem	—			
2. Implicit self-esteem	.10*	—		
3. Adaptive perfectionism	.11**	.07	—	
4. Maladaptive perfectionism	−.41***	.03	.25***	—
M	33.21	1.83	2.75	1.62
SD	4.88	2.70	0.69	0.69

Note: *$p < .05$; **$p < .01$; ***$p < .001$.

implicit self-esteem and explicit self-esteem, $r = .10$, $p < .02$, the strength of the relationship was very weak. This is consistent with previous research showing that implicit and explicit self-esteem are, at best, only moderately correlated with each other (e.g., Bosson et al., 2000). Significant gender differences emerged for both implicit and explicit self-esteem. Consistent with previous research (Block & Robins, 1993; Kling, Hyde, Showers, & Buswell, 1999; Major, Barr, Zubek, & Babey, 1999; Robins, Trzesniewski, Tracy, Gosling, & Potter, 2002), men reported higher levels of explicit self-esteem than women, $t'(512.96) = -2.61$, $p < .01$. In contrast, women reported marginally higher levels of implicit self-esteem than men, $t'(442.69) = 1.94$, $p < .06$. Explicit self-esteem was negatively correlated with maladaptive perfectionism, $r = -.41$, $p < .001$, and a weak correlation also emerged between explicit self-esteem and adaptive perfectionism, $r = .11$, $p < .01$. Implicit self-esteem was not correlated with either adaptive or maladaptive perfectionism, $rs < .07$, *ns*. Consistent with previous research (e.g., Kawamura & Frost, 2004), adaptive and maladaptive perfectionism were positively correlated, $r = .25$, $p < .001$.

Data Analytic Strategy

Hypotheses concerning discrepant self-esteem and perfectionism were tested through the use of hierarchical multiple regression analyses. All continuous predictors were first centered on their respective means (Aiken & West, 1991). On Step 1, the main effect terms for explicit self-esteem, implicit self-esteem, and gender (female = 0 and male = 1) were entered. Although no predictions were made concerning interactions involving gender, these interactions were examined for exploratory purposes. However, preliminary results found no significant interactions involving gender, so these terms were trimmed. Thus, the only term entered on Step 2 was the interaction of explicit self-esteem and implicit self-esteem. Because hypotheses concerned the interaction of main effect terms, these regression analyses were followed by the simple slopes tests recommended by Aiken and West (1991) to describe the interaction of continuous variables.

Discrepant Self-esteem and Maladaptive Perfectionism

This analysis examined the relationship between discrepant self-esteem and maladaptive perfectionism. Main effects emerged for explicit self-esteem ($\beta = -.43$, $p < .001$), implicit self-esteem ($\beta = .08$, $p < .05$), and gender ($\beta = .09$, $p < .03$). However, the main effects of implicit and explicit self-esteem were qualified by their interaction, $\beta = -.11$, $p < .01$. Predicted values for this interaction are shown in Figure 1. Simple slopes tests (Aiken & West, 1991) were conducted to probe the pattern of this interaction. These simple slopes tests revealed that individuals with high explicit self-esteem reported lower levels of maladaptive perfectionism than individuals with congruent low self-esteem ($\beta = -.33$, $p < .001$) or discrepant low self-esteem ($\beta = -.54$, $p < .001$). Finally, individuals with discrepant low self-esteem reported higher levels of maladaptive perfectionism than individuals with congruent low self-esteem ($\beta = .18$, $p < .001$). Thus, individuals with discrepant low self-esteem possessed the highest levels of maladaptive perfectionism, whereas individuals with congruent low self-esteem possessed moderate levels of maladaptive perfectionism. Individuals with high explicit self-esteem—regardless of their level of implicit self-esteem—reported the lowest levels of maladaptive perfectionism.

Discrepant Self-esteem and Adaptive Perfectionism

This analysis examined the relationship between discrepant self-esteem and adaptive perfectionism. A main effect emerged for explicit self-esteem, $\beta = .11$, $p < .01$. However, the main effect of explicit self-esteem was qualified by its interaction with implicit self-esteem, $\beta = -.09$, $p < .04$. Predicted values for this interaction are shown in Figure 2. Simple slopes tests revealed that implicit self-esteem was not a significant predictor of adaptive perfectionism among individuals with high explicit self-esteem, $\beta = -.03$, *ns*. In addition, these tests revealed that explicit self-esteem was a significant predictor of adaptive perfectionism among those with low implicit

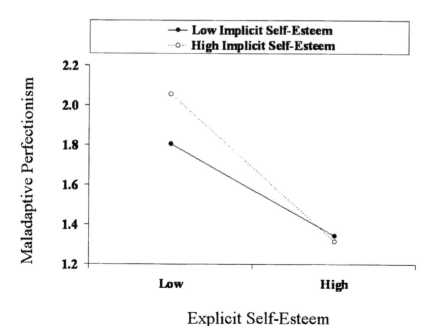

FIGURE 1 Maladaptive perfectionism: Predicted values for the interaction between implicit and explicit self-esteem.

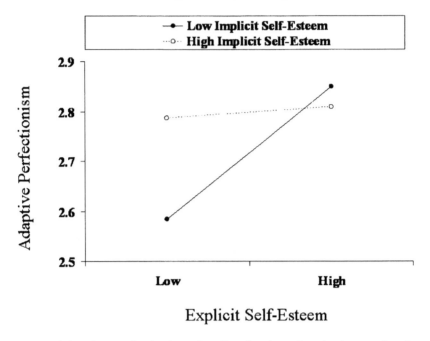

FIGURE 2 Adaptive perfectionism: Predicted values for the interaction between implicit and explicit self-esteem.

self-esteem, $\beta = .19$, $p < .001$. As expected, individuals with discrepant low self-esteem reported higher levels of adaptive perfectionism than individuals with congruent low self-esteem, $\beta = .15$, $p < .02$. The reported level of adaptive perfectionism did not differ between individuals with discrepant low self-esteem and those with congruent high self-esteem, $\beta = .02$, *ns*. Thus, individuals with discrepant low self-esteem possessed higher levels of adaptive perfectionism than individuals with congruent low self-esteem. In fact, the adaptive perfectionism of individuals with discrepant low self-esteem was no different from the levels of adaptive perfectionism found among those individuals with high explicit self-esteem.

Discussion

In the present research, we sought to examine the moderating role that implicit self-esteem may play in the relationship between perfectionism and explicit self-esteem. We were guided in this process by the glimmer of hope hypothesis, which proposes that the high levels of implicit self-esteem found among individuals with discrepant low self-esteem (i.e., low explicit self-esteem but high implicit self-esteem) may result in higher levels of optimism and less self-protection than is typically seen among individuals with low explicit self-esteem (Spencer et al., 2005). We proposed that high implicit self-esteem may serve as a motivation for individuals with low explicit self-esteem to adopt perfectionistic standards. More specifically, we predicted that individuals with discrepant low self-esteem would report higher levels of perfectionism than individuals with congruent low self-esteem. The results of the study were consistent with our hypothesis that implicit self-esteem would moderate the relationship between explicit self-esteem and perfectionism. That is, individuals with discrepant low self-esteem reported higher levels of both adaptive and maladaptive perfectionism than individuals with congruent low self-esteem. When compared with individuals with high levels of explicit self-esteem, individuals with discrepant low self-esteem had higher levels of maladaptive perfectionism and similar levels of adaptive perfectionism.

One of the more interesting questions to emerge from the present study concerns the reason discrepant low self-esteem is associated with perfectionism; that is, why do individuals with discrepant low self-esteem experience a drive to be perfect? Although the present study was based on a process model that assumed that discrepant low self-esteem precedes perfectionism, the results of the present study do not allow us to determine the direction of causation. However, we suggest three possible answers to this lingering question. First, as our process model assumed, it is possible that discrepant low self-esteem causes individuals to develop perfectionistic standards. This explanation is derived from the idea that individuals with discrepant low self-esteem are motivated to resolve the attitudinal ambivalence toward the self resulting from the inconsistency of their conscious and nonconscious feelings of self-worth when their implicit attitudes enter into consciousness (Newby-Clark et al., 2002; Spencer et al., 2005). That is, high implicit self-esteem may serve as a source of motivation for individuals with low explicit self-esteem to resolve the discrepancy between their implicit self-esteem and explicit self-esteem by raising their level of explicit self-esteem. In order for individuals with discrepant low self-esteem to raise their explicit self-esteem, it may be necessary for them to maintain the belief that they *can* be successful while acknowledging their current faults and weaknesses so that these limitations may eventually be overcome (rather than merely being ignored). Thus, individuals with discrepant low self-esteem may adopt perfectionistic standards in an attempt to raise their level of explicit self-esteem and resolve their inconsistent attitudes toward the self. Future research is needed to determine whether individuals with discrepant low self-esteem who adopt perfectionistic standards actually report higher levels of explicit self-esteem over time. However, it is also possible that their high implicit self-esteem may lead individuals to adopt standards that are too high and that the failure to meet these unrealistic standards may ironically serve to maintain (or intensify) their low levels of explicit self-esteem. In addition, research should also examine other potential mechanisms that individuals with discrepant low self-esteem could employ to enhance their conscious feelings of self-worth.

Second, perfectionism may cause discrepancies to develop between implicit and explicit self-esteem. That is, the demanding standards of the perfectionist—especially those with maladaptive perfectionism—may artificially lower the individual's conscious feelings of self-worth while having a negligible impact on implicit self-esteem. This possibility is based on the assumption that implicit self-esteem is either a highly stable construct that is relatively immune to everyday experiences or, at the very least, that it is not influenced by the failure to live up to perfectionistic standards.

Third, both discrepant low self-esteem and perfectionism may result from the influence of some other variable. One possibility is that both may be the result of individuals' childhood interactions with their parents. For example, Hamachek (1978) discussed the possibility that perfectionism may develop in response to parental love and approval that is contingent upon perfect—or nearly perfect—behavior (see Jordan et al., 2003a, for findings concerning the association between implicit self-esteem and contingent self-esteem). Similarly, discrepant low self-esteem could have its origin in these early interactions with demanding parents as well.

In fact, initial evidence has shown that adult levels of implicit self-esteem are related to their early interactions with their caregivers (DeHart, Pelham, & Tennen, 2006). That is, individuals who reported higher levels of implicit self-esteem also reported that their parents were more nurturing and less overprotective compared with those individuals who reported lower implicit self-esteem. In addition to these general parenting styles, future research should examine the association between implicit self-esteem (and explicit self-esteem) and the standards that parents set for their children.

The present findings may also have implications for psychological adjustment. Although previous research has shown that low explicit self-esteem is associated with depressive symptoms (see Ingram, Miranda, & Segal, 1998, or Tennen & Affleck, 1993, for a review), it is possible that the fragile or secure nature of an individual's self-esteem may be at least as important as their level of self-esteem. For example, a number of studies have found strong relationships between self-esteem instability and depressive symptoms such that individuals who report more fluctuations in their state self-esteem also tend to report more depressive symptoms (Butler, Hokanson, & Flynn, 1994; de Man, Gutierrez, & Sterk, 2001; Hayes, Harris, & Carver, 2004; Kernis et al., 1998; Roberts & Gotlib, 1997; Roberts & Kassel, 1997; Roberts & Monroe, 1992). Given the conceptual and empirical similarities between the models of self-esteem instability and discrepant self-esteem (e.g., Zeigler-Hill, 2006), it is certainly possible that implicit self-esteem may also play a role in psychological adjustment. One possibility is that high implicit self-esteem may protect individuals from negative psychological outcomes such as depression (Logel, Spencer, & Zanna, 2005). However, it is also possible that high levels of implicit self-esteem may be an indicator of current distress among those with low levels of explicit self-esteem. That is, current psychological distress may be associated with a decline in explicit self-esteem while leaving implicit self-esteem relatively unscathed resulting in discrepant low self-esteem. Consistent with this idea, previous research has found that both depressed and formerly depressed individuals possess positive implicit self-esteem (De Raedt, Schacht, Franck, & De Houwer, 2006; Gemar, Segal, Sagrati, & Kennedy, 2001).

The present study is certainly not without limitations. One limitation is that only a single measure of implicit self-esteem was employed in the present study. Because the measurement of implicit self-esteem is still in its earliest stages, it is helpful when multiple measures of implicit self-esteem are included in research so that similarities and differences in these measures may be observed. This is especially important given that there is no clear consensus at the present time as to which, if any, of the methods that are currently employed accurately measure implicit self-esteem. A second limitation is that follow-up measures of psychological adjustment were not collected as part of the present study. The inclusion of adjustment measures would have allowed for the examination of whether the glimmer of hope that is believed to characterize individuals with discrepant low self-esteem resulted in positive or negative psychological adjustment over time. A third limitation of the present study is that the interactions of implicit and explicit self-esteem that emerged from these analyses were relatively weak and would only have been detected with a large sample of participants.

Conclusion

The findings of the present study complement and extend previous findings concerning discrepant low self-esteem. In previous studies, individuals with discrepant low self-esteem have been found to be keenly aware of their flaws (Bosson et al., 2003, Study 2), yet they remain optimistic (Bosson et al., 2003, Study 1). Consistent with these previous findings, individuals with discrepant low self-esteem in the present study reported high levels of both adaptive and maladaptive perfectionism, which suggests that they establish very high standards for their performance and are highly self-critical following failure. However, the high level of adaptive perfectionism found among these individuals suggests that they may still be able to find some degree of satisfaction in their accomplishments.

References

Aiken, L. S., & West, S. G. (1991). *Multiple regression: Testing and interpreting interactions.* London: Sage.

Ashby, J. S., & Rice, K. G. (2002). Perfectionism, dysfunctional attitudes, and self-esteem: A structural equations analysis. *Journal of Counseling and Development, 80,* 197–203.

Baumeister, R. F., Bushman, B. J., & Campbell, W. K. (2000). Self-esteem, narcissism, and aggression: Does violence result from low self-esteem or from threatened egotism? *Current Directions in Psychological Science, 9,* 141–156.

Baumeister, R. F., Campbell, J. D., Krueger, J. I., & Vohs, K. D. (2003). Does high self-esteem cause better performance, interpersonal success, happiness, or healthier lifestyles? *Psychological Science in the Public Interest, 4,* 1–44.

Baumeister, R. F., Heatherton, T. F., & Tice, D. M. (1993). When ego threats lead to self-regulation failure: Negative consequences of high self-esteem. *Journal of Personality and Social Psychology, 64,* 141–156.

Baumeister, R. F., Smart, L., & Boden, J. M. (1996). Relation of threatened egotism to violence and aggression: The dark side of high self-esteem. *Psychological Review, 103,* 5–33.

Baumeister, R. F., Tice, D. M., & Hutton, D. G. (1989). Self-presentational motivations and personality differences in self-esteem. *Journal of Personality, 57,* 547–579.

Blaine, B., & Crocker, J. (1993). Self-esteem and self-serving biases in reactions to positive and negative events: An integrative review. In R. F. Baumeister (Ed.), *Self-esteem: The puzzle of low self-regard* (pp. 55–85). New York: Plenum Press.

Blaskovich, J., & Tomaka, J. (1991). Measures of self-esteem. In J. P. Robinson, P. R. Shaver, & L. S. Wrightsman (Eds.), *Measures of personality and social psychological attitudes* (Vol. 1, pp. 115–160). New York: Academic.

Blatt, S. J. (1995). The destructiveness of perfectionism: Implications for the treatment of depression. *American Psychologist, 50,* 1003–1020.

Blatt, S. J., Quinlan, D. M. Pilkonis, P. A., & Shea, M. T. (1995). Impact of perfectionism and need for approval on the brief treatment of depression: The National Institute of Mental Health Treatment of Depression Collaborative Research Program revisited. *Journal of Consulting and Clinical Psychology, 63,* 125–132.

Block, J., & Robins, R. W. (1993). A longitudinal study of consistency and change in self-esteem from early adolescence to early adulthood. *Child Development, 64,* 909–923.

Bosson, J. K., Brown, R. P., Zeigler-Hill, V., & Swann, W. B., Jr. (2003). Self-enhancement tendencies among people with high explicit self-esteem: The moderating role of implicit self-esteem. *Self and Identity, 2,* 169–187.

Bosson, J. K., Swann, W. B., Jr., & Pennebaker, J. W. (2000). Stalking the perfect measure of implicit self-esteem: The blind men and the elephant revisited? *Journal of Personality and Social Psychology, 79,* 631–643.

Brouwers, M., & Wiggum, C. D. (1993). Bulimia and perfectionism: Developing the courage to be perfect. *Journal of Mental Health Counseling, 15,* 141–149.

Brown, J. D. (1993). Self-esteem and self-evaluation: Feeling is believing. In J. M. Suls (Ed.), *The self in social perspective* (pp. 27–58). Hillsdale, NJ: Lawrence Erlbaum Associates, Inc.

Butler, A. C., Hokanson, J. E., & Flynn, H. A. (1994). A comparison of self-esteem lability and low trait self-esteem as vulnerability factors for depression. *Journal of Personality and Social Psychology, 66*, 166–177.

Crocker, J., Thompson, L., McGraw, K., & Ingerman, C. (1987). Downward comparison, prejudice, and evaluation of others: Effects of self-esteem and threat. *Journal of Personality and Social Psychology, 52*, 907–916.

Crocker, J., & Wolfe, C. T. (2001). Contingencies of self-worth. *Psychological Review, 108*, 593–623.

Davis, C. (1997). Normal and neurotic perfectionism in eating disorders: An interactive model. *International Journal of Eating Disorders, 22*, 421–426.

de Man, A. F., Gutierrez, B. I. B., & Sterk, N. (2001). Stability of self-esteem as moderator of the relationship between level of self-esteem and depression. *North American Journal of Psychology, 3*, 303–308.

De Raedt, R., Schacht, R., Franck, E., & De Houwer, J. (2006). Self-esteem and depression revisited: Implicit positive self-esteem in depressed patients? *Behaviour Research and Therapy, 44*, 1017–1028.

Deci, E. L., & Ryan, R. M. (1995). Human autonomy: The basis for true self-esteem. In M. H. Kernis (Ed.), *Efficacy, agency, and self-esteem* (pp. 31–49). New York: Plenum Press.

DeHart, T., Pelham, B. W., & Tennen, H. (2006). What lies beneath: Parenting style and implicit self-esteem. *Journal of Experimental Social Psychology, 42*, 1–17.

Demo, D. H. (1985). The measurement of self-esteem: Refining our methods. *Journal of Personality and Social Psychology, 48*, 1490–1502.

Diener, E. (1984). Subjective well-being. *Psychological Bulletin, 95*, 542–575.

Dunkley, D. M., & Blankstein, K. R. (2000). Self-critical perfectionism, coping, hassles, and current distress: A structural equation modeling approach. *Cognitive Therapy and Research, 24*, 713–730.

Dunkley, D. M., Zuroff, D. C., & Blankstein, K. R. (2003). Self-critical perfectionism and daily affect: Dispositional and situational influences on stress and coping. *Journal of Personality and Social Psychology, 84*, 234–252.

Epstein, S. (1994). Integration of the cognitive and the psychodynamic unconscious. *American Psychologist, 49*, 709–724.

Epstein, S., & Morling, B. (1995). Is the self motivated to do more than enhance and/or verify itself? In M. H. Kernis (Ed.), *Efficacy, agency, and self-esteem* (pp. 9–29). New York: Plenum.

Farnham, S. D., Greenwald, A. G., & Banaji, M. R. (1999). Implicit self-esteem. In D. Abrams & M. A. Hogg (Eds.), *Social identity and social cognition* (pp. 230–248). Oxford, UK: Blackwell.

Fazio, R. H., & Olson, M. A. (2003). Implicit measures in social cognition research: Their meaning and uses. *Annual Review of Psychology, 54*, 297–327.

Fein, S., & Spencer, S. J. (1997). Prejudice as self-image maintenance: Affirming the self through derogating others. *Journal of Personality and Social Psychology, 73*, 31–44.

Fitch, G. (1970). Effects of self-esteem, perceived performance, and choice on causal attributions. *Journal of Personality and Social Psychology, 16*, 311–315.

Frost, R. O., Heimberg, R. G., Holt, C. S., Mattia, J. I., & Neubauer, A. L. (1993). A comparison of two measures of perfectionism. *Personality and Individual Differences, 14*, 119–126.

Frost, R. O., Marten, P., Lahart, C., & Rosenblate, R. (1990). The dimensions of perfectionism. *Cognitive Therapy and Research, 14*, 449–468.

Frost, R. O., Steketee, G., Cohn, L., & Griess, K. (1994). Personality traits in subclinical and non-obsessive-compulsive volunteers and their parents. *Behaviour Research and Therapy, 32*, 47–56.

Gemar, M. C., Segal, Z. V., Sagrati, S., & Kennedy, S. J. (2001). Mood-induced changes on the Implicit Association Test in recovered depressed patients. *Journal of Abnormal Psychology, 110*, 282–289.

Greenwald, A. G., & Banaji, M. R. (1995). Implicit social cognition: Attitudes, self-esteem, and stereotypes. *Psychological Review, 102,* 4–27.

Greenwald, A. G., & Farnham, S. D. (2000). Using the implicit association test to measure self-esteem and self-concept. *Journal of Personality and Social Psychology, 79,* 1022–1038.

Grzegorek, J. L., Slaney, R. B., Franze, S., & Rice, K. G. (2004). Self-criticism, dependency, self-esteem, and grade point average satisfaction among clusters of perfectionists and nonperfectionists. *Journal of Counseling Psychology, 51,* 192–200.

Hamachek, D. E. (1978). Psychodynamics of normal and neurotic perfectionism. *Psychology, 15,* 27–33.

Hayes, A. M., Harris, M. S., & Carver, C. S. (2004). Predictors of self-esteem variability. *Cognitive Therapy and Research, 28,* 369–385.

Hetts, J. J., Sakuma, M., & Pelham, B. W. (1999). Two roads to positive regard: Implicit and explicit self-evaluation and culture. *Journal of Experimental Social Psychology, 35,* 512–559.

Hewitt, P. L., & Flett, G. L. (1991). Perfectionism in the self and social contexts: Conceptualization, assessment, and association with psychopathology. *Journal of Personality and Social Psychology, 60,* 456–470.

Horney, K. (1950). *Neurosis and human growth.* New York: Norton.

Ingram, R. E., Miranda, J., & Segal, Z. V. (1998). *Cognitive vulnerability to depression.* New York: Guilford Press.

Jones, J. T., Pelham, B. W., Mirenberg, M. C., & Hetts, J. J. (2002). Name letter preferences are not merely mere exposure: Implicit egotism as self-regulation. *Journal of Experimental Social Psychology, 38,* 170–177.

Jordan, C. H., Logel, C., Spencer, S. J., Zanna, M. P., & Whitfield, M. L. (in press). The heterogeneity of self-esteem: Exploring the interplay between implicit and explicit self-esteem. In R. E. Petty, R. H. Fazio, & P. Brinol (Eds.), *Attitudes: Insights from the new implicit measures.* Mahwah, NJ: Lawrence Erlbaum Associates, Inc.

Jordan, C. H., Spencer, S. J., & Zanna, M. P. (2003a). "I love me... I love me not": Implicit self-esteem, explicit self-esteem, and defensiveness. In S. J. Spencer, S. Fein, M. P. Zanna, & J. M. Olson (Eds.), *Motivated social perception: The Ontario symposium,* (Vol. 9, pp. 117–145). Mahwah, NJ: Lawrence Erlbaum Associates, Inc.

Jordan, C. H., Spencer, S. J., & Zanna, M. P. (2005). Types of high self-esteem and prejudice: How implicit self-esteem relates to ethnic discrimination among high explicit self-esteem individuals. *Personality and Social Psychology Bulletin, 31,* 693–702.

Jordan, C. H., Spencer, S. J., Zanna, M. P., Hoshino-Browne, E., & Correll, J. (2003b). Secure and defensive high self-esteem. *Journal of Personality and Social Psychology, 85,* 969–978.

Jordan, C. H., Whitfield, M., & Zeigler-Hill, V. (2006). *Intuition and the correspondence between implicit and explicit self-esteem.* Manuscript submitted for publication.

Kawamura, K. Y., & Frost, R. O. (2004). Self-concealment as a mediator in the relationship between perfectionism and psychological distress. *Cognitive Therapy and Research, 28,* 183–191.

Kernberg, O. F. (1970). Factors in the psychoanalytic treatment of narcissistic personalities. *Journal of the American Psychoanalytic Association, 18,* 51–85.

Kernis, M. H. (2003). Toward a conceptualization of optimal self-esteem. *Psychological Inquiry, 14,* 1–26.

Kernis, M. H., Grannemann, B. D., & Barclay, L. C. (1989). Stability and level of self-esteem as predictors of anger arousal and hostility. *Journal of Personality and Social Psychology, 56,* 1013–1023.

Kernis, M. H., & Paradise, A. W. (2002). Distinguishing between fragile and secure forms of high self-esteem. In E. L. Deci & R. M. Ryan (Eds.), *Self-determination: Theoretical issues and practical applications* (pp. 339–360). Rochester, NY: University of Rochester Press.

Kernis, M. H., Whisenhunt, C. R., Waschull, S. B., Greenier, K. D., Berry, A. J., Herlocker, C. E., et al. (1998). Multiple facets of self-esteem and their relations to depressive symptoms. *Personality and Social Psychology Bulletin, 24,* 657 – 668.

Kitayama, S., & Karasawa, M. (1997). Implicit self-esteem in Japan: Name letters and birthday numbers. *Personality and Social Psychology Bulletin, 23,* 736 – 742.

Kling, K. C., Hyde, J. S., Showers, C. J., & Buswell, B. N. (1999). Gender differences in self-esteem: A meta-analysis. *Psychological Bulletin, 125,* 470 – 500.

Kohut, H. K. (1971). *The analysis of the self.* Madison, WI: International Universities Press.

Koole, S. L., Dijksterhuis, A., & van Knippenberg, A. (2001). What's in a name: Implicit self-esteem and the automatic self. *Journal of Personality and Social Psychology, 80,* 669 – 685.

Koole, S. L., & Pelham, B. W. (2003). On the nature of implicit self-esteem: The case of the name letter effect. In S. J. Spencer, S. Fein, M. P. Zanna, & J. M. Olson (Eds.), *Motivated social perception: The Ontario symposium* (Vol. 9, pp. 93 – 116). Mahwah, NJ: Lawrence Erlbaum Associates, Inc.

Koole, S. L., Smeets, K., van Knippenberg, A., & Dijksterhuis, A. (1999). The cessation of rumination through self-affirmation. *Journal of Personality and Social Psychology, 77,* 111 – 125.

Logel, C., Spencer, S., & Zanna, M. (2005). *Implicit self-esteem and depression: A longitudinal study.* Poster presented at the meeting of the Society for Personality and Social Psychology, New Orleans, LA.

Major, B., Barr, L., Zubek, J., & Babey, S. H. (1999). Gender and self-esteem: A meta-analysis. In W. B. Swann, Jr., J. H. Langlois, & L. A. Gilbert (Eds.), *Sexism and stereotypes in modern society: The gender science of Janet Taylor Spence* (pp. 223 – 253). Washington, DC: American Psychological Association.

McGregor, I., & Marigold, D. C. (2003). Defensive zeal and the uncertain self: What makes you so sure? *Journal of Personality and Social Psychology, 85,* 838 – 852.

McGregor, I., Nail, P. R., Marigold, D. C., & Kang, S.-J. (2005). Defensive pride and consensus: Strength in imaginary numbers. *Journal of Personality and Social Psychology, 89,* 978 – 996.

Miller, D. T., & Ross, M. (1975). Self-serving biases in the attribution of causality: Fact or fiction? *Psychological Bulletin, 82,* 213 – 225.

Newby-Clark, I. R., McGregor, I., & Zanna, M. P. (2002). Thinking and caring about cognitive inconsistency: When and for whom does attitudinal ambivalence feel uncomfortable? *Journal of Personality and Social Psychology, 82,* 157 – 166.

Nuttin, J. M. (1985). Narcissism beyond Gestalt awareness: The name letter effect. *European Journal of Social Psychology, 15,* 353 – 361.

Nuttin, J. M. (1987). Affective consequences of mere ownership: the name letter effect in twelve European languages. *European Journal of Social Psychology, 17,* 381 – 402.

Papps, B. P., & O'Carroll, R. E. (1998). Extremes of self-esteem and narcissism and the experience and expression of anger and aggression. *Aggressive Behavior, 24,* 421 – 438.

Pelham, B. W., & Hetts, J. J. (1999). Implicit and explicit personal and social identity: Toward a more complete understanding of the social self. In T. Tyler & R. Kramer (Eds.), *The psychology of the social self* (pp. 115 – 143). Mahwah, NJ: Lawrence Erlbaum Associates, Inc.

Pelham, B. W., Koole, S. L., Hardin, C. D., Hetts, J. J., Seah, E., & DeHart, T. (2005). Gender moderates the relation between implicit and explicit self-esteem. *Journal of Experimental Social Psychology, 41,* 84 – 89.

Rice, K. G., Ashby, J. S., & Slaney, R. B. (1998). Self-esteem as a mediator between perfectionism and depression: A structural equations analysis. *Journal of Counseling Psychology, 45,* 304 – 314.

Roberts, J. E., & Gotlib, I. H. (1997). Temporal variability in global self-esteem and specific self-evaluations as prospective predictors of emotional distress: Specificity in predictors and outcome. *Journal of Abnormal Psychology, 106,* 521 – 529.

Roberts, J. E., & Kassel, J. D. (1997). Labile self-esteem, stressful life events, and depressive symptoms: Prospective data testing a model of vulnerability. *Cognitive Therapy and Research, 21,* 569 – 589.

Roberts, J. E., & Monroe, S. M. (1992). Vulnerable self-esteem and depressive symptoms: Prospective findings comparing three alternative conceptualizations. *Journal of Personality and Social Psychology, 62,* 804 – 812.

Robins, R. W., Hendin, H. M., & Trzesniewski, K. H. (2001). Measuring global self-esteem: Construct validation of a single-item measure and the Rosenberg Self-Esteem Scale. *Personality and Social Psychology Bulletin, 27,* 151 – 161.

Robins, R. W., Trzesniewski, K. H., Tracy, J. L., Gosling, S. D., & Potter, J. (2002). Global self-esteem across the life span. *Psychology and Aging, 17,* 423 – 434.

Rosenberg, M. (1965). *Society and the adolescent self-image.* Princeton, NJ: Princeton University Press.

Shimizu, M., & Pelham, B. W. (2004). The unconscious cost of good fortune: Implicit and explicit self-esteem, positive life events, and health. *Health Psychology, 23,* 101 – 105.

Silber, E., & Tippett, J. S. (1965). Self-esteem: Clinical assessment and measurement validation. *Psychological Reports, 16,* 1017 – 1071.

Slaney, R. B., Rice, K. G., & Ashby, J. S. (2002). A programmatic approach to measuring perfectionism: The Almost Perfect Scales. In G. L. Flett & P. L. Hewitt (Eds.), *Perfectionism: Theory, research, and treatment* (pp. 63 – 88). Washington, DC: American Psychological Association.

Smith, E. R., & DeCoster, J. (2001). Dual-process models in social and cognitive psychology: Conceptual integration and links to underlying memory systems. *Personality and Social Psychological Review, 4,* 108 – 131.

Spalding, L. R., & Hardin, C. D. (1999). Unconscious unease and self-handicapping: Behavioral consequences of individual differences in implicit and explicit self-esteem. *Psychological Science, 10,* 535 – 539.

Spencer, S. J., Jordan, C. H., Logel, C. E. R., & Zanna, M. P. (2005). Nagging doubts and a glimmer of hope: The role of implicit self-esteem in self-image maintenance. In A. Tesser, J. V. Wood, & D. A. Stapel (Eds.), *On building, defending and regulating the self: A psychological perspective* (pp. 153 – 170). New York: Psychology Press.

Strack, F., & Deutsch, R. (2004). Reflective and impulsive determinants of social behavior. *Personality and Social Psychology Review, 8,* 220 – 247.

Suddarth, B. H., & Slaney, R. B. (2001). An investigation of the dimensions of perfectionism in college students. *Measurement and Evaluation in Counseling and Development, 34,* 157 – 165.

Tennen, H., & Affleck, G. (1993). The puzzles of self-esteem: A clinical perspective. In R. F. Baumeister (Ed.), *Self-esteem: The puzzle of low self-regard* (pp. 241 – 262). New York: Plenum Press.

Tice, D. M. (1991). Esteem protection or enhancement? Self-handicapping motives and attributions differ by trait self-esteem. *Journal of Personality and Social Psychology, 60,* 711 – 725.

Tyrka, A. R., Waldron, I., Graber, J. A., & Brooks-Gunn, J. (2002). Prospective predictors of the onset of anorexic and bulimic syndromes. *International Journal of Eating Disorders, 32,* 282 – 290.

Verkuyten, M. (1996). Personal self-esteem and prejudice among ethnic majority and minority youth. *Journal of Research in Personality, 30,* 248 – 263.

Verkuyten, M., & Masson, K. (1995). "New racism," self-esteem, and ethnic relations among minority and majority youth in the Netherlands. *Social Behavior and Personality, 23,* 137 – 154.

Weinstein, N. D. (1980). Unrealistic optimism about future life events. *Journal of Personality and Social Psychology, 39,* 806 – 820.

Wilson, T. D., Lindsey, S., & Schooler, T. Y. (2000). A model of dual attitudes. *Psychological Review, 107,* 101 – 126.

Zeigler-Hill, V. (2006). Discrepancies between implicit and explicit self-esteem: Implications for narcissism and self-esteem instability. *Journal of Personality, 74,* 119 – 143.

Self and Identity, 6: 154–172, 2007
http://www.psypress.com/sai
ISSN: 1529-8868 print/1529-8876 online
DOI: 10.1080/15298860601128255

When "They" Becomes "We": Multiple Contrasting Identities in Mixed Status Groups

AMY K. SANCHEZ
CRISTINA ZOGMAISTER
LUCIANO ARCURI

University of Padova, Padova, Italy

The present research investigated the development of multiple in-group identities among minority group members within a higher status majority. Explicit and implicit identification with the in-group (Southern Italy), out-group (Northern Italy), and a superordinate category (Italy) was examined in 29 Southern Italian students living in Northern Italy. On average, participants strongly identified with the in-group, and those who had spent more time in the north simultaneously displayed increased implicit identification with the out-group. As predicted, incorporation of the out-group into the self occurred only in participants who were not already strongly identified with the superordinate category. Implications for intergroup relations and well being of minority group members are discussed.

The current research examines the potential influence of intergroup contact with a higher status majority on the resulting identification processes of members of low-status groups. According to social identity theory (SIT), the desire to maintain a positive self-concept motivates people to identify with positively viewed social groups (Tajfel & Turner, 1979, 1986). However, in the case of members of stigmatized minority groups, this causes a conflict to arise between one's desire for a positive social identity and the reality of one's own in-group status (Ellemers, Van Rijswijk, Roefs, & Simons, 1997). To remedy this conflict SIT suggests that low-status group members rely on coping strategies including, when possible, leaving the original in-group in favor of a higher status group (Karasawa, Karasawa, & Hirose, 2004; Tajfel & Turner, 1986).

In many cases, the ties to one's in-group lie not only in social identity but also in concrete indicators including family name, accent, and factual information such as one's city of origin. Canceling out an in-group identity based on such factors would therefore require rejecting realistic information about oneself. With the present work we suggest that in these cases a viable strategy may be for the minority member to

The research was supported in part by a grant to the first author in May 2004 from the Fulbright Program. Portions of the research discussed in the current paper were presented at the Meeting of the European Social Cognition Network in Vitznau, Switzerland, in September 2005 and at the Congresso Nazionale AIP della Sezione di Psicologia Sociale in Genoa, Italy, in September 2006.

Correspondence should be addressed to: Amy Sanchez, 46 Central Street, Waltham, MA 02453, USA. E-mail: asanchez@wesleyan.edu incorporate a new out-group identity into the self-concept, or essentially to join the majority, without rejecting the existing in-group.

Identification at the Superordinate Level

An alternative option for restoring one's threatened identity would be to recategorize oneself at a superordinate level, which encompasses both the minority in-group and the majority out-group. The common in-group identity model (Gaertner, Rust, Dovidio, Bachman, & Anastasio, 1994), suggests that intergroup differences may be made less salient and a new, comprehensive identity may be developed that includes both groups, such that former out-group members can be considered part of one's in-group. Through this process, feelings of in-group favoritism are extended to include both the majority and the minority under the overarching classification of the superordinate identity, encouraging a positive attitude towards both groups (Dovidio, Gaertner, Niemann, & Snider, 2001; Dovidio, Gaertner, & Validzic, 1998). Accordingly, it can be speculated that the positive social status of the superordinate group helps reduce the negative impact on the social identity of the original lower status group. Existing research on the interaction between superordinate identity and in-group identity, in fact, supports the idea that simultaneous identification does occur (Dovidio et al., 2001) and that focusing on the superordinate level of identification can enhance the social identities of lower status group members (Mummendey, Klink, Mielke, Wenzel, & Blanz, 1999).

However, this status increase may come at a cost. In fact, according to the model of optimal distinctiveness (Brewer, 1991), optimal social identity is achieved through a balance between similarity to and distinctiveness from others, and that this balance is a defining motivation in one's identification with various social groups. By reaching equilibrium between social distinctiveness and social inclusiveness, one can protect the self-concept from threats of isolation (in the case of too much distinctiveness) or lack of individuality (in the case of too much inclusiveness). The model of optimal distinctiveness predicts that individuals will seek groups that provide a balance between the two extremes. Applied to the common in-group identity model, this implies that the new, common identity category would run the risk of being too broad and inclusive to induce strong identification from its in-group members.

Providing partial support to the common in-group identity model, recent studies show that the lower that subgroup members consider their in-group status to be the more frequently they rely on the superordinate category to identify themselves. This indicates that superordinate identification serves a compensatory function for aspects in which the in-group identity compares negatively to other subgroups (Hornsey & Hogg, 2002). Nevertheless, this effect emerges only when the superordinate and subgroup identities are activated simultaneously and personal distinctiveness is therefore maintained. In addition, research shows that simultaneous activation of both a sub- and superordinate category helps reduce bias more than the superordinate category alone (Hornsey & Hogg, 2000). Thus, though prompting recategorization among low- and high-status groups to form one cohesive in-group eliminates the status disparity, exclusively embracing a superordinate identity at the expense of one's original in-group eliminates an important facet of minority members' identity, which results in a threatening reduction of personal distinctiveness (Brewer, 1991; Brewer & Miller, 1996).

Another Possibility: Incorporating the Positive Effects of a Common In-group Identity Without Forfeiting the Original In-group

The preceding discussion suggests that, in order for identification at the higher level to have positive consequences for a group member, it must occur without a disidentification from the lower status group that maintains personal distinctiveness. The possibility of a coping strategy that incorporates the positive effects of a common in-group identity without the adverse loss of personal distinctiveness rests on the assertion that " ... the self concept is *expandable and contractable* across different levels of social identity with associated *transformations* [italics in original] in the definition of self and the basis for self-evaluation" (Brewer, 1991, p. 476). The idea, consistent with self-categorization theory (Turner, Oakes, Haslam, & McGarty, 1994), that identity development is fluid and context dependent allows for the possibility of identification with new groups as new contexts arise. Depending on the limitations or advantages in a given social context, members' identification with the in-group may be effected by situational factors, such as expectations of future interaction with the group (Veenstra, Haslam, & Reynolds, 2004).

Among low-status minorities entering the context of a higher status majority, for example in the case of immigration, fluid identity development would allow for identification adjustments to adapt to changes in the social framework. Research indicates that among low-status groups, in-group attitudes correlate positively with in-group identification (Bratt, 2002). Importantly, Bratt (2002) also found that there is an absence of negative correlation between in-group and out-group attitudes, suggesting that it is possible to develop a positive attitude towards both one's in-group and the out-group. If this is the case, then it is at least conceivable that an analogous effect could be observed on the identification processes: that is, minority group members could develop a positive out-group identification, which would not negatively impact in-group attitudes and in-group identification. Taking into account the tendency among minority groups to display increasingly favorable attitudes towards a higher status majority over time (e.g., Hetts, Sakuma, & Pelham, 1999; Livingston, 2002), the question emerges as to whether these changes can accompany parallel adjustments in identification. In other words, can increased identification with a high-status out-group over time occur without a negative influence on the original, low-status in-group, as in the case of multiple in-group identity development?

While much of the research regarding identity development focuses on interactions between a single in-group and out-group, in a field setting there are often several groups overlapping and interacting simultaneously. A person can easily consider, for example, the in-groups of women, psychologists, and soccer fans as equally pertinent to her social identity depending on context and relevant comparison groups (Brewer, 1991). Some recent research has begun to explore the processes involved in multiple in-group identification, specifically regarding the interaction between status difference and identity development. Consistent with the coping strategies presented by SIT, Roccas (2003) found that individuals are more likely to show increased identification with high-status groups if they are already members of a distinct lower status group. There is, however, very little literature on the incorporation of an out-group that is in direct conflict with a pre-existing in-group identity—in essence, identifying with the high-status group without ever abandoning the original identity of the low-status group.

Yet Another Possibility: Identification with Both the In-group and the Out-group

Thus far, we have discussed the possibility of abandoning the in-group in favor of the majority out-group, and the possibility of identifying (without abandoning the in-group, in order to maintain optimal distinctiveness) with a more comprehensive superordinate group that encompasses both the in- and out-groups. There remains, however, still another possibility: to identify simultaneously with the majority out-group *and* with the minority in-group. While a superordinate category reduces the salience of in- and out-group boundaries by recategorizing them both into one, broad "umbrella" identity (such as Black and White Americans focusing on their shared national identity as opposed to their racial identity), identification with both the in-group and the out-group requires the simultaneous development of two potentially contradictory identities, such as a minority member who considers herself both part of the minority and part of the majority of a given population. According to the self-expansion model (Wright, Aron, & Tropp, 2002), out-group identification, or the tendency of members of one group to take on the out-group as a reference point and encompass it into their social identity, can occur independently of existing in-group identification. The model maintains that self-expansion, or this process of including the out-group in the self, occurs because the desire for self-enhancement and increased self-efficacy motivates people to incorporate into their self-concept the " ... material and social resources, perspectives, and identities that will facilitate achievement of goals" (Wright et al., 2002, p. 344). Consistent with the view of a context dependant social identity, the model suggests that when confronted with a new situation, people may respond by incorporating into the self other people or groups that successfully cope with the situation. Therefore, for low-status group members, a high-status group could be perceived as particularly successful in coping and would likely become a target of introjection. Unlike the common in-group identity model, this does not necessitate recategorization (and therefore lack of distinctiveness) but instead implies concurrent identification with both the in-group and the out-group. Similar to research indicating that low-status members engage in the preservation of positive, status-irrelevant in-group traits (Cadinu & Cerchioni, 2001; Karasawa et al., 2004), by *expanding* the social identity, the original in-group distinctiveness and identification can remain intact and accessible for situations in which relevant minority group traits are more adaptive than majority traits. Simultaneously, minority group members can draw on the positive social identity associated with the high-status majority once it is incorporated into the self. The inherent theoretical implication is that it is possible to develop additional in-group identifications to protect oneself in situations that threaten existing in-groups, without disidentifying with one's existing in-group, even if the two in-groups appear mutually exclusive.

Because intergroup conflict often occurs between groups that share an overriding common identity (for example, native and immigrant citizens sharing the same national identity) it is important to examine how the superordinate category effects out-group identification. While the self-expansion model does not directly address the interaction between expansion of the in-group and identification with a pre-existing superordinate category, it maintains that one of the motivating factors for out-group identification lies in the ability to incorporate and draw on characteristics that differ from pre-existing aspects of one's self-concept and which assist in coping with various situations. Therefore, the drive for self-expansion will be highest in the absence of a pre-existing, potentially relevant identity that would enable coping in a given situation. Consequently, it can be surmised that strong identification with a relevant superordinate category would act as a buffer and thereby obviate the need or motivation to incorporate the out-group into one's self-concept.

The Present Study

In the present study, our main objective was to investigate the processes involved in the development of multiple in-group identities, focusing on the identification of minority group members within the context of a higher status majority. More specifically, a direct test of the hypothesis proposed in the self-expansion model was carried out with regards to the identity development of Southern Italians living within a higher status Northern Italian majority, in relation to identification with the in-group (Southern Italy), out-group (Northern Italy) and a superordinate category (Italy). Due to the long history of deeply defined, distinct regional cultures within Italy, regional differences often hold more weight than national similarities. As such, many Italians identify primarily with their region of origin, and view those from other areas of Italy as part of the out-group. This distinction is most pronounced in the existence of stereotypes and prejudice between northern and southern regions, and the resulting discrepancy in regional status. Previous research shows that Northern Italians are viewed more positively by both groups and are judged as having a higher status than Southern Italians (Battacchi, 1972; Capozza, Bonaldo, & DiMaggio, 1982).

In line with our hypothesis of the development of an identification of low-status group members to the higher status out-group as a consequence of increased contact with the out-group, recent research by Zogmaister, Arcuri, and Modena (2006) on Southern Italians living in the north indicates that Southern Italians do indeed develop more favorable out-group attitudes in relation to the length of time spent in the north, as measured by performance on implicit attitude scales. This result is coherent with the possibility of the development of an identification with the out-group. Notably, this correlation did not emerge with more traditional measures of explicit identification. As social norms increasingly expect the expression of in-group pride among minority members, effect size using explicit measures of out-group favoritism or bias towards the in-group has diminished (Zogmaister et al., 2006). Unfortunately, given the persistence of prejudice and intergroup tension in real-world settings, there is reason to believe that intergroup biases go under detected in research due to self-presentation efforts by participants (see Karpinski & Steinman, 2006; Maass, Castelli, & Arcuri, 2000; Nosek, 2005; Zogmaister et al., 2006, for a general discussion).

Recent research shows that implicit measures, on the other hand, are more resistant to these self-presentation controls. Implicit measures examine reactions that occur too quickly for participants to modify their responses consciously, and in addition may reflect automatic processes or perspectives of which the participant is not consciously aware. For this reason, implicit as opposed to explicit measures of identification were used as the basis for determining participants' in-group, out-group, and national identification levels. In particular, the present research employed the Go/No-Go Association Task (Nosek & Banaji, 2001) as a measure of self–group association, which should record the ease with which participants succeed in associating the self with a given group. Additionally, we utilized a self–group overlap measure created by Smith and Henry (1996), which should instead assess how much participants see their own characteristics as similar to the characteristics of a certain group and to what degree perceived incongruence between the self and group characteristics result in greater difficulty (and therefore slower responses) in classifying these characteristics. In this procedure, participants are requested first to classify adjectives as descriptive/nondescriptive of themselves in a dichotomous way, and they are subsequently asked to evaluate the level of group-descriptiveness of these same adjectives on a Likert scale. What usually emerges is that participants are faster in the "congruent" cases, i.e., when an adjective is shared by self and in-group, or not shared by both, as compared to the incongruent cases, in which an adjective is considered as representative of the self, but not the in-group, or vice-versa. This pattern of results can be considered as an indirect and automatic effect of group membership.

To summarize, the three main questions examined in the current study were:

1. Whether Southern Italians in Northern Italy would incorporate the out-group (Northern Italy) into their social identity, as evidenced by performance on implicit identification measures.
2. Whether this process would be moderated by the existence of a superordinate national identity.
3. Whether this process would effect participants' original in-group identification.

We predicted that Southern Italians who had spent more time in the north would display higher levels of implicit identification with the high-status out-group. We expected this process to occur without a concurrent negative correlation between in-group identification on the one hand and either out-group identification or national identification on the other hand, suggesting the development of multiple in-group identities as opposed to a binary switch from the low- to high-status in-group. This prediction was made despite that northern and southern regional identities are generally viewed as mutually exclusive. Finally, we hypothesized that the increase in out-group identification would occur only in those participants characterized by low identification with the superordinate category (Italy), indicating that the super-ordinate category acts as a buffer that offers a positive in-group identity with regard to the status-relevant traits and, when activated alongside the existing subgroup identity, reduces the need to incorporate a separate, external in-group identity. We did not expect to find any influence of the permanence in the north on the level of explicit identification with the higher status out-group. The effect of the stay in the north on identification does not necessarily need to be a conscious effect, and because social norms would request low-status group members not to betray the in-group by stating an identification with the out-group, we believed this would induce most participants to maintain a proffered identification with the original in-group category.

Method

Participants

Twenty-nine (14 male, 15 female) undergraduate and graduate students with Southern Italian origins volunteered to participate. All participants were born in regions of Southern Italy and at the time of the experiment were enrolled at the University of Padova and living in the northern *Veneto* region. Participants ranged in age from 18 to 29 years ($M = 23.1$) and had spent between 12 and 180 months living in the north ($M = 59.31$).

Materials

Self–group Overlap Measure.   The first exercise was an adaptation of the task used by Smith and Henry (1996) to examine identification with in-group-relevant traits. Adjectives typically associated with stereotypes of Northern and Southern Italians were ascertained during a pretest in which 10 students at the University of Padova were asked to list descriptors that they believed could be used to classify Northern and Southern Italians. An initial list of adjectives that were stereotypical either of Northern or Southern Italians was compiled through this pretest, and was further integrated using adjectives from a pretest conducted by Maass, Milesi, Zabbini, and Stahlberg (1995). In the final list, 30 adjectives were chosen with 10 seen as typically northern traits (e.g., ambitious, individualistic), 10 seen as typically southern traits (e.g., generous, impulsive), and 10 "ambiguous" traits that were not correlated with stereotypes of either region (e.g., honest, arrogant). For each of the two target categories, a total of 7 positive and 3 negative traits were presented; 8 positive and 2 negative traits were used for the "ambiguous" group. A full list of the adjectives is available from the authors.

The self–group overlap measure consisted of two separate phases. In the first phase, participants were presented with the adjectives, one after the other in random order, centered at the top of the computer screen beneath the question, "Does this adjective describe you?" Participants were instructed to press one of two keys to indicate whether they considered the Multiple Identities 16 adjectives descriptive or not descriptive of themselves (A = *describes me*, 5 = *does not describe me*), at which point the subsequent adjective appeared on the screen. Response time was automatically recorded in milliseconds. Two practice traits (*elegant, gluttonous*) with no relevance to northern or southern stereotypes were also included at the start of the implicit overlap task to reduce error in initial responses. Both participants' responses and reaction times in milliseconds were recorded.

The second phase consisted of three blocks of trials. In each of these blocks, participants were presented with one the following questions: "How much does this adjective describe Southern Italians?" "How much does this adjective describe Northern Italians?" and "How much does this adjective describe you?" The question remained on the screen during the whole block, and the same adjectives discussed above were presented again, one after the other in randomized order. Underneath the adjective a 7-point Likert scale ranging from 1 (*Not at all*) to 7 (*Extremely*) remained on the screen. Participants used the mouse to click on the number that they felt most accurately classified the adjective for each of the three questions. Once participants clicked on a number, the next adjective appeared on the screen. Participants' number responses were recorded.

Go/No-go Association Task.   In order to examine implicit identification with the in-group (Southern Italy), out-group (Northern Italy), and superordinate category (Italy), the Go/No-go Association Task was used (GNAT; Nosek & Banaji, 2001). Participants were presented with a series of stimuli on a monitor. For each stimulus they were requested to react, by pressing the space bar, only if it belonged to a certain category. For instance, in a block of trials they were presented with personal pronouns and asked to react only to those related to the first person singular and to do nothing to the other pronouns. Responses were to be given within 660 ms. In critical blocks participants were requested to react simultaneously to two categories, and the ease of the task was considered an index of automatic association between the categories. The learning phase, presented first, consisted of five blocks in random order in which the target categories were *Self* (represented by pronouns like *me, myself*), *Others* (e.g., *them, themselves*), *Italy* (represented by central Italian cities like *Rome* and *Florence*), *Southern Italy* (represented by southern Italian cities like *Lecce* and *Catania*), and *Northern Italy* (represented by northern Italian cities like *Padua* and *Venice*). This was followed by the assessment phase, which consisted of six blocks in random order in which the target categories were *Self and Italy, Self and Southern Italy, Self and Northern Italy, Others and Italy, Others and Southern Italy*, and *Others and Northern Italy*. Each block in the assessment phase consisted of 12 practice trials and 24 test trials, generated randomly, so that each city was presented a total of three times per block, and reaction time and errors were automatically recorded. The concepts and categories relevant to each trial remained at the top of the computer screen for the duration of that trial, and the space bar was used for all responses. Cities were chosen as associated with Northern, Southern, and Central Italy based on a pretest in which 10 Southern Italian students at the University of Padova listed the cities they considered most representative of each of the three regions. During the trials examining northern regional identity, Northern Italian cities were presented against a background of foreign cities and Southern and Central Italian cities. During the trials examining southern regional identity, Southern Italian cities were presented against a background of foreign cities and Northern and Central Italian cities. During the trials examining Italian identity, centrally located Italian cities were presented against a background of foreign cities. A complete list of the stimuli used in this task is available from the authors.

Explicit Identification Questionnaire. The experimenters also included an explicit measure of national and regional identification. This consisted of three questions, which appeared separately in the center of the computer screen, in random order, described as following: "To what degree do you consider yourself Italian?" "To what degree do you consider yourself Southern Italian?" and "To what degree do you consider yourself Northern Italian?" Underneath the question a 5-point Likert scale ranging from 1 (*Not at all*) to 5 (*Very much*) remained on the screen, and the preceding on-screen directions instructed participants to use the mouse to click on the number that they felt most accurately classified their level of identification for each category.

Procedure

Participants took part in the experiment individually. The experiment was administered by the first author, who spoke in standard Italian but with a subtle American accent, and hence could be easily categorized as belonging neither to the in-group, nor to the out-group. Participants were presented, in this order, with the first phase of the self–group overlap measure, the GNAT, the second phase of the self–group overlap measure, and the computer-administered self-report on explicit identification. These measures were integrated into a single sequence of tasks administered using Inquisit 2.0 (Millisecond Software) and each measure was preceded by on-screen instructions, which enabled participants to self-administer the exercises using a keyboard once the program had begun. Upon completion of the computer-based tasks, participants were administered another questionnaire not relevant for the present purposes and then they filled out a brief one-page questionnaire regarding age; amount of time spent in Northern Italy; reason for moving to Northern Italy; future plans to stay in Northern Italy, return to Southern Italy, or other, etc. This concluded the experiment and participants were thanked and fully debriefed.

Results

Go/No-go Association Task

We computed the implicit index of identification with the in-group (Southern Italians), the out-group (Northern Italians), and the superordinate category (Italians), based on the GNAT. More specifically, we conducted a signal detection on the accuracy of participants in recognizing cities representing each target group (i.e., Southern Italians, Northern Italians, Italians), in the task in which they were associated with pronouns related to the self, and in the task in which they were associated with pronouns related to others. The index of automatic identification with Northern Italians was computed as the difference between the sensitivity of participants (d'') in these two tasks. Similar indexes were computed for the automatic identification of participants with Southern Italians and with the higher level in-group of Italians. Our participants displayed, on average, a significant level of automatic identification with the in-group of Southern Italians, $t(28) = 2.79, p < .001$ ($M = 0.48$, $SD = 0.93$). The mean level of automatic identification with the superordinate category of Italians ($M = -0.04$, $SD = 0.99$), and with the out-group category ($M = -0.13$, $SD = 0.96$) were both non-significant, $ts < 0.73, ps > .47$. The correlations between the three GNAT automatic identification indexes were negligible and non-significant, all $ps > .44$.

Impact of Length of Stay in North

How did the length of the stay in the north influence identification levels of our participants? To answer this question, we computed a logarithmic regression analysis, as we expected the influence of the stay in the north to be more pronounced during the first period of the stay, and to grow progressively less important for longer stays. Results indicated that the permanence in the north significantly influenced the level of identification with the north, $R^2 = .18, F(27) = 5.95, p = .02$; as depicted in Figure 1. Southern Italians that had spent only a few months in the north were the most disidentified, while those that had spent several months in the north were more neutral or even positively identified with the north. Additionally, the impact of the length of stay in the north was much higher during the first few years of the stay. No effects of the length of stay in the north were observed on either the identification with the south, $R^2 = .06, F(27) = 1.77, p = .20$, or the identification with Italians, $R^2 = .01, F(27) < 1, p = .65$.

Impact of Identification with the Superordinate Category

Our hypothesis of a possible moderating effect of identification with the super-ordinate category on the described process was subsequently analyzed. Participants

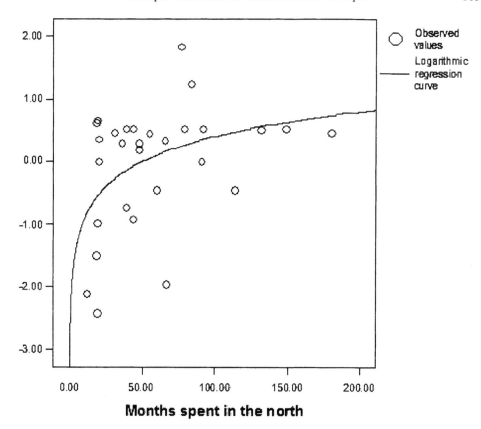

FIGURE 1 Regression analysis of all participants' identification with Northern Italy based on months in the north.

were classified as low-identifiers or high-identifiers with the superordinate category according to their level of identification with Italians computed through the GNAT. Participants whose level of identification with Italians was lower than the median of the group (i.e., participants with a level of automatic identification with the out-group from the lowest observed level to $-.45$) were considered low-identifiers, whereas those with values higher than the median (i.e., participants with a level of automatic identification from $-.07$ through the highest observed value) were considered high-identifiers. We then computed two separate logarithmic regression analyses, one for low-identifiers, and one for high-identifiers, in order to investigate the effect of the stay in the north on the identification with the out-group. For low-identifiers with the superordinate category, the stay in the north significantly influenced the level of identification with the out-group, $R^2 = .34$, $F(1, 13) = 6.80$, $p = .02$; as depicted in Figure 2. For high-identifiers, on the contrary, the stay in the north had no significant impact on the level of implicit identification with the north: $R^2 = .02$, $F(1, 12) < 1$, $p = .64$, as depicted in Figure 3.

Self–Group Overlap

We subsequently analyzed results from the measure of self–group overlap (Smith & Henry, 1996). The adjectives were categorized as stereotypical of Northern and

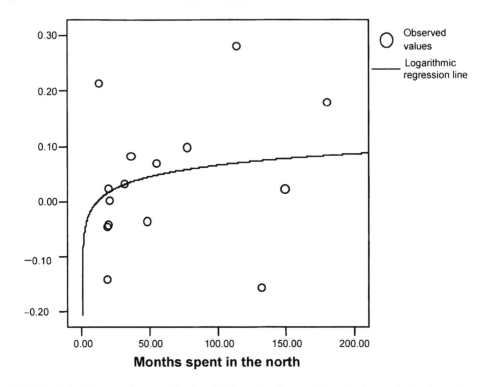

FIGURE 2 Regression analysis of identification with Northern Italy, based on months in the north, among participants characterized by low national identification.

Southern Italians, by comparing the evaluations provided by participants in the blocks that explicitly asked them how much they considered each adjective descriptive of Southern Italians, and Northern Italians, respectively. Nine adjectives (e.g., *reserved, individualistic*) were chosen as stereotypic of Northern Italians according to the following rules: (a) they were valued as significantly more descriptive of Northern as compared to Southern Italians; (b) their mean values were significantly higher than the midpoint of the scale for their evaluation as typical of Northern Italians; and (c) they were valued as neutral or counter-stereotypical for Southern Italians (i.e., they received mean evaluations equal to or lower than the midpoint of the scale, for the question of how descriptive they were considered of Southern Italians). Analogous rules were applied for selecting adjectives as stereotypic of Southern Italians (13 were chosen, e.g., *open, jealous*): (a) they were valued as significantly more descriptive of Southern as compared to Northern Italians; (b) their mean values were significantly higher than the midpoint of the scale for their evaluation as typical of Southern Italians; and (c) they were valued as neutral or counter-stereotypical for Northern Italians. Using this classification, we computed the automatic overlap measure, based on answers to the first task of the self–group overlap measure, in which participants classified adjectives as applying or not applying to themselves in a dichotomous way, by pressing one of two separate keys.[1]

Latencies for responses occurring between −3 standard deviations and +3 standard deviations from the mean reaction times were selected for analysis and submitted to a log transformation to reduce skew (Fazio, 1990). For each participant the mean reaction time in answering "yes" to stereotypical southern traits, the mean

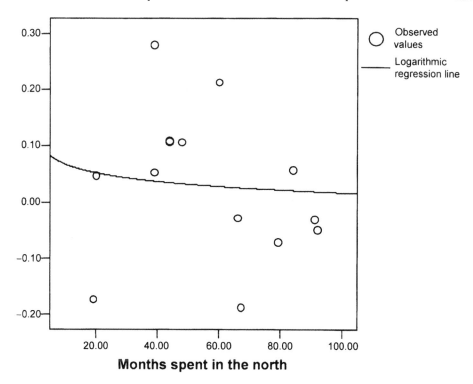

Months spent in the north

FIGURE 3 Regression analysis of identification with Northern Italy, based on months in the north, among participants characterized by high national identification.

reaction time in answering "no" to stereotypical southern traits, the mean reaction time in answering "yes" to stereotypical northern traits, and the mean reaction time in answering "no" to stereotypical northern traits were computed. Data from six participants could not be used because they failed to answer "no" to any of the adjectives considered as stereotypical of Southern Italians. These indexes were first submitted to a two-way ANOVA, with Type of Adjective (stereotypic northern vs. stereotypic southern) and Type of Response (no vs. yes) as the two within-participant factors. This analysis revealed a main effect of Type of Adjective, $F(1, 22) = 11.97$, $p = .002$, indicating that participants were faster in responding to adjectives that were typical of Southern, as compared to Northern, Italians. A main effect of Type of Answer also emerged: participants were faster in answering "yes" as compared to "no", $F(1, 22) = 15.44$, $p = .001$. More interestingly, an interaction qualified the main effects, $F(1, 22) = 5.83$, $p = .02$, indicating that the difference between the "yes" and "no" reactions was higher for adjectives stereotypical of Southern as compared to Northern Italians. Two separate t-tests revealed that the difference between reaction times to "yes" and "no" answers was significant for adjectives stereotypic of Southern Italians, $t(22) = 4.66$, $p < .001$, whereas this same difference was not significant for adjectives stereotypic of Northern Italians, $t(22) = 1.45$, $p = .16$. Hence, we observed the self–in-group overlap effect, described by Smith and Henry (1996), in relation to the group of Southern Italians, whereas no self–out-group overlap effect was observed. An index of self–in-group overlap was computed as the difference in reaction times in "no" and "yes" answers provided for adjectives typical of Southern Italians, and a similar index of self–out-group overlap was computed as the difference in reaction times in "no" and "yes" answers provided for adjectives typical of Northern Italians.

These indexes of self–in-group and self–out-group overlap did not correlate with each other, $r(23) = .18$, $p = .40$. Mean values, based on a re-transformation of the means computed on the log-transformed latencies, are presented in Table 1.

We subsequently investigated whether the self–group overlap measure was influenced by the length of the stay in the north. A regression analysis was computed, which revealed no effect of the length of the stay on the self–out-group overlap, $R^2 = .00$, $p = .95$, and no effect on the self–in-group overlap, $R^2 = .05$, $p = .31$. Self–group overlap measures did not correlate with automatic identification measures from the GNAT, all $ps > .22$.

Explicit Identification Measures

Participants were explicitly asked how much they identified as Southern Italians, Northern Italians, and the more general category of Italians, on a 5-point Likert scale. Analyses revealed that, on average, the explicit identification with Southern Italians was significantly higher than the midpoint of the scale, $t(28) = 14.22$, two-tailed, $p < .001$, as was the mean level of explicit identification with Italians, $t(28) = 19.33$, two-tailed, $p < .001$. Conversely, the mean level of identification with Northern Italians was significantly lower than the midpoint of the scale, $t(28) = 2.22$, two-tailed, $p < .05$. See Table 2 for the mean explicit identification levels. None of these indexes of explicit identification was influenced by the stay in the north; all R^2s $< .09$, all $ps > .11$.

Future Plans

We asked our participants about their plans for the future. Among them, 10 had plans to stay in Northern Italy (34.5%), 6 had plans to go back to Southern Italy (20.7%), and 13 had other plans for the future (44.8%). The one-way ANOVA revealed a significant difference between the mean level of automatic identification of these three groups with Northern Italians, $F(2, 26) = 5.65$, $p < .01$ (see Table 3). In

TABLE 1 Mean Reaction Time latencies to Northern and Southern Traits

	Type of Adjective	
Response	Northern Italian	Southern Italian
Yes	1665.96	1319.66
No	1813.83	1715.01

TABLE 2 Explicit Identification as Northern Italian, Southern Italian, and Italian

Category*	Minimum	Maximum	Mean (SD)
Italians	4.00	5.00	4.69 (0.47)
Northerners	1.00	5.00	2.55 (1.09)
Southerners	3.00	5.00	4.52 (0.57)

*$n = 29$ for each category.

TABLE 3 Mean Level of Identification with the North (GNAT Index) in Relation to Future Plans

Future plans	Mean	SD	N
Stay in north	−0.0320	0.88815	10
Return to south	−1.0200	1.23567	6
Other	0.4023	0.60523	13
Total	−0.0417	0.98987	29

particular, participants planning to go back to Southern Italy displayed a higher level of disidentification with Northern Italy as compared to participants who were planning to stay in the north, $t(14) = 1.86$, $p < .05$, one-tailed. No significant difference between participants depending on plans for the future emerged on their level of automatic identification with Southern Italy. A larger number of participants would be necessary for more detailed analyses, but these results do provide some support to the validity of our automatic out-group identification measure as an indicator of important processes regulating intergroup behaviors.

Discussion

Identification and Implications for Intergroup Relations/Coping Strategies

Consistent with our hypotheses and with the predictions of the self-expansion model (Wright et al., 2002), results from the present research evidenced that members of a low-status minority (Southern Italians) who had spent more time living within the context of a high-status majority (Northern Italians) displayed higher levels of automatic identification with the high-status out-group. More specifically, results from the GNAT showed a significant correlation between the duration of the participants' stay in the north and their level of identification with Northern Italy, particularly within the first several months of the stay, such that longer stays correlated with higher levels of implicit identification with the north. Therefore, participants who had spent more time in the north developed an automatic association between the self and the out-group on the implicit identification measure, indicating the incorporation of the out-group into their social identity.

As expected, this effect was not revealed at the explicit level. Participants expressed positive explicit identification with Southern Italy and with the superordinate national category, and did not express identification with the out-group. Explicit identification was not influenced by the permanence in the north. Additionally, permanence in Northern Italy had no effect on participants' performance on the self–group overlap measure.

The absence of an effect on explicit identification is not surprising for two reasons. First, it deals with a process that develops over time and which therefore manifests itself at the level of spontaneous reactions before that of conscious reactions, such that a person can be unaware of changes in his or her own identification. Second, among members of a minority group strong social pressures can exist that condemn the expression of identification with the out-group because it could be viewed as a betrayal of one's original identity. The capacity to overcome these limitations stemming from participants' concerns for self-presentation and from difficulties with introspection are the specific motivations for which implicit measures were chosen for this study.

The dissociation that emerges between the two measures examining implicit identification, however, is particularly interesting. Specifically, an effect of the duration of stay in the north emerges in the GNAT but does not emerge in the self–group overlap measure. What does this divergence mean? Both measures examine spontaneous aspects of group identification. The GNAT illustrates that our participants spontaneously identify, on average, with the in-group, while the self–group overlap measure indicates that it is in-group characteristics that facilitate or interfere with the attribution of characteristics to the self. Still, the absence of correlations between the two measures suggests that they examine two distinct aspects of group identification.

In particular the GNAT is presented as a measure of association between the self and the group: it should record the ease with which people are able to associate the self with a specific group. The self–group overlap measure, on the other hand, is presented as a measure of how much participants see their own characteristics as similar to those of a certain group and how much difficulty (demonstrated by slower response times) is caused by incongruence between the way in which participants see themselves and the way they view the group.

An increase in participants' implicit identification with the north on the GNAT over time therefore indicates a strengthening in participants' implicit association with the out-group. The absence of a change in participants' performance on the self–group overlap measure, however, indicates that they continued to view their original in-group (Southern Italy) as a frame of reference for their personal traits. These results suggest that our participants, apparently, are not simply reconceptualizing themselves as members of the out-group, as it appears that they are not abandoning their southern identity. Instead, they begin to encompass or bring the out-group closer to themselves.

Consistent with this idea and with our second hypothesis, this finding was accompanied by high identification levels with the in-group on both implicit and explicit identification measures, and results showed no effect of time spent in the north on identification with the in-group. The steadily high levels of in-group identification among participants who had spent several months in the north, paired with increased identification with the out-group, indicates that participants simultaneously associated the in- and out-groups with the self. This provides support for the incorporation of a new identity without rejection of the original in-group, indicating the emergence of multiple in-group identities.

As predicted, the above effect was moderated by participants' level of identification with the superordinate category. On average, our participants did not display implicit identification with the superordinate category, but a high degree of variability was observed between participants: approximately half of them displayed a positive identification, and the other half a disidentification, from the superordinate category. According to their implicit identification with Italy, as measured by performance on the GNAT, participants were classified as low-identifiers or high-identifiers with the superordinate category. For those participants with high national identification, time spent in the north had no impact on out-group identification. For participants with low national identification, on the other hand, more time spent in the north was significantly correlated with increased identification with the out-group.

This finding provides direct support for the prediction in the self-expansion model that acquiring an external social identity is more likely when that identity provides relevant coping tools (for example, positive group traits) that offer the possibility for increased self-efficacy and self-enhancement. The results show that members of a lower status group can incorporate the out-group into their social identity independently of their continued in-group identification. However, high-identifiers already possess a strong national identity, which includes both Northern and Southern Italians. Hence, in situations threatening their in-group, they are already equipped with an inclusive, higher level identity, or buffer, through which they can draw on positive coping tools not present in the low-status in-group identity. This is consistent with the common in-group identity model (Gaertner et al., 1994) and with previous support for self-enhancement of social identity among low-status groups when the superordinate category is emphasized (Mummendey et al., 1999). Low-identifiers, on the other hand, lack this relevant, pre-existing social identity. Acquiring an external identity (in this case, the high-status north) therefore allows for the expansion of the self to include a group that can provide the positive image or traits lacking from the original identity, as postulated in SIT, without abandoning the original in-group identification.

The findings of the current study are encouraging in their implications for intergroup relations and coping strategies among low-status groups. Participants' tendency to identify with the out-group at an implicit level could help alleviate some of the negative effects that previous research shows to be correlated with discrimination and low-status group membership, such as elevated stress (e.g., Pak, Dion, & Dion, 1991). In addition, our analysis of participants' future plans shows that disidentification with the north was higher for participants who planned to permanently return to Southern Italy than for those who planned to stay in the north. This suggests that an elevated level of out-group identification is correlated with low-status group members' tendency to remain among (and presumably integrate into) the high-status out-group community. Meanwhile, participants' implicit identification with the south did not differ depending on their future plans. Because participants' identification with the original in-group was simultaneously sustained, regardless of how much time they had spent (and planned to spend in the future) in the context of the northern majority, stress reduction and increased integration for the low-status group would not be diminished by the loss of personal distinctiveness proposed by Brewer (1991) in her theory of optimal distinctiveness.

Limitations and Questions for Future Research

The most important question left open from our research concerns the direction of causality. From the data, we cannot tell whether participants developed a stronger association with the northern out-group over time (because of their stay) or whether, on the contrary, those characterized by a lower level of association with the north were more likely to leave after a shorter stay while those more highly identified with the north remained. Both explanations are congruent with our data, and only a longitudinal study could disentangle these two possibilities. The observed buffering effect of the identification with Italians, though, is in favor of our explanation in terms of in-take of the out-group into the self. Specifically, if disidentification from the north caused low-identified participants to return home, this should have happened independently of the identification with the superordinate category. In the future, a longitudinal study measuring participants' identification levels upon first arrival in the north, and then again several months into their stay, could clarify these results.

Also, as demonstrated in previous research on this population (Zogmaister et al., 2006), this pattern of identification change over time is consistent with attitude change toward the out-group over time among Southerners in the north. Zogmaister et al. found that Southern Italian participants who had spent more time in Northern Italy expressed a higher level of out-group favoritism than southerners who had spent only a short time in the north. As discussed above, the present research indicates that among this population a second transformation in cognitive representations, consisting of an increase in identification with the out-group, accompanies this attitude change. Because these two phenomena are most likely related, further research that investigates the relationship between intergroup attitude change and intergroup identification could help shed light on both processes and on their mutual impact on minority members' relationship with the out-group.

Finally, the division evidenced in our participants, between incorporation of the out-group into the self or strong identification with the superordinate category, raises certain questions regarding the relative effectiveness of these coping strategies in buffering against the negative effects of the low-status in-group. Specifically, which strategy correlates more strongly to reduced stress among low-status minority members living amidst a high-status majority, and better integration with the majority? More importantly, how can the development of multiple in-group identities be facilitated for purposes of easing integration and lowering stress and feelings of alienation? The results of the present study highlight several important processes involved in out-group identification and multiple identity development. Support is provided for the process of simultaneous identification with the out-group and in-group, where out-group identification increased over time and was moderated by the presence of a strong superordinate identity. Nevertheless, continued examination of out-group identification, specifically in context of a superordinate identity, is necessary to help clarify these questions and to better understand what factors contribute to increased identification with both categories.

Note

1. Our procedure of classification of adjectives as stereotypical of the in-group and stereotypical of the out-group differs from the idiographic one proposed by Smith and Henry (1996). The original procedure bases the differentiation of adjectives as descriptive and non-descriptive of the group on the responses of the participant in the second phase of the task and hence, the adjectives that are considered descriptive are potentially different for each participant. We were forced to base the classification of adjectives as stereotypic and nonstereotypic on the group's responses, instead of the responses of the single participant, because a large number of participants made great use of the midpoint of the scale, making it impossible to compute the index in the traditional manner. Only for eight participants could we compute the self–north overlap measure according to Smith and Henry's original proposal, and only for five the self–south overlap measure. For those participants, the correlation between the traditional method and our index of self–north overlap, was $r(8) = .67$, and the self–south overlap had a correlation of $r(5) = .93$, which made us reasonably confident with the method we chose.

References

Battacchi, M. W. (1972). *Meridionali e settentrionali nella struttura del pregiudizio etnico in Italia [Southerners and Northerners in the structure of ethnic prejudice in Italy]* (2nd ed.). Bologna, Italy: Il Mulino.

Bratt, C. (2002). Contact and attitudes between ethnic groups: A survey-based study of adolescents in Norway. *Acta Sociologica, 45*, 107–125.

Brewer, M. B. (1991). The social self: On being the same and different at the same time. *Personality and Social Psychology Bulletin, 17*, 475–482.

Brewer, M. B., & Miller, N. (1996). *Intergroup relations*. Oxford, UK: Open University Press.

Cadinu, M. R., & Cerchioni, M. (2001). Compensatory biases after in-group threat: "Yeah, but we have a good personality". *European Journal of Social Psychology, 31*, 353–367.

Capozza, D., Bonaldo, E., & DiMaggio, A. (1982). Problems of identity and social conflict: Research on ethnic groups in Italy. In H. Tajfel (Ed.), *Social identity and intergroup relations* (pp. 299–334). Cambridge, UK: Cambridge University Press.

Dovidio, J. F., Gaertner, S. L., Niemann, Y. F., & Snider, K. (2001). Racial, ethnic, and cultural differences in responding to distinctiveness and discrimination on campus: Stigma and common group identity. *Journal of Social Issues, 57*, 167–188.

Dovidio, J. F., Gaertner, S. L., & Validzic, A. (1998). Intergroup bias: Status, differentiation, and a common in-group identity. *Journal of Personality and Social Psychology, 75*, 109–120.

Ellemers, N., Van Rijswijk, W., Roefs, M., & Simons, C. (1997). Bias in intergroup perceptions: Balancing group identity with social reality. *Personality and Social Psychology Bulletin, 23*, 186–198.

Fazio, R. H. (1990). A practical guide to the use of response latency in social psychological research. In C. Hendrick & M. Clark (Eds.), *Research methods in personality and social psychology: Review of personality and social psychology* (Vol. 11, pp. 74–97). Thousand Oaks, CA: Sage.

Gaertner, S. L., Rust, M. C., Dovidio, J. F., Bachman, B. A., & Anastasio, P. A. (1994). The contact hypothesis: The role of a common in-group identity on reducing intergroup bias. *Small Group Research, 25*, 224–249.

Hetts, J. J., Sakuma, M., & Pelham, B. W. (1999). Two roads to positive regard: Implicit and explicit self-evaluation and culture. *Journal of Social Psychology, 35*, 512–559.

Hornsey, M. J., & Hogg, M. A. (2000). Subgroup relations: A comparison of the mutual intergroup differentiation and common in-group identity models of prejudice reduction. *Personality and Social Psychology Bulletin, 26*, 242–256.

Hornsey, M. J., & Hogg, M. A. (2002). The effects of status on subgroup relations. *British Journal of Social Psychology, 41*, 203–218.

Karasawa, M., Karasawa, K., & Hirose, Y. (2004). Homogeneity perception as a reaction to identity threat: Effects of status difference in a simulated society game. *European Journal of Social Psychology, 34*, 613–625.

Karpinski, A., & Steinman, R. B. (2006). The single category implicit association test as a measure of implicit social cognition. *Journal of Personality and Social Psychology, 91*, 16–32.

Livingston, R. W. (2002). The role of perceived negativity in the moderation of African Americans' implicit and explicit racial attitudes. *Journal of Experimental Social Psychology, 38*, 405–413.

Maass, A., Castelli, L., & Arcuri, L. (2000). Measuring prejudice: Implicit versus explicit techniques. In R. Brown & D. Capozza (Eds.), *Social identity processes: Trends in theory and research* (pp. 96–116). London: Sage.

Maass, A., Milesi, A., Zabbini, S., & Stahlberg, D. (1995). Linguistic intergroup bias: Differential expectancies or in-group protection? *Journal of Personality and Social Psychology, 68*, 116–126.

Mummendey, A., Klink, A., Mielke, R., Wenzel, M., & Blanz, M. (1999). Sociostructural characteristics of intergroup relations and identity management strategies: Results from a field study in East Germany. *European Journal of Social Psychology, 29*, 259–285.

Nosek, B. A. (2005). Moderators of the relationship between implicit and explicit evaluation. *Journal of Experimental Psychology, 134,* 565–584.

Nosek, B. A., & Banaji, M. R. (2001). The Go/No-go Association Task. *Social Cognition, 19,* 625–666.

Pak, A. W., Dion, K. L., & Dion, K. K. (1991). Social-psychological correlates of experienced discrimination: Test of the double jeopardy hypothesis. *International Journal of Intercultural Relations, 15,* 243–254.

Roccas, S. (2003). The effect of status on identification with multiple groups. *European Journal of Social Psychology, 33,* 351–366.

Smith, E. R., & Henry, S. (1996). An in-group becomes part of the self: Response time evidence. *Personality and Social Psychology Bulletin, 22,* 635–642.

Tajfel, H., & Turner, J. C. (1979). An integrative theory of intergroup conflict. In W. Austin & S. Worchel (Eds.), *The social psychology of intergroup relations.* Monterey, CA: Brooks/ Cole.

Tajfel, H., & Turner, J. C. (1986). The social identity theory of intergroup behavior. In S. Worchel & W. Austin (Eds.), *Psychology of intergroup relations* (pp. 7–24). Chicago: Nelson Hall.

Turner, J. C., Oakes, P. J., Haslam, S. A., & McGarty, C. (1994). Self and collective: Cognition and social context. *Personality and Social Psychology Bulletin, 20,* 454–463.

Veenstra, K., Haslam, S. A., & Reynolds, K. J. (2004). The psychology of casualization: Evidence for the mediating roles of security, status and social identification. *British Journal of Social Psychology, 43,* 499–514.

Wright, S. C., Aron, A., & Tropp, L. R. (2002). Including others (and groups) in the self: Self-expansion and intergroup relations. In J. Forgas & K. Williams (Eds.), *The social self: Cognitive, interpersonal, and intergroup perspectives* (pp. 343–363). New York: Psychology Press.

Zogmaister, C., Arcuri, L., & Modena, S. (2006). La percezione di gruppi caratterizzati da status sociale asimmetrico. Rapporto tra processi impliciti ed espliciti [The perception of groups characterized by asymmetrical social status. The relationship between implicit and explicit processes]. *Rassegna di Psicologia, 13,* 93–121.

Self and Identity, 6: 173–188, 2007
http://www.psypress.com/sai
ISSN: 1529-8868 print/1529-8876 online
DOI: 10.1080/15298860601115328

The Malleability of Men's Gender Self-concept

CADE MCCALL

University of California, Santa Barbara, California, USA

NILANJANA DASGUPTA

University of Massachusetts, Amherst, Massachusetts, USA

The present study tested the influence of social status and gender salience on the malleability of men's gender self-concepts at an automatic versus controlled level. Male participants were placed in a superior or subordinate role relative to a male or female confederate for a joint task; subsequently their automatic and controlled beliefs about themselves were measured. We predicted first, that men placed in a subordinate role would protect against the threat to their self-concept by automatically self-stereotyping more than men placed in a superior role. As a secondary hypothesis, we predicted that the presence of a female interaction partner would increase the situational salience of gender, which in turn would evoke gender stereotypic self-descriptions. Results confirmed these hypotheses. These data suggest that men's gender self-concepts are malleable and that situational cues differentially affect self-conceptions at an automatic and controlled level.

Over the past fifty years gender norms in American society have changed dramatically. As noted by psychologists and feminist theorists alike, more of these changes have occurred with respect to women's gender roles (Diekman & Eagly, 2000; Steinem, 2000). Men's roles, however, have stayed far more consistent. For example, while women's participation in the work force has nearly doubled since 1950 (Diekman & Eagly, 2000; US Department of Labor, 2002), men's participation in domestic work has increased only marginally (Biernat & Wortman, 1991). Perhaps as a result, stereotypes about women tend to be various and dynamic while stereotypes about men tend to be more limited and stable (Deaux, Winton, Crowley, & Lewis, 1985; Diekman & Eagly, 2000). Along the same lines, men's attitudes about gender tend to be more traditional than women's attitudes (Jackson, Hodge, & Ingram, 1994) and some evidence suggests that men comply more closely with gender stereotypes than do women (Burris, Branscombe, & Klar, 1997; Hogg & Turner, 1987).

This research was Cade McCall's Master's thesis conducted under the supervision of Nilanjana Dasgupta when both authors were at New School University. Data collection was supported by grants from the National Institute of Mental Health (R03 MH66036-01) and from New School University to the second author.

We are indebted to Abraham Greenwald and Maile O'Hara for serving as confederates, and to January Massin for serving as the experimenter in this study.

Correspondence should be addressed to: Cade McCall, Department of Psychology, University of California, Santa Barbara, CA 93106-9660, USA. E-mail: mccall@psych.ucsb.edu

Despite these data, other evidence suggests that men's gender-related self-conceptions show some degree of malleability across contexts (Deaux & Major, 1987). Depending on the social situation and the degree to which their gender is distinctive, men are differentially likely to endorse stereotypically masculine traits in describing themselves (Cota & Dion, 1986; Dailey & Rosenzweig, 1988; Hogg & Turner, 1987). For example, when men are the minority sex in mixed-sex groups, they are more likely to mention gender-related qualities in self-descriptions (Cota & Dion, 1986). Moreover, men's self-perceptions of their roles vary across different settings, with contexts such as the workplace prompting more stereotypically masculine self-descriptions and sexual situations prompting less masculine self-descriptions (Dailey & Rosenzweig, 1988). When are men's self-conceptions malleable and when are they stable? What is the best way to capture this flexibility? The overarching goal of the present study was to specify and test two conditions under which men's gender self-conceptions ought to show flexibility. Our primary focus was on men's automatic (implicit) self-conceptions, but for comparison purposes, we also examined their controlled (explicit) self-perceptions.

Compensatory Cognition and the Working Self-concept

For many years, research on the self-concept followed two separate lines: one wherein the self was conceptualized as a stable and enduring mental representation and one wherein the self was conceptualized as a fluid and malleable mental representation (Markus & Kunda, 1986). On the one hand, research on the consistency of the self-concept has demonstrated that people actively seek out information and situations that confirm their existing self-concept and misinterpret or ignore information that contradicts their dominant beliefs about themselves (Shrauger & Lund, 1975; Swann, 1997). On the other hand, research on the malleability of the self-concept has also provided considerable evidence that beliefs about the self expressed at any given time or situation depend on their relevance in that particular situation (Cota & Dion, 1986; Daily & Rosenzweig, 1988; Devos & Banaji, 2003; Greenberg & Pyszczynski, 1985; McGuire, McGuire, Child, Fujioka, 1978; McGuire, McGuire, & Winton, 1979; Moskowitz, 2002; Steele, 1988; Turner, Oakes, Haslam & McGarty, 1994).

In an attempt to integrate these lines of research, Markus and colleagues proposed a model of the working self-concept, which consists of individuals' self-relevant attributes that are activated or elicited by a particular event or a situation (Markus & Kunda, 1986). The working self-concept is also shaped by challenges to the self. Threat to self-esteem, threat to one's social status, and threat to one's membership in important groups are all countered by malleable self-conceptions (Markus & Wurf, 1987; Moskowitz, 2001).

Compensatory cognition is one way in which the working self-concept changes when confronted by threats (Greenberg & Pyszczynski, 1985; Markus & Wurf, 1987; Moskowitz, 2001; Steele, 1988; Wicklund & Gollwitzer, 1981). This psychological response is of particular interest to us in the present study. Compensatory cognition appears to protect valued beliefs about the self when those beliefs are threatened by contradicting information (Markus & Wurf, 1987; Moskowitz, 2002; Wicklund & Gollwitzer, 1981).

Some researchers contend that people may not be aware when various self-enhancing mechanisms and behaviors are at work (Markus & Kunda, 1986; Markus & Wurf, 1987; Moskowitz, 2001, 2002; Rudman, Dohn, & Fairchild, 2006;

Tesser, 2000). In one study that supports this point (Markus & Kunda, 1986), participants were made to feel either extremely unique or extremely similar to others. Subsequently, they were asked to select self-descriptive adjectives from a given list and the speed at which they responded was measured. While participants did not differ in the words they chose, they did differ in their speed of response. Participants made to feel extremely similar to others were faster at endorsing "unique" traits while participants made to feel dissimilar from others were faster at endorsing "similar" traits. Markus and Kunda (1986) argued that this compensatory effect was automatic based on the evidence that participants' explicit self-descriptions were the same across conditions, but what varied was the speed with which those traits were attributed to the self.

More recent work by Moskowitz (2001, 2002) provides similar evidence. In one study, Moskowitz (2002, Experiment 1) asked athletes to describe either an experience of success or failure in their athletic careers (a self-affirming or self-threatening experience). Subsequently, they completed a Stroop task in which words relevant to the goal of athleticism (e.g., "athletic", "strong") and words irrelevant to that goal (e.g., "studious", "smart") were presented in various colors. When asked to identify the color of athleticism-relevant words, participants who had been threatened were significantly slower than others who had been affirmed suggesting that threat to their athletic prowess automatically drew participants' attention to the semantic meaning of goal-relevant words and interfered with their ability to name the colors of those words. When the words were irrelevant to athleticism, however, response latencies for self-threatened and self-affirmed participants were not significantly different. A second study provided a conceptual replication using participants whose egalitarian goals had been threatened (Moskowitz, 2002, Experiment 2). These data suggest that participants automatically attended to words relevant to threatened goals. Importantly, as in Markus and Kunda's (1986) study, participants were unaware that their compensatory responses were influenced by the experimental manipulation. Together, this evidence suggests that compensatory cognition occurs automatically and without people's awareness, a point that has been made by other self-concept theories as well (Tesser, 2000).

Past research suggests that affect-laden situations and experiences have a particularly potent effect on the malleability of automatic attitudes and beliefs about others and the self. For example, studies have found that White participants show increased automatic race bias when placed in a situation where they receive negative feedback from a Black supervisor rather than positive feedback from the same individual (Sinclair & Kunda, 1999). Similarly, men show greater automatic bias against women when they anticipate playing a subordinate role rather than a superior role in an interaction with a woman (Richeson & Ambady, 2001). Moreover, White participants show greater automatic bias against African Americans on a reaction time task when their egalitarian self-conceptions are threatened because the task is framed as a measure of their personal attitudes rather than a measure of cultural stereotypes (Frantz, Cuddy, Burnett, Ray, & Hart, 2004). Finally, when automatic evaluations of the self are the focus of investigation, automatic self-esteem has been found to increase in response to self-relevant threats (Rudman et al., 2006). All of these instances show that negative affective experiences are particularly effective in modulating automatic attitudes and beliefs expressed in those situations.

Based on the evidence described above, we predict that threat to self-relevant beliefs will shift men's automatic beliefs about themselves in a compensatory fashion.

We do not, however, expect these shifts to be reflected in controlled self-descriptions. On the contrary, if compensatory cognition quickly and successfully protects the self from threatening information, then subsequent explicit accounts of the self may survive unscathed. In other words, compensatory cognition may be captured more easily using indirect measures that assess automatic self-related beliefs whereas direct measures that assess controlled beliefs may fail to do so (Markus & Kunda, 1986; Moskowitz, 2001).

Threat to One's Social Status and Its Effect on the Self-concept

Different events or situational variables may threaten people's self-conceptions and trigger compensatory cognition as a way of countering the threat. In our research we focused on threats to men's gender-related beliefs about themselves as agentic, authoritative, and masterful. We chose agency as the masculine trait dimension given the abundance of research demonstrating that men describe themselves as, and are stereotyped as, more agentic than women (Eagly & Karau, 2002; Eagly & Steffen, 1984; Eagly & Wood, 1991; Hosoda & Stone, 2000). Similarly on implicit measures of gender self-concept, men and women show even stronger gender differences, sometimes as much as three times the difference they show on explicit measures (Greenwald & Farnham, 2000). Thus, we believed that placing men in a low status (non-agentic) position would challenge their masculine self-beliefs.

Men are particularly likely to be invested in masculine self-conceptions given the fact that they belong to a high-status group. Typically, members of high-status groups identify more strongly with their in-group than members of low-status groups (Ellemers, Doosje, Van Knippenberg, de Vries, & Wilke, 1988), and they tend to think and act in ways that maintain their group membership (Depret & Fiske, 1999; Ellemers, Doosje, Van Knippenberg, & Wilke, 1992; Fiske, 2001; Operario, Goodwin, & Fiske, 1998). Threatening masculine self-conceptions may be particularly important to men because deviation from agentic norms is likely to challenge the justification for their in-group's high status and the privilege associated with it (Burris et al., 1997; Hogg & Turner, 1987). As a result it seems reasonable to predict that when agentic self-beliefs are threatened, men will compensate by expressing even more masculine self-beliefs to preserve their privilege.

Thus, the first goal of the present research was to test whether men, when unexpectedly placed in a counterstereotypic low-status role involving little authority and agency, will compensate for their loss of agency by bolstering masculine attributes associated with the self and distancing themselves from feminine attributes associated with the self, compared to other men placed in a stereotypic high-status role. Given the evidence that compensatory cognition functions outside of awareness, we predicted that shifts in men's gender self-conceptions as a function of their status would emerge more clearly in terms of automatic self-related beliefs rather than controlled beliefs.

Situational Salience of Gender and Its Effect on the Self-concept

In addition to social status, other situational cues may also affect people's self-conceptions. Cues that draw attention to gender, such as the sex of one's interaction partners, may make people think about themselves in a more gender schematic manner (James, 1993). In the presence of out-group members one's own group membership may become salient, leading people to mention in-group traits and behaviors more frequently in self-descriptions (Cota & Dion, 1986; Hogg & Turner, 1987; McGuire, McGuire, & Cheever, 1986).

In line with this evidence, some researchers contend that people's in-group identities are most likely to affect their judgment and behavior under two conditions—when situational cues (a) render in-group identity distinctive, and (b) make people consciously reflect on themselves (Abrams, 1994). By integrating self-categorization theory (Turner, Hogg, Oakes, Reicher, & Wetherell, 1987) and self-attention theory (Wicklund, 1975), Abrams (1994) argues that self-focus or self-awareness enhances the influence of salient group membership on judgment and behavior. This claim is supported by evidence that when placed into minimal groups, people who are self-aware base their behavior on in-group standards and act to preserve their in-group's distinctiveness more than others who are less self-aware (Abrams & Brown, 1989). Likewise, when group membership is made salient, highly self-aware individuals express a stronger sense of belonging to the in-group as well as greater pride in their in-group than less self-aware individuals (Abrams, 1985).

It is not clear, however, whether group-related distinctiveness will have equivalent effects in the absence of self-focus or self-reflection. In other words, while the effect of gender salience on controlled self-beliefs is robust (Cota & Dion, 1986; Hogg & Turner, 1987), the same may not be true for automatic self-beliefs. To the extent that automatic attitudes and beliefs are particularly sensitive to threat or other affect-laden contexts (e.g., Rudman et al., 2006), comparatively neutral contexts created by varying gender salience may not be sufficient to alter automatic beliefs about the self. Based on these arguments, we do not expect gender salience by itself to play a strong role when participants' self-related beliefs are measured indirectly using a reaction-time measure. However, we predict that gender salience will play a role in participants' self-reported descriptions of themselves. That is, male participants who interact with a female partner will be more likely to describe themselves in terms of stereotypically masculine traits than male participants who interact with a male partner.

Method

Overview

The primary purpose of this study was to investigate the role of social status and gender salience on the malleability of men's gender self-conceptions. To that end, male participants were placed in a superior or subordinate role relative to a male or female confederate for a joint task on public speaking. Subsequently we assessed participants' automatic and controlled beliefs about themselves. We predicted first that participants placed in a low-status role would automatically emphasize their stereotypically masculine agentic qualities significantly more than those placed in a high-status role. As a secondary hypothesis, we predicted that participants who had to interact with a female partner would subsequently describe themselves using more masculine agentic qualities than those who had to interact with a male partner.

Participants

A community sample of 58 men participated in exchange for $10 each. Participant's age ranged from 17 to 68 years old with a mean age of 32. In terms of ethnicity,

51% of participants identified as White, 20% identified as Hispanic, 13% identified as Black, 7% identified as multiracial, 3% identified as Asian, 1% as Native American, and 5% did not specify their race. Participants were recruited with flyers posted in Manhattan, as well as postings on the Internet (www.craigslist.org, www.loot.com, and www.nypress.com).

Independent and Dependent Variables

Manipulation of social status.   Participants were told that they would engage in a public speaking task for fifteen minutes. In reality, this task was designed to manipulate the social status of the participant in relation to the confederate. The high-status role was designed to be the control condition, requiring more agentic and authoritative behaviors (stereotypically masculine qualities). The low-status role was designed to require more compliant and accepting behaviors (that are stereotypically feminine qualities; see Eagly & Karau, 2002). Specifically, in the "subordinate participant" condition, participants were led to believe that the confederate was a professor of public speaking and as such possessed the expertise and authority to evaluate the public speaking performance of the participant.[1] To enhance the effect of the confederate's superior status, the confederate was dressed in a business suit and sat at the front of a lecture-style classroom at the teacher's desk whereas the participant was asked to sit at a student desk. The confederate told the participant that he or she was currently conducting research on public speaking with a particular focus on people's ability to read aloud fluently from teleprompters. The confederate then asked participants to read aloud a short script (taken from "The Testimony of Sculpture" by Harold Haydon) so that he or she could collect some new data on ordinary people's public speaking abilities. As the participant read, the superior confederate observed closely and took notes. When the participant was done, the confederate gave him some general feedback including a number of suggestions the participant could use to improve his public speaking.

In the "superior participant" condition, participants were given the authority to evaluate the performance of the confederate and to determine the resources that should be allocated to him or her (i.e., the confederate was ostensibly "outcome dependent" on the participant; see Fiske, 2001; Operario et al., 1998; Raven, 1993). Specifically, participants were told that the confederate was a graduate student training to become a teaching assistant (TA). To underscore the confederate's subordinate status, he or she was dressed casually like a graduate student, and sat at one of the student desks in a lecture-style classroom while the participant sat at the teacher's desk in front of the classroom. Additionally, participants were told that as part of the TA selection process, the selection committee required that each graduate student read aloud a given passage in front of an unfamiliar audience and have his or her performance evaluated by a member of the audience. The ostensible goal of this exercise was to get "objective feedback" from the audience (i.e., the participant) about the confederate's speaking style, confidence, and his/her potential to be an effective lecturer. This feedback would determine whether the confederate would get a teaching assistantship the following semester. Accordingly, the confederate (the "prospective TA") read aloud, making some common mistakes along the way including some speech errors and mispronunciations, occasional fidgeting, failing to make frequent eye contact, and standing with poor posture. Afterward, participants completed a written evaluation for the "TA Training Committee."

Manipulation of gender salience in the situation. The salience of participant gender was manipulated by alternating the sex of the confederate. In the high gender salience condition, male participants interacted with a female confederate while in the low gender salience condition male participants interacted with a male confederate.

Measurement of automatic beliefs about the self. Participants' automatic beliefs about the self were assessed with the Implicit Association Test (IAT; Greenwald, McGhee, & Schwartz, 1998). The IAT is a computerized task that measures the relative strength with which two target concepts (e.g., self vs. not self) are associated with two types of attributes using response latency to operationalize belief strength. The stronger the mental association between a target and attribute, the more quickly people should be able to categorize them together in a speeded reaction-time task. In the present experiment, the two target concepts in the IAT were the self and non-self, which were represented by pronouns such as "I" and "me," versus "they" and "them," respectively. The two attribute dimensions of interest were "leader" and "learner" represented by words such as "influential" and "knowledgeable," versus "apprentice" and "novice," respectively (see Appendix for all stimuli used in the IAT). These two attribute dimensions were chosen because they capture qualities typically associated with people in superior versus subordinate social roles and because these qualities clearly map onto masculine stereotypes about authority and leadership versus feminine stereotypes about compliance and deference (Eagly & Karau, 2002; Eagly & Steffen, 1984). All attributes chosen for this study were positive and thus were not confounded by variance in valence.

During the IAT, after some practice, participants were exposed to four types of stimuli presented one at a time on a computer screen (leader, learner, self and non-self words). Their task was to categorize each word using one of two designated response keys as quickly and accurately as possible. In two critical blocks of the IAT, participants were instructed to categorize leader words and self-related pronouns using the same key but learner words and non-self pronouns using a different key (abbreviated as me + leader and not-me + learner, respectively). In two other blocks of the IAT, response key assignment was reversed such that now participants were instructed to categorize learner words and self-related pronouns using the same key but leader words and non-self pronouns using a different key (abbreviated as me + learner and not-me + leader, respectively). The order in which the IAT blocks were presented was counterbalanced between participants.

Typically, when a target concept and an attribute sharing the same response key are strongly associated in participants' mind, they classify them quickly and easily whereas when they are weakly associated, participants classify them more slowly and with greater difficulty. If a participant associates himself more strongly with leader than learner attributes, he ought to be faster at categorizing me + leader and not-me + learner and slower at categorizing me + learner and not-me + leader. The difference in response latency (in milliseconds) for the two types of blocks, is referred to as the IAT effect and is a measure of participants' automatic self-conceptions. Given our prediction that men in a low-status position would automatically bolster stereotypically masculine attributes and distance themselves from stereotypically feminine attributes, we expected their responses to be significantly faster during the me + leader/not-me + learner block than the me + learner/not-me + leader block.

By comparison, we expected participants in the high-status position to express less self-stereotypic beliefs by responding equally fast to both blocks.

Measurement of controlled beliefs about the self.   Participants also completed a questionnaire concerning their beliefs about the self. Specifically, they rated the extent to which the 12 leader- and learner-related attributes (e.g., knowledgeable, beginner) described themselves using 7-point scales (1 = *Does not describe me at all* to 7 = *Describes me very well*). These attributes were the same ones used in the IAT (see Appendix for the complete list). We expected men in the high gender salience condition (who interacted with a female confederate) to endorse more leader traits and fewer learner traits compared to men in the low gender salience condition (who interacted with a male confederate).

Demographic measure.   Participants also completed a general demographic questionnaire that included questions about their age, ethnicity, and occupation.

Procedure

Male volunteers were scheduled to participate in the study one at a time. A female experimenter greeted participants and led them to believe that they were participating in two separate and unrelated activities. The "first activity" was, in fact, the status manipulation and the "second activity" involved the administration of the automatic and explicit belief measures. The experimenter told participants that since her experiment would only take half an hour, she was "loaning" some of her experimental time to another ostensibly unrelated project, which would be administered first. After participants were done participating in that project, they would begin her experiment.

   At this point, the experimenter took the participant to a classroom, introduced him to the confederate and left the room. Depending upon the experimental condition, participants were either introduced to a female or male confederate who was either in a subordinate or superior role relative to participants. The confederate identified himself or herself as either a professor of public speaking or a graduate student and introduced the public speaking task (see materials section for details). This task took about twenty minutes. Afterwards, the confederate told the participant that the first activity was over and led him to a different room where the original experimenter was waiting.

   At this time, the experimenter administered the IAT and the self-report questionnaire. Finally, participants completed the demographic questionnaire, after which they were probed for suspicion, debriefed, thanked and paid for their participation.

Results

Effect of Status and Confederate Sex on Automatic Self-concept

IAT data were prepared using the revised algorithm recommended by Greenwald, Nosek, and Banaji (2003). In keeping with this new procedure, the two blocks of the IAT that required simultaneous categorization of me/not-me pronouns and leader/learner attributes were retained and the practice blocks were eliminated. The four data collection blocks were used to calculate an automatic self-belief score (or IAT effect) for each participant. This score represented the differential speed with which participants completed the me + leader block compared to the me + learner block in terms of effect size or modified Cohen's *d* (IAT *D*; see Greenwald et al., 2003, for details). Large effect sizes indicate more stereotypic automatic self-beliefs for male participants whereas effect sizes close to zero indicate less stereotypic automatic self-beliefs for male participants.

In order to test whether participants' status or the sex of their interaction partner influenced their automatic self-related beliefs, we conducted a Participant Status (low vs. high) × Confederate Sex (male vs. female) Analysis of Variance (ANOVA) using IAT effect size (*D*) as the dependent variable. As predicted, the ANOVA revealed a significant main effect of participants' status, $F(1, 58) = 4.26$, $p = .04$.[2] Specifically, as shown in Figure 1, male participants in the subordinate condition were significantly faster at associating themselves with leader-like traits than learner-like traits (IAT effect = 142 ms; IAT $D = .26$) whereas male participants in the superior condition were equally fast at associating themselves with leader and learner traits (IAT effect = −25 ms; IAT $D = −.07$). Mean response latencies for the me + leader versus me + learner blocks showed that participants in the subordinate condition were substantially slower at associating themselves with learner attributes ($M = 1122$ ms) than leader attributes ($M = 980$ ms), whereas participants in the superior condition were equally fast at associating themselves with both learner and leader attributes (Ms = 971 and 996 ms, respectively). In other words, the data suggest that men in the subordinate role automatically compensated by distancing themselves from stereotypically feminine qualities compared to stereotypically masculine qualities whereas men in the superior role were equally likely to associate themselves with both types of qualities.

Effect of Status and Confederate Sex on Controlled Self-concept

Controlled self-related beliefs were derived from the self-description questionnaire in the following manner. Each participant's self-ratings on the six "leader" words were

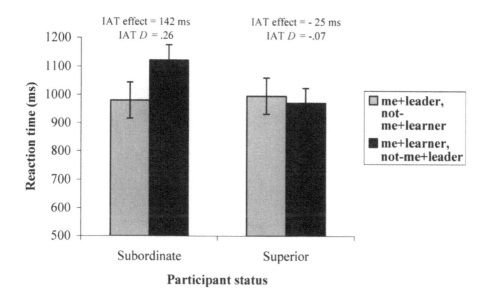

FIGURE 1 The influence of social status on men's automatic beliefs about the self.

averaged together to produce a self-concept score for leadership traits ($\alpha = .83$). The six "learner" words were also averaged together to produce a self-concept score for learner-like traits ($\alpha = .67$). A Confederate Sex × Participant Status × Trait Type ANOVA with self-ratings as the dependent variable revealed a significant main effect of trait type indicating that, overall, male participants identified themselves more strongly with leadership qualities ($M_{leader} = 5.18$) than with learner-like qualities ($M_{learner} = 3.99$); $F(1, 58) = 47.68$, $p < .0009$. More importantly, as predicted, this main effect was qualified by a significant interaction between Confederate Sex × Trait Type, $F(1, 59) = 4.09$, $p = .05$; see Figure 2. T-tests showed that participants who had encountered a female confederate were more likely to self-stereotype than those who had encountered a male confederate. In the female confederate condition, the difference between men's endorsement of leadership qualities ($M_{leader} = 5.37$) versus learner-like qualities ($M_{learner} = 3.82$, $t(31) = 6.03$, $p = 10^{-6}$) was larger than the difference in the male confederate condition, $M_{leader} = 4.99$, $M_{learner} = 4.15$, $t(30) = 3.79$, $p = .001$. The ANOVA did not reveal any other effects (all $ps > .20$).

Relation between Automatic and Controlled Self-beliefs

To examine the relationship between automatic and controlled self-beliefs, we first calculated a difference score for self-reported trait ratings to make them comparable to the IAT effect by subtracting ratings for learner-like traits from ratings for leadership traits. Thus, larger positive difference scores indicate that participants described themselves as possessing more leadership qualities than learner-like qualities. To test if the relationship between automatic and controlled self-beliefs was moderated by manipulated status or confederate gender, we conducted a regression analysis using IAT scores as the outcome variable. In the first step of this regression, confederate gender, participants' status and self-related beliefs (difference score) were entered as predictor variables. In the second step, we added the first-order

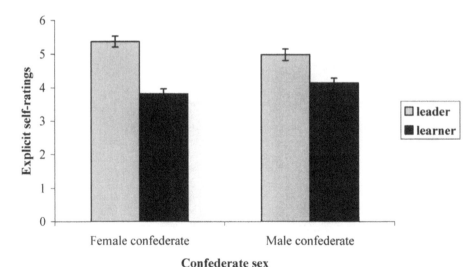

FIGURE 2 The influence of confederate sex on men's controlled beliefs about the self.

interaction terms between our predictor variables. In the third step, we added the second-order interaction term (confederate gender × participant status × self-related beliefs).

Results revealed that automatic self-beliefs (IAT effect) were significantly related to participant status and to self-reported beliefs, $F(3, 54) = 2.90, p = .04$. As expected, participants placed in a low-status role automatically compensated by exhibiting more leader-like self-beliefs than others placed in a high-status role ($ß = .27, p = .04$). Additionally, participants who described themselves using more leadership traits were also more likely to exhibit automatic leader-like self-conceptions ($ß = .26, p = .05$). All other effects were nonsignificant.

General Discussion

The present study offers new evidence suggesting that men's gender self-conceptions are malleable in response to situational cues. Different situational factors, however, evoke shifts in automatic self-conceptions compared to controlled self-conceptions.

Threat to One's Social Status and its Effect on the Self-concept

The experimental manipulation of social status yielded evidence that, in general, men automatically compensate for an experience of subordination. Participants in the low-status condition expressed a more stereotypically masculine pattern of automatic self-beliefs than participants in the high-status position. This pattern appears to be driven by one or both of the following when men were placed in a low-status role: (a) a weakening of the association between the self-concept and stereotypically feminine attributes, or (b) a weakening of the association between other people and masculine attributes. We interpret these data to suggest that when placed in a counterstereotypically subordinate role, male participants' agentic and authoritative masculine self-concepts were threatened. They responded to this threat by automatically rejecting feminine attributes in themselves and/or automatically rejecting the notion that masculine attributes may be present in other people. The result of both types of compensatory cognitions is to protect one's own masculine self-conception in a relative sense. These data fall in line with other research suggesting that threats to the self may be particularly potent in altering implicit cognition (e.g., Rudman et al., 2006) and that threat to their masculinity may make men particularly motivated to distance themselves from femininity (Kilianski, 2003; McCreary, 1994).

Interestingly, the effects of compensatory cognition did not appear in participants' conscious and reflective descriptions of themselves. The evidence that self-regulation emerged more clearly at an automatic level fits nicely with other researchers' argument that people are often not conscious of compensatory cognition as it occurs (Markus & Wurf, 1987; Moskowitz, 2002; Tesser, 2000). We interpret these findings to suggest that the automatic compensatory response functions as a regulatory process that might preempt the need for changes in one's conscious self-conceptions. If the compensation is effective, one would not expect any changes in descriptions of the self.

While our data support these claims, future research should clarify a few ambiguities in our findings. First, the IAT results for the men in the lower status position suggest that the differences in the IAT effect were driven by slower response latencies for the counterstereotypic associations, which includes both the "me + learner" pairing and the "not me + leader" pairing. As such, we cannot determine from these data which of these pairings drove the effect when men were placed in the lower status role. It is possible that the compensatory reaction is as much about rejecting the association of others with masculine traits as it is about rejecting the association of the self with feminine traits. Future research might use a different reaction-time task that allows for the disaggregation of these associations to clarify this point.

A second ambiguity in the study stems from the manipulation of status. The nature of our manipulation is such that participants in the low-status condition were in a position to be criticized while the participants in the high-status position were not (and were, in fact, given the opportunity to criticize others). As such, participants' compensatory reaction may have been driven by the threat of criticism and not the threat to social status per se. Future research should create a social status manipulation that is able to decouple these interpretations. However such a decoupling may be difficult given that low status and being subject to critical evaluation often go hand in hand.

More generally, questions remain about the psychological mechanism that causes threat-induced compensatory cognition. Some researchers argue that a discrepancy between individuals' self-defining goals and their actual performance arouses negative affect, which in turn, triggers self-regulation (Moskowitz, 2001; cf. Tesser, 2000). Applying this theory to our study, the low-status position is likely to have contradicted participants' self-definition as agentic, assertive, and authoritative. This contradiction may have aroused negative affect, which in turn triggered compensatory protection of the threatened beliefs. While evidence supports the claim that counterstereotypic behavior evokes negative affect (e.g., Rudman & Fairchild, 2004) and that negative affect can be countered with implicit bolstering of self-esteem (Rudman et al., 2006), the attribution of a similar mechanism to our findings is speculative and requires direct exploration.

Questions also remain as to whether women would react similarly to counterstereotypic experiences. Whereas low-status roles are counterstereotypic for men, high-status roles are counterstereotypic for women. We expect women to be less threatened by counterstereotypic experiences of high status than men are to counterstereotypic experiences of low status based on the evidence that women's gender roles tend to be more dynamic than men's gender roles (Diekman & Eagly, 2000), and that more than a few women aspire to agentic roles (Rudman & Glick, 1999). As such, we do not expect women in high-status roles to compensate by bolstering stereotypically feminine attributes or by distancing themselves from masculine attributes in the self. In fact, some evidence suggests that women placed in high-status roles find it easier to associate masculine attributes with the self compared to other women placed in low-status roles (Haines & Kray, 2005). However, if stereotypically feminine yet strongly positive self-beliefs are challenged, we predict that this might be particularly threatening to women and might, in turn, elicit automatic compensatory reactions to protect one's femininity.

Given individual variations in the strength of in-group identification and the effects that such variations have on self-stereotyping and intergroup behavior (Schmitt & Branscombe, 2001; Verkuyten & Nekuee, 1999), we believe that compensatory reactions observed in the present study are likely to be moderated by individual differences. Specifically, we anticipate that the degree to which men identify as masculine is likely to moderate their compensatory cognitions in response to threat. Along the same lines, we predict that women with more masculine or agentic self-conceptions might compensate in a fashion similar to that observed in the present study.

Finally, we found no significant effect of confederate sex on participants' automatic beliefs about themselves. Participants in the subordinate condition automatically distanced themselves from feminine self-conceptions regardless of whether the individual in the superior role was male or female. As such, it appears that automatic self-stereotyping was dependent on the experience of subordination alone and not on the stereotypicality of the superior individual's sex and role combined. To the extent that compensatory reactions are primarily focused on maintaining self-related beliefs in an automatic fashion, the sex of the superior may be less important in this context. Future research should investigate the degree to which this pattern holds true in other social contexts.

Situational Salience of Gender and Its Effect on the Self-concept

In terms of the situational manipulation of gender salience, the present study found that participants who interacted with a female confederate described themselves using more stereotypically masculine traits compared to participants who interacted with a male confederate. As in earlier research (Cota & Dion, 1986; Hogg & Turner, 1987), self-related beliefs became more gendered when attention was directed to the self via the solicitation of explicit self-descriptions. In line with earlier research, we interpret our data to suggest that male participants' gender identity became more salient when their attention was focused on the self in the presence of the female confederate. As suggested by Abrams (1994), distinctiveness influenced people's self-related beliefs only when self-descriptions were solicited directly. While the data only allow for conjecture, we suggest that the manipulation of gender distinctiveness, in contrast to the manipulation of social status, was not sufficiently affect-laden to alter the implicit beliefs about the self.

Conclusion

In conclusion, the present research demonstrates that people's self-concepts are flexible and sensitive to contextual cues. At the same time, this flexibility works to keep people's beliefs about themselves aligned with prototypical in-group characteristics. In the case of men, when their high-status masculine self-beliefs are threatened, the self-regulatory system automatically and subtly works to validate their masculine self-conceptions. Furthermore, when gender is relevant in a given situation, men describe themselves using more in-group stereotypes. Together these findings demonstrate how the malleability of the working self-concept works differentially at the automatic versus controlled level to preserve one's in-group identity and related beliefs about the self.

Notes

1. The confederates were about 30 years old; thus both status manipulations (professor and student) were believable.
2. The ANOVA did not reveal any other significant effects ($Fs < 1$).

References

Abrams, D. (1985). Focus of attention in minimal intergroup discrimination. *British Journal of Social Psychology, 24*, 65 – 74.

Abrams, D. (1994). Social self-regulation. *Personality and Social Psychology Bulletin, 20*, 473 – 483.

Abrams, D., & Brown, R. (1989). Self-consciousness and social identity: Self-regulation as a group member. *Social Psychology Quarterly, 52*, 311 – 318.

Biernat, M., & Wortman, C. B. (1991). Sharing of home responsibilities between professionally employed women and their husbands. *Journal of Personality and Social Psychology, 60*, 844 – 860.

Burris, C. T., Branscombe, N. R., & Klar, Y. (1997). Maladjustment implications of self and group gender-role discrepancies: An ordered-discrepancy model. *European Journal of Social Psychology, 27*, 75 – 95.

Cota, A. A., & Dion, K. L. (1986). Salience of gender and sex composition of ad hoc groups: An experimental test of distinctiveness theory. *Journal of Personality and Social Psychology, 50*, 770 – 776.

Dailey, D. M., & Rosenzweig, J. (1988). Variations in men's psychological sex role self-perception as a function of work, social and sexual life roles. *Journal of Sex and Marital Therapy, 14*, 225 – 240.

Deaux, K., & Major B. (1987). Putting gender into context: An interactive model of gender-related behavior. *Psychological Review, 94*, 369 – 389.

Deaux, K., Winton, W., Crowley, M., & Lewis, L. L. (1985). Level of categorization and content of gender stereotypes. *Social Cognition, 3*, 145 – 167.

Depret, E., & Fiske, S. T. (1999). Perceiving the powerful: Intriguing individuals versus threatening groups. *Journal of Experimental Social Psychology, 35*, 461 – 480.

Devos, T., & Banaji, M. R. (2003). Implicit self and identity. *Annals New York Academy of Sciences, 1001*, 177 – 211.

Diekman, A. B., & Eagly, A. H. (2000). Stereotypes as dynamic constructs: Women and men of the past, present, and future. *Personality and Social Psychology Bulletin, 26*, 1171 – 1188.

Eagly, A. H., & Karau, S. J. (2002). Role congruity theory of prejudice toward female leaders. *Psychological Review, 109*, 573 – 598.

Eagly, A. H., & Steffen, V. J. (1984). Gender stereotypes stem from the distribution of women and men into social roles. *Journal of Personality and Social Psychology, 46*, 735 – 754.

Eagly, A. H., & Wood, W. (1991). Explaining sex differences in social behavior: A social role perspective. *Personality and Social Psychology Bulletin, 17*, 306 – 315.

Ellemers, N., Doosje, B., Van Knippenberg, A. V., & Wilke, H. (1992). Status protection in high status minority groups. *European Journal of Social Psychology, 22*, 123 – 140.

Ellemers, N., Doosje, B., Van Knippenberg, A. V., de Vries, N., & Wilke, H. (1988). Social identification and permeability of group boundaries. *European Journal of Social Psychology, 18*, 497 – 513.

Fiske, S. T. (2001). Effects of power on bias: Power explains and maintains individual, group, and societal disparities. In A. Y. Lee-Chai & J. A. Bargh (Eds.), *The use and abuse of power: Multiple perspectives on the causes of corruption* (pp. 181 – 193). Philadelphia: Psychology Press.

Frantz, C. M., Cuddy, A. J., Burnett, M., Ray, H., & Hart, A. (2004). A threat in the computer: The race Implicit Association Test as a stereotype threat experience. *Personality and Social Psychology Bulletin, 30*, 1611 – 1624.

Greenberg, J., & Pyszczynski, T. (1985). Compensatory self-inflation: A response to threat to the self-regard of public failure. *Journal of Personality and Social Psychology, 49*, 273 – 280.

Greenwald, A. G., & Farnham, S. D. (2000). Using the Implicit Association Test to measure self-esteem and self-concept. *Journal of Personality and Social Psychology, 79*, 1022 – 1038.

Greenwald, A. G., McGhee, D. E., & Schwartz, J. L. K. (1998). Measuring individual differences in implicit cognition: The Implicit Association Test. *Journal of Personality and Social Psychology, 74*, 1464 – 1480.

Greenwald, A. G., Nosek, B. A., & Banaji, M. R. (2003). Understanding and using the Implicit Association Test: 1. An improved scoring algorithm. *Journal of Personality and Social Psychology, 85,* 197–216.

Haines, E. L., & Kray, L. J. (2005). Self-power associations: The possession of power impacts women's self-concepts. *European Journal of Social Psychology, 35,* 643–662.

Hogg, M. A., & Turner, J. C. (1987). Intergroup behavior, self-stereotyping and the salience of social categories. *British Journal of Social Psychology, 26,* 325–340.

Hosoda, M., & Stone, D. L. (2000). Current gender stereotypes and their evaluative content. *Perceptual and Motor Skills, 90,* 1283–1294.

Jackson, L. A., Hodge, C. N., & Ingram, J. M. (1994). Gender and self-concept: A re-examination of stereotypic differences and the role of gender attitudes. *Sex Roles, 30,* 615–630.

James, K. (1993). Conceptualizing self with in-group stereotypes: Context and esteem precursors. *Personality and Social Psychology Bulletin, 18,* 117–121.

Kilianski, S. E. (2003). Explaining heterosexual men's attitudes toward women and gay men: The theory of exclusively masculine identity. *Psychology of Men & Masculinity, 4*(1), 37–56.

Markus, H. R., & Kunda, Z. (1986). Stability and malleability of the self-concept. *Journal of Personality and Social Psychology, 51,* 858–866.

Markus, H. R., & Wurf, E. (1987). The dynamic self-concept: A social psychological perspective. *Annual Reviews in Psychology, 38,* 299–237.

McCreary, D. R. (1994). The male role and avoiding femininity. *Sex Roles, 31,* 517–531.

McGuire, W. J., McGuire, C. V., & Cheever, J. (1986). The self in society: Effects of social contexts on the sense of self. *British Journal of Social Psychology, 25,* 259–270.

McGuire, W. J., McGuire, C. V., Child, P., & Fujioka, T. (1978). Salience of ethnicity in the spontaneous self-concept as a function of one's ethnic distinctiveness in the social environment. *Journal of Personality and Social Psychology, 36,* 511–520.

McGuire, W. J., McGuire, C. V., & Winton, W. (1979). Effects of household sex composition on the salience of one's gender in the spontaneous self-concept. *Journal of Experimental Social Psychology, 15,* 77–90.

Moskowitz, G. B. (2001). Preconscious control and compensatory cognition. In G. B. Moskowitz (Ed.), *Cognitive social psychology: The Princeton symposium on the legacy and future of social cognition* (pp. 353–358). Hillsdale, NJ: Lawrence Erlbaum Associates, Inc.

Moskowitz, G. B. (2002). Preconscious effects of temporary goals on attention. *Journal of Experimental Social Psychology, 38,* 397–404.

Operario, D., Goodwin, S. A., & Fiske, S. T. (1998). Power is everywhere: Social control and personal control both operate at stereotype activation, interpretation, and response. In R. S. Wyer (Ed.), *Stereotypic activation and inhibition: Advances in social cognition* (Vol. 11, pp. 163–175). Mahwah, NJ: Lawrence Erlbaum Associates, Inc.

Raven, B. H. (1993). The bases of power: Origins and recent developments. *Journal of Social Issues, 49,* 227–252.

Richeson, J. A., & Ambady, N. (2001). Who's in charge? Effects of situational roles on automatic gender bias. *Sex Roles, 44,* 493–512.

Rudman, L. A., Dohn, M. C., & Fairchild, K. (2006). *Implicit self-esteem compensation: Automatic threat defense.* Manuscript submitted for publication.

Rudman, L. A., & Fairchild, K. (2004). Reactions to counterstereotypic behavior: The role of backlash in cultural stereotype maintenance. *Journal of Personality and Social Psychology, 87,* 157–176.

Rudman, L. A., & Glick, P. (1999). Feminized management and backlash toward agentic women: The hidden costs to women of a kinder, gentler image of middle managers. *Journal of Personality and Social Psychology, 77,* 1004–1010.

Schmitt, M. T., & Branscombe, N. R. (2001). The good, the bad, and the manly: Threats to one's prototypicality and evaluations of fellow in-group members. *Journal of Experimental Social Psychology, 37,* 510–517.

Shrauger, J. S., & Lund, A. K. (1975). Self-evaluation and reactions to evaluations from others. *Journal of Personality, 43*, 94–108.

Sinclair, L., & Kunda, Z. (1999). Reactions to a Black professional: Motivated inhibition and activation of conflicting stereotypes. *Journal of Personality and Social Psychology, 77*, 885–904.

Steele, C. M. (1988). The psychology of self-affirmation: Sustaining the integrity of the self. *Advances in experimental social psychology. Vol. 21. Social psychological studies of the self: Perspectives and programs* (pp. 261–302). San Diego, CA: Academic Press.

Steinem, G. (2000, June 30), Envisioning the future: Gloria Steinem. *Off Our Backs, 30*, 8.

Swann, W. B. (1997). The trouble with change: Self-verification and allegiance to the self. *Psychological Science, 8*, 177–180.

Tesser, A. (2000). On the confluence of self-esteem maintenance mechanisms. *Personality and Social Psychology Review, 4*, 290–299.

Turner, J. C., Hogg, M. A., Oakes, P. J., Reicher, S. D., & Wetherell, M. (1987). *Rediscovering the social group: A self-categorization theory.* Oxford, UK: Blackwell.

Turner, J. C., Oakes, P. J., Haslam S. A., & McGarty, C. (1994). Self and collective: Cognition and social context. *Personality and Social Psychology Bulletin, 20*, 454–463.

US Department of Labor Bureau of Labor Statistics. (2002). Labor force statistics from the current population survey. (Retrieved 6 November 2002 from http://data.bls.gov)

Verkuyten, M., & Nekuee, S. (1999). Ingroup bias: the effect of self-stereotyping, identification and group threat. *European Journal of Social Psychology, 29*, 411–418.

Wicklund, R. A. (1975). Objective self-awareness. In L. Berkowitz (Ed.), *Advances in experimental social psychology* (Vol. 8). New York: Academic Press.

Wicklund, R. A., & Gollwitzer, P. M. (1981). Symbolic self-completion, attempted influence, and self-deprecation. *Basic and Applied Social Psychology, 2*, 89–114.

Appendix

IAT stimuli

Leader words	*Learner words*
Influential	Beginner
Knowledgeable	Learning
Authority	Willing
Assertive	Apprentice
Confident	Novice
Leader	Learner
Self-related pronouns	*Other related pronouns*
I	They
Me	Them
Mine	Their
My	Theirs
Myself	Other

Self and Identity, 6: 189–208, 2007
http://www.psypress.com/sai
ISSN: 1529-8868 print/1529-8876 online
DOI: 10.1080/15298860601118769

Autonomy and Control Motivation and Self-esteem

HOLLEY S. HODGINS

Skidmore College, Saratoga Springs, New York, USA

ARIEL B. BROWN

Boston University, Boston, Massachusetts, USA

BARBARA CARVER

Skidmore College, Saratoga Springs, New York, USA

Two studies examined the hypothesis that primed autonomy and control motivations would influence self-esteem (SE) in the direction of autonomy increasing and control decreasing SE. Explicit, implicit, and defensive (i.e., the discrepancy between implicit and explicit) SE were measured. Results confirmed the hypothesis for implicit and for defensive SE. There were substantial sex differences, with men showing greater reactivity to motivation priming and threat than women. Results are interpreted in terms of a self-determination theory view of motivation and SE (Deci & Ryan, 2000).

According to self-determination theory (SDT), when individuals' basic psychological needs for autonomy, competence, and relatedness are satisfied, they are motivated *autonomously*: They tend to choose behaviors based on interests, integrated values and goals; to endorse their own activities; and to experience feedback, outcomes, and other events as informational rather than as threatening (Deci & Ryan, 2000). Autonomy motivation allows individuals to approach others in a non-controlling manner; those high on autonomy orientation report open, honest, and satisfying daily interpersonal interactions (Hodgins, Koestner, & Duncan, 1996a). Moreover, basic need satisfaction and autonomous motivation allow for genuine or noncontingent self-esteem (SE), a sense of self-worth that is based on simply being who one *is*, rather than on achieving success or obtaining particular outcomes (Deci & Ryan, 1995; Reis, Sheldon, Gable, Roscoe, & Ryan, 2000; Ryan & Deci, 2004). Genuine SE is relatively stable, and individuals with genuine SE do not engage in a lot of "esteeming," that is, the incessant process of assessing and protecting self-worth (Ryan & Brown, 2003). Additionally, Hodgins and Knee (2002) propose that

This research was supported by National Science Foundation Grant BCS 0338749 to the first author.

The authors wish to thank David Lahna, Kendra Kavanaugh, and Kate Villanova for collecting data for Study 2.

Correspondence should be addressed to: Holley S. Hodgins, Department of Psychology, Skidmore College, 815 North Broadway Avenue, Saratoga Springs, NY 12866, USA. E-mail: hhodgins@skidmore.edu genuine SE is important for the way individuals approach their everyday experiences, both intrapersonal and interpersonal. They suggest that the genuine SE that is associated with autonomy is one critical factor that allows individuals to experience emotions and events nondefensively, with relatively little distortion and bias. That is, to the extent that individuals are autonomously motivated and experience secure self-worth, they have less need to protect themselves by avoiding the implications of information that is contained in experiences.

When intrinsic psychological needs are unmet, however, individuals become control motivated, which is characterized by an orientation toward contingencies. This can include sensitivity to external pressures (i.e., from situations and other people), and from internally controlling imperatives (e.g., one's own "shoulds" and "oughts"). Highly control oriented individuals tend to see the entire social world in terms of control, both controlling others and being controlled (Hodgins et al., 1996a), and organize their behavior on the basis of sensitivity to pressure. Hence, they experience and react to events (even potentially neutral ones) as coercive, initiate behavior on the basis of demands from others and themselves (i.e., "shoulds") rather than from genuine interest or integrated goals, and generally feel like pawns rather than originators of their activities and feelings, which can result in a tendency to be controlling toward others (Deci & Ryan, 2000). Furthermore, when basic needs are unsatisfied and motivation is control-oriented, self-worth is called into question, and individuals develop SE that is contingent on performance outcomes as a result of experiencing past contingent regard from important others (Assor, Roth, & Deci, 2004). When SE is contingent, maintaining high SE is tied directly to whether one is successful in important domains. However, even if high SE is maintained by achieving success, contingent SE is always tenuous because the entire basis of self-regard is continually at stake—whether one is worthy is a salient question that must be answered repeatedly, and simply asking the question results in a pressured and driven experience. Accordingly, Hodgins and Knee (2002) hypothesized that the contingent SE that is associated with control motivation is an important underlying cause of the generalized defensiveness toward experience that results from control motivation. To the extent that individuals are control motivated and therefore experience contingent SE, they must defend against all information, thoughts, and emotions that do not support SE in order to maintain a sense of self-worth.

Kernis and his colleagues introduced the concept of SE stability, which refers to whether SE fluctuates across time and situations, and which is associated with contingent self-worth (see Kernis & Paradise, 2002, for a review). They suggest that all high SE is not the same: High and stable SE allows for healthy functioning, whereas high unstable SE creates vulnerability to numerous problems. Empirically, they have shown that high, unstable SE is correlated with having strivings that are more control motivated (Kernis, Paradise, Whitaker, Wheatman, & Goldman, 2000), and with self-regulation that is based on contingent SE (Waschull & Kernis, 1996).

Research also shows that contingent SE is associated with negative outcomes. For example, contingent SE mediates the positive correlation between control motivation and alcohol consumption (Neighbors, Larimer, Geisner, & Knee, 2004), predicts greater vulnerability to appearance-based social comparisons (Patrick, Neighbors, & Knee, 2004), predicts worse outcomes among women who misperceive what men find attractive (Bergstrom, Neighbors, & Lewis, 2004), and has costs across various domains including learning, relationships, and health (Crocker & Park, 2004).

In summary, past SDT theory and research has focused predictions about SE on the *type* of SE (secure versus contingent, and stable versus unstable) rather than the *level* of SE. We predicted, however, that the motivations and their accompanying SE types also have implications for SE *level*. If the continual "esteeming" that is required by contingent SE undermines SE level (Ryan & Brown, 2003), then control motivation, which is accompanied by contingent SE, should decrease SE level. In contrast, autonomy motivation and the accompanying genuine SE should allow individuals' attentional focus to be on interests and activities, rather than defending and maintaining self-worth; thus, autonomy motivation should promote a higher level of SE.

Defensive Self-esteem

Can the differential influence of control and autonomy motivations on SE level be measured explicitly, using self-reports? The difficulty here is that considerable research has documented that high scores on explicit SE measures can be associated with defensive and self-protective behavior—so much so that they have been used as a proxy for defensiveness (e.g., Pyszczynski, Greenberg, Solomon, Arndt, & Schimel, 2004). For example, individuals who report high SE may also make unrealistically positive claims about the self (Roth, Snyder, & Pace, 1986), and use self-handicapping to enhance success (Tice, 1991) or for strategic self-presentation (Tice & Baumeister, 1990). They may also engage in nonproductive persistence on unsolvable puzzles (McFarlin, Baumeister, & Blascovich, 1984), use compensatory self-enhancement in self-descriptions (Baumeister, 1982), and set risky and inappropriately high goals under ego threat (Baumeister, Heatherton, & Tice, 1993). Indeed, it is now widely accepted that high self-esteem (SE) is heterogeneous, has multiple origins, and can be adaptive or maladaptive. Various terms have been used for this distinction, including defensive versus genuine SE (Schneider, 1969; Schneider & Turkat, 1975; see also Hewitt & Goldman, 1974), defensive versus healthy SE (Raskin, Novacek, & Hogan, 1991), and defensive versus secure SE (Jordan, Spencer, & Zanna, 2003a). Individuals with defensive SE manifest other signs of defensiveness, including trait narcissism, ingroup bias, and dissonance reduction (Jordan, Spencer, Zanna, Hoshino-Browne, & Correll, 2003b). They may also engage in more ethnic discrimination (Jordan, Spencer, & Zanna, 2005) and use more compensatory self-enhancement (Bosson, Brown, Zeigler-Hill, & Swann, 2003).

In short, simply reporting high SE is not sufficient evidence for positive self-evaluation, nor is it a good predictor of positive psychological adjustment. Explicit SE measures are problematic because they do not discriminate between: (1) genuine self-regard; (2) impression management and need for approval (e.g., social desirability bias; Schneider & Turkat, 1975); and (3) self-deception about self-regard (Farnham, Greenwald, & Banaji, 1999; Raskin et al., 1991). Although measuring stability along with level of SE may address this problem partially (Kernis & Paradise, 2002), it does not avoid self-deception entirely and, furthermore, researchers are not always able to assess SE stability.

Implicit Self-esteem

Recently, *implicit* SE measures have been introduced that circumvent many problems associated with self-reports. In contrast to deliberative self-evaluation, implicit measures tap self-evaluative processes that are believed to be relatively automatic (i.e., well-learned to the point of routinization). Implicit SE methods are diverse; they include the assessment of: (1) the name letter effect (NLE), which yields preferences for own name letters and birthday dates (Nuttin, 1985, 1987); (2) the automatic association between self and pleasant or unpleasant words in the Implicit Association Test (IAT; Farnham et al., 1999); and automatic attitude activation using either (3) supraliminal primes (Hetts, Sakuma, & Pelham, 1999) or (4) subliminal primes (Spalding & Hardin, 1999). These measures all purport to assess implicit SE with minimal influence from impression management and self-deception biases. Two recent articles have noted, however, that some implicit SE measures are more indirect than others, and therefore tap attitudes that are more implicit. For example, Bosson, Swann, and Pennebaker (2000) consider the Spalding and Hardin (1999) measure to be less direct than either the name letter or IAT tasks. To the extent that the purpose of a task is masked, a measure can be considered indirect (Dijksterhuis, 2004). By this logic, the Spalding and Hardin (1999) measure is the most indirect measure of SE because it is the only one that uses subliminal exposure to stimuli. In other words, it is less plausible for impression management or self-deception to influence responses when the primes are subliminal.

Another issue about implicit measures is whether they measure stable trait SE or momentary state SE. Bosson et al. (2000) take the view that implicit measures should assess a stable dimension: They criticize measures with low test–retest reliability (e.g., the Spalding & Hardin subliminal priming measure) and recommend that researchers avoid them in favor of measures with high test–retest reliability, which they claim should be better at predicting behavior. And, indeed, research that uses implicit SE measures as a stable trait has contributed interesting insights (e.g., Jordan et al., 2003a, 2005; Bosson et al., 2003). However, there also is evidence that implicit attitudes are malleable (Blair, 2002) and respond to experimental manipulations in theoretically meaningful ways. For example, implicit SE can be raised through classical conditioning (Baccus, Baldwin, & Packer, 2004) and subliminal conditioning (Dijksterhuis, 2004). Hence, research that examines momentary state SE also provides important theoretical contributions. When implicit SE is used as a state outcome measure, high test–retest reliability could be a liability, indicating a lack of sensitivity to contextual manipulations. In the current studies we used the subliminal Spalding and Hardin (1999) task as an outcome measure because: (1) it is the most indirect of the implicit SE measures; and (2) based on Bosson et al.'s (2003) observation of its low test–retest reliability, we suspect it is more of a state than a trait measure, and therefore sensitive to context. In support of its convergent and discriminant validity, Spalding and Hardin (1999) showed that scores on their implicit measure correlated with a nonverbal measure of anxiety, whereas self-reported SE did not, and self-reported SE related to self-handicapping, a deliberate self-presentational strategy, whereas implicit SE did not.

Motivation Orientations and Priming

Self-determination theory (SDT) postulates that everyone has both autonomous and control motivational orientations to some degree, but that individuals differ regarding the strengths of these orientations (Deci & Ryan, 2000). Thus, individuals with strong autonomy motivation orientation tend to respond autonomously in many situations, whereas those with strong control motivation orientation tend to interpret and respond to events in their environments in a controlled way. Nonetheless, situations that activate control motivation can lead people to act in a more controlled manner than they typically would and, likewise, autonomy-supportive environments can awaken autonomy motivation and allow the existing proclivity for autonomy to manifest (Deci & Ryan, 2000; Vallerand & Ratelle, 2002). Indeed, recent empirical evidence shows that motivation orientations can be temporarily primed and subsequently influence motivation-relevant outcomes, including self-reported intrinsic motivation, interest and enjoyment of a task, perceived choice, and free-choice behavior (Levesque & Pelletier, 2003). The results of the motivation priming studies are consistent with much other research demonstrating that nonconsciously primed concepts can operate automatically, outside of awareness, including attitudes (e.g., Fazio, Sanbonmatsu, Powell, & Kardes, 1986), prejudice and stereotypes (e.g., Dovidio, Kawakami, Johnson, Johnson, & Howard, 1997), attachment styles (Mikulincer & Shaver, 2001) and goals and motives (Bargh, Gollwitzer, Lee-Chai, Barndollar, & Trotschel, 2001), and that primed concepts influence subsequent perception and behavior in prime-consistent directions.

The Current Studies

The current studies used a priming task modeled after that of Bargh and his colleagues (Bargh, Chen, & Burrows, 1996) and similar to that of Levesque and Pelletier (2003) to induce participants in the direction of either autonomy or control motivation orientation, and to provide a causal test of the effect of motivation on SE. We expected that the prime would increase the cognitive accessibility of the motivation prime and make salient the self-aspects that underlie each motivation orientation. Hence, for autonomy-primed participants, the secure aspects of SE would become activated and level would remain high, whereas among control-primed participants, the contingent aspects of SE would become activated, which would lead to a focus on self-worth assessment that would undermine SE level.

We examined the effect of primed autonomous and control motivations on three outcome variables—implicit SE, explicit SE, and SE defensiveness (the difference between these). Because we believe the subliminal priming measure assesses automatic self-evaluations that are sensitive to context, we hypothesized that the control prime would result in lower implicit SE relative to the autonomy prime. In contrast, explicit SE scores can reflect defensive and other motivational biases. Based on this tendency, and our belief that defensiveness underlies control motivation (Hodgins & Knee, 2002), we hypothesized that explicit SE would show the opposite pattern and would be defensively higher under control priming than under autonomy priming.

Finally, we examined defensive SE, defined as the discrepancy between high explicit and low implicit SE. Although this discrepancy has been called various names, including defensive SE (Bosson et al., 2003; Jordan et al., 2003b) and defensive pride (McGregor, Nail, Marigold, & Kang, 2005), we chose defensive SE because, as described above, it predicts various defensive behaviors. Consistent with the defensiveness that accompanies control motivation, we expected that control priming would lead to higher defensive SE than autonomy priming would.

The studies also included a threat manipulation because we expected that SE differences would be most likely to show up under threat. Hence, we hypothesized that threat would magnify the effect of control motivation priming on implicit SE (in essence, a double whammy effect). If so, the questioning of self-worth that occurs when contingent SE is salient should lead to a larger decrease in SE when threat also is present. In contrast, the secure SE that accompanies autonomy motivation should buffer the effect of threat.

Past research has not reported sex differences in either implicit or defensive SE (e.g., Bosson et al., 2003; Jordan et al., 2003a, 2003b, 2005), so we did not expect main effects for gender. However, when sex differences in motivation orientation occur, they tend to be in the direction of men being higher on control motivation and women higher on autonomy (Deci & Ryan, 1985a), and past research shows that control motivation is associated with interpersonal defensiveness (Hodgins et al., 1996a). Finally, being male and being control-oriented both independently predict self-defensive accounts for bad behavior (Hodgins, Liebeskind, & Schwartz, 1996b). Hence, although we did not have a strong a priori empirical basis for expecting sex differences in implicit, explicit, or defensive SE, past sex differences in control motives and defensiveness suggest that if sex differences occurred, they would be in the direction of greater male defense.

Study 1

Method

Participants

Seventy-seven undergraduates (61 women), ages 17–22, the majority of whom (89%) were White, participated in partial fulfillment of a course requirement. Two participants (1 woman) who identified the theme of control motivation primes were eliminated from analyses, resulting in a final sample of 75 participants.

Materials

Motivation prime.   Following the procedure of Bargh et al. (1996), materials were developed to prime autonomy and control motivation. There were two versions, one for each motivation, and each version had 30 items (15 targets and 15 fillers). Each item had five words from which participants were instructed to construct a grammatically correct four-word sentence (see Appendix). In order to strengthen the priming, separate instructions were given for autonomy and control that emphasized the quality of motivation without referring to performance level. Instructions for the control version specifically aimed to increase the sense of coercion and pressure that defines control motivation by stating that: "the measure correlates with verbal intelligence in adults," and that "most college students should be able to complete it." In contrast, autonomy instructions specifically aimed to emphasize interest without pressure by stating that: "many people find the task enjoyable and interesting," and that "we need to obtain norms." In keeping with similar tasks, a manipulation check was not included because priming effects depend on participants remaining unaware of the prime (Bargh, 1992); however, participants were probed for suspicions during debriefing.

Threat manipulation.   Participants read one of two versions of a fictitious local newspaper account reporting a survey of local residents' opinions. The parts critical to the threat manipulation were:

> [threat version]...76% of downtown business owners "agreed somewhat" or "agreed strongly" with the statement, "Skidmore students can be quite difficult to deal with." Furthermore, 80% of the business owners "agreed somewhat" or "agreed strongly" with the statement, "Skidmore students are a major cause of damage to downtown night-time establishments."

[non-threat version]... 76% of downtown business owners "agreed somewhat" or "agreed strongly" with the statement, "Skidmore students usually are very friendly and polite." Furthermore, 80% of the residents polled "agreed somewhat" or "agreed strongly" with the statement, "The high level of volunteer work among Skidmore students greatly benefits Saratoga Springs residents."

Explicit SE. Heatherton and Polivy's (1991) State Self-Esteem Scale (SSES) was used to measure self-reported (i.e., explicit) SE. The scale includes 20 items; participants respond using 5-point Likert-type scales. In Study 1, scores ranged from 45.5 to 95.0 ($M = 74.6$, $SD = 10.3$). Internal reliability in a large sample (Heatherton & Polivy, 1991) was $\alpha = .92$; in the current study the reliability was $\alpha = .87$.

Implicit SE. Spalding and Hardin's (1999) implicit SE measure was used in which participants categorize positive target words (e.g., worthy, winner) and negative target words (e.g., weak, loser) as quickly as possible. Each target word is preceded by a subliminal prime that is either self-relevant (i.e., me, myself) or self-irrelevant (i.e., two, manners). Each of the 12 target words (6 negative, 6 positive) appears twice after each of the four primes, for a total of 96 trials, presented in random order. The test was administered on a Macintosh computer running PsychLab V1.0–103.2 software (Gum, 1997). Participants responded on keys labeled with "+" and "–" symbols, counterbalanced to appear on the right and left sides of the keyboard for equal numbers of participants. Each trial consisted of a 54 ms forward mask letter string, 13 ms blank, 13 ms prime, 13 ms blank, 54 ms backward mask letter string, 94 ms blank, and a target word.

Following Spalding and Hardin (1999), incorrect trials were omitted, latencies below 300 ms were recoded to 300, and latencies above 2000 ms were recoded to 2000. Response latencies were log transformed to correct for positive skew, and implicit SE scores were calculated by creating two difference scores: (1) the mean latency for positive targets and self-relevant primes was subtracted from the mean latency for negative targets and self-relevant primes; and (2) the mean latency for positive targets and self-irrelevant primes was subtracted from the mean latency for negative targets and self-irrelevant primes. The difference score for self-irrelevant trials was then subtracted from the difference score for self-relevant trials; hence, higher scores indicate higher implicit SE.[1] Log transformed scores ranged from −.15 to .25 ($M = 0.02$, $SD = 0.07$). Spalding and Hardin (1999) did not report internal reliability; in our sample, $\alpha = .90$.

Procedure

Participants were run in small groups in a study described as three unrelated tasks. Participants were randomly assigned to prime and threat conditions. They completed the priming task, received the threat manipulation, and completed a linguistic intergroup bias (LIB) task that was included for a separate study and was unrelated to the current study. The LIB task involved choosing verbal descriptions of stick figure drawings of people depicted in everyday situations from among options that varied in their level of abstractness. Although the LIB task occurred between the priming task and the SE measures, the task was emotionally neutral and did not disrupt our expected findings. Participants then completed the implicit SE measure, explicit SE measure, a follow-up questionnaire, and were debriefed.

Results

Data analysis. Analyses of variance (ANOVAs) were performed with between-subjects factors of Primed Motivation (autonomous or control), Threat (threat or no threat), and Sex. Dependent variables included explicit SE, implicit SE, and defensive SE scores (computed as described below). Pearson r was computed as an estimate of effect size (Rosenthal & Rosnow, 1984). According to Cohen and Cohen (1983, p. 61) rs of .10, .30, and .50 correspond to small, medium, and large effects, respectively.

Explicit SE. Men self-reported higher state SE ($M = 80.5$, $SD = 9.7$) than did women ($M = 73.1$, $SD = 10.0$), $F(1, 74) = 7.63$, $p < .01$, $r = .31$.[2] The means for the Threat variable were in the direction of a defensive response (threat: $M = 76.9$, $SD = 10.0$; no threat: $M = 72.5$, $SD = 10.2$), but did not reach significance, $F(1, 74) = 1.69$, $p < .20$, $r = .15$. The Motivation Prime × Threat interaction was weak and not significant, $F(1, 74) = 2.32$, $p < .14$, $r = .17$. There was no effect of Motivation Prime, $F < 1$.

Implicit SE. In contrast to explicit scores, implicit SE showed no effect of sex, $F < 1$. As expected, participants primed with control motivation exhibited lower implicit SE ($M = -0.010$, $SD = 0.068$) than those primed with autonomy ($M = 0.035$, $SD = 0.063$), $F(1, 74) = 5.47$, $p < .03$, $r = .26$, showing that activated control motivation undermines implicit SE compared to autonomy motivation. There was a trend for men to have lower implicit SE under threat ($M = -0.019$, $SD = 0.078$) compared to under no threat ($M = 0.026$, $SD = 0.079$) and compared to women (threat: $M = 0.027$, $SD = 0.068$; no threat: $M = 0.014$, $SD = 0.061$), but the Threat × Sex interaction did not reach significance, $F(1, 74) = 2.27$, $p < .14$, $r = .17$. The main effect of Threat and the Motivation Prime × Threat interaction were both weak, Fs < 1.

Defensive SE. As in other research, implicit and explicit SE scores were unreliably correlated, $r = -.13$, $p < .28$. We examined the discrepancy between implicit and explicit SE by calculating defensive SE scores. Standardized implicit scores were subtracted from standardized explicit scores, so that higher numbers indicate a tendency to self-report higher SE relative to the implicit measure. On this difference score, men showed higher defensive SE ($M = 0.82$, $SD = 1.62$) than did women ($M = -0.18$, $SD = 1.43$), $F(1, 74) = 5.64$, $p < .02$, $r = .27$.[3] However, the sex difference was moderated by a significant Sex × Primed Motivation × Threat interaction, $F(1, 74) = 6.22$, $p < .02$, $r = .28$. As seen in Table 1, the greater defensiveness of men was a result of very high defensiveness among men who were primed with control motivation and received threat. Simple effects tests showed that the Motivation × Threat interaction was significant for men, $F(1, 14) = 4.57$, $p < .056$, $r = .50$, but not women, $F(1, 59) < 1.61$, $p < .21$, $r = .16$. Thus, only men supported the double-whammy hypothesis.

Discussion

As expected, control-primed participants showed lower implicit SE compared to autonomy-primed participants, suggesting that merely being exposed to cues of control motivation is sufficient to cause more negative automatic self-associations.

TABLE 1　Mean Defensive SE Scores as a Function of Threat, Motivation Prime, and Sex (Study 1)

	Threat		No threat	
	Autonomy	Control	Autonomy	Control
Females				
M	0.19_a	-0.24_a	-0.59_a	-0.07_a
SD	1.18	1.91	1.77	0.60
Males				
M	0.04_a	2.48_b	0.77_a	-0.03_a
SD	1.26	0.32	2.45	0.32

Note: Means with different subscripts differ at $p < .05$.

In contrast, Motivation Prime did not show the expected reverse main effect on explicit SE, with control prime leading to defensively higher explicit SE. It is possible that the explicit measure is less sensitive to our manipulations than the implicit measure is.

As noted earlier, although sex differences in defensive SE have not been reported previously, male defensiveness on other outcome measures allowed a tentative prediction of greater male defense. Accordingly, men showed more defensive SE (i.e., a greater tendency to report high explicit SE when implicit SE was low) than did women. Furthermore, the Prime × Threat × Sex interaction suggests that control-primed men under threat were the most defensive of all. That is, men responded to a two-pronged threat (i.e., primed with control motivation, and threatened by an insult to their school identity) by increasing their explicit SE when their implicit SE was low. This suggests that although the threat manipulation alone did not influence defensive SE, threat in conjunction with motivation prime was effective, but only for men.

The low number of men in Study 1, however, brings the reliability of the sex differences into question, so they require replication. Study 2 therefore sought to replicate Study 1 with an adequate distribution of participants by sex. Additionally, sex differences in motivational orientation could have contributed to the sex differences, as men sometimes are higher on control motivation and women on autonomy motivation (e.g., Deci & Ryan, 1985a). Hence, Study 2 included a trait measure of motivation orientation that would allow us to examine the effects of primed motivation and gender on SE, and to tease apart the combined contribution of gender and individual differences, by controlling for individual differences in motivation orientation.

Finally, Study 1 did not include a neutral motivation prime condition, so the results do not address whether autonomy raises implicit SE or control motivation lowers it, relative to a control group comparison. In order to examine this question, a neutral condition was included in Study 2 in which participants were exposed only to motivationally neutral words. The Study 2 procedure also specifically omitted Study 1's intervening task between the prime and SE outcome variables.

Study 2

In Study 2, our main objective was to further investigate the effect of primed motivation orientations, threat, and gender on explicit, implicit, and defensive SE. We predicted that motivation orientations would influence implicit SE such that autonomy-primed participants would show more positive and control-primed participants less positive automatic self associations, relative to a neutral prime condition. We also expected to replicate the gender difference of greater male defensiveness under conditions of control priming and threat.

Method

Participants

One hundred five undergraduates (57 women, 48 men), the majority of whom (91%) were White, participated in partial fulfillment of a psychology course requirement.

Materials

General Causality Orientations Questionnaire (GCOS). The GCOS (Deci & Ryan, 1985a) consists of three subscales measuring individual differences in autonomy, control, and impersonal motivational orientations. As noted earlier, autonomy and control orientations differ from one another in that autonomy includes a sense of self-determination about behavior, whereas control does not. However, both autonomy and control motivation orientation involve a sense of competence or agency that allows for effective functioning. In contrast, impersonal orientation refers to having beliefs of noneffectance, that is, that one cannot attain desired outcomes. In past research, impersonal motivation was associated with social anxiety, self-derogation, depression (Deci & Ryan, 1985b) and restrictive anorexia (Strauss & Ryan, 1987). We used the 17-vignette (51 item) GCOS (Ryan, 1989). Each vignette describes a situation and has three items, one each for autonomy, control, and impersonal. Participants use 7-point (1 to 7) scales to rate the likelihood of responding in each way. An example of a vignette and its items is as follows:

> You have been offered a new position in a company where you have worked for some time. The first question that is likely to come to mind is (a) I wonder if the new work will be interesting? (the autonomous response), (b) Will I make more money at this position? (the controlled response), and (c) What if I can't live up to the new responsibility? (the impersonal response).

Responses are summed, resulting in scores representing the strength of each of the three motivational orientations. The GCOS subscales have been unrelated in past research (Deci & Ryan, 1985b); in our sample, the only intercorrelation that approached significance was that between autonomy and impersonal, $r = -.17$, $p < .09$. Men were significantly higher on control motivation, $r = .22$, $p < .03$, and lower on autonomy motivation, $r = -.19$, $p < .05$, a sex difference noted before (Deci & Ryan, 1985a). In the past, GCOS subscales have shown good internal reliability ($\alpha s = .75$ to .90) and test–retest reliability ($rs = .75$ to .85; Blustein, 1988; Deci & Ryan, 1985b; Vallerand, Blais, LaCouture, & Deci, 1987). Internal consistencies were .81, .70, and .81 for the autonomy, control, and impersonal subscales, respectively.

Motivation prime. The same sentence scramble task was used as in Study 1, with the addition of a neutral condition (see Appendix). Instructions for the neutral priming task stated that the test: "has not been used in college students, therefore, we need to obtain norms."

Threat manipulation.   The same threat manipulation was used as in Study 1.

Explicit SE.   The SSES measure was used as in Study 1. Scores ranged from 39 to 96 ($M = 72.3$, $SD = 13.1$); $\alpha = .91$.

Implicit SE.   Implicit SE was measured as in Study 1. Log transformed scores ranged from $-.13$ to .08 ($M = -0.01$, $SD = 0.04$); $\alpha = .93$.

Procedure

Participants were randomly assigned to condition and run in small groups in a study that was described as three unrelated experiments. They completed the GCOS, the priming task, received the threat manipulation, completed the implicit and explicit SE measures, completed a follow-up questionnaire, and were debriefed.

Results and Discussion

Data analysis.   Preliminary regression analyses showed that the GCOS did not interact with prime or threat, all $Fs < 1.5$. Impersonal motivation orientation correlated negatively with explicit SE, $r = -.63$, $p < .001$, and with defensive SE, $r = -.45$, $p < .001$. As noted above, being female predicted higher autonomy and lower control motivation, therefore, GCOS scores were covaried in an ANOVA in order to control for sex differences in pre-existing motivational orientation, and to rule them out as an explanation for effects of sex on the manipulated variables. Thus, analyses included between-subjects factors of Primed Motivation (autonomous, neutral, or control), Threat (threat or no threat), and Sex, and the three GCOS sub-scales as covariates. Dependent variables again included explicit SE, implicit SE, and SE defense scores. All means reported for Study 2 are adjusted for the covariates.

Following Rosenthal and Rosnow (1984; see also Zuckerman, Hodgins, Zuckerman, & Rosenthal, 1993), planned contrasts were performed to test whether the three levels of prime yielded the predicted linear pattern. Planned contrasts test the significance of the precise predicted pattern of differences among the levels of the outcome variable by assigning contrast weights that sum to zero. When a prediction is linear, as ours was, the appropriate contrast weights are $+1$, 0, and -1 assigned to the autonomy, neutral, and control primes to test the precise prediction that autonomy-primed participants will show the highest implicit SE, neutral-primed participants a moderate level, and control-primed the lowest level (Rosenthal & Rosnow, 1984, pp. 346–352).

Explicit SE.   Men again reported higher explicit SE ($M = 74.9$, $SD = 13.0$) than women ($M = 70.4$, $SD = 12.9$), $F(1, 103) = 4.48$, $p < .04$, $r = .20$, and there were no effects of Motivation Prime or Threat, all $Fs < 1$.

Implicit SE.   As in Study 1, and again in contrast to explicit scores, implicit SE showed no effect of sex, $F < 1$. New to Study 2, there was a main effect of threat such that threatened participants had implicit SE that was lower ($M = -0.022$, $SD = 0.04$) than those not threatened ($M = -0.001$, $SD = 0.04$), $F(1, 104) = 7.07$, $p < .01$, $r = .25$.[4] However, the marginal Threat × Sex interaction found in Study 1 was reliable in Study 2, $F(1, 104) = 6.38$, $p < .01$, $r = .24$, such that threatened men had the lowest implicit SE (see Table 2). Simple effects showed an effect of threat for

TABLE 2 Mean Implicit SE Scores as a Function of Threat and Sex (Study 2)

	Threat	No threat
Females		
M	-0.008_a	-0.007_a
SD	0.035	0.041
Males		
M	-0.036_b	0.006_a
SD	0.049	0.043

Note: Means with different subscripts differ at $p < .05$.

men, $F(1, 47) = 10.04$, $p < .01$, $r = .42$, but not women, $F(1, 56) < 1$. The significance of the Study 2 result lends confidence to the sex difference that appeared as a trend in Study 1; together they suggest that the implicit SE of men, but not women, was decreased when threatened.

Replicating Study 1, and consistent with the primary hypothesis, there was a main effect of Motivation Prime, linear contrast $F(1, 104) = 4.88$, $p < .04$, $r = .21$. The significant linear contrast indicates that participants primed with control motivation had relatively lower implicit SE ($M = -0.027$, $SD = 0.05$) and those primed with autonomy had relatively higher implicit SE ($M = -0.001$, $SD = 0.04$), compared to neutral-primed ($M = -0.006$, $SD = 0.03$). Although the linear contrast was significant, inspection of the means shows that the largest difference in implicit SE was between control-primed and neutral-primed participants. Simple effects confirmed that autonomy did not differ from neutral, $F < 1$, autonomy was higher than control, $F(1, 71) = 5.21$, $p < .03$, $r = .26$, and neutral was higher than control, $F(1, 67) = 4.26$, $p < .05$, $r = .24$. Hence, control priming lowered implicit SE, but autonomy priming did not increase it, relative to neutral priming.

Defensive SE.   As in past research and in Study 1, implicit and explicit SE scores were unreliably correlated, $r = -.05$. Replicating Study 1, men showed higher defensive SE ($M = 0.47$, $SD = 1.45$) than did women ($M = -0.02$, $SD = 1.24$), $F(1, 103) = 3.78$, $p < .055$, $r = .19$. In contrast to Study 1, the Sex × Primed Motivation × Threat interaction was nonsignificant, $F(1, 74) = 1.85$, $p < .17$. Instead, there was a main effect for motivation prime that approached significance such that autonomy-primed participants tended to have the least defensive SE ($M = 0.00$, $SD = 1.21$), neutral-primed participants were in the middle ($M = 0.13$, $SD = 1.22$), and control-primed participants tended to have the highest defensive SE ($M = 0.54$, $SD = 1.62$) linear contrast, $F(1, 103) = 3.16$, $p < .09$, $r = .17$. It was only marginally significant, however, and the simple effects were not significant. The means of the Threat variable showed somewhat greater defensiveness for threatened participants (threat: $M = 0.38$, $SD = 1.32$, no threat: $M = 0.06$, $SD = 1.37$), but did not reach significance, $F(1, 103) = 1.83$, $p < .18$, $r = .13$.

In sum, Study 2 replicates Study 1 in showing that motivation priming influences implicit SE on a measure that is unlikely to be influenced by deliberative intentions. It also extends Study 1's results by showing that control motivation undermines implicit SE more than autonomy increases it, relative to our neutral prime condition. Hence, both studies show support for the primary hypothesis, namely, that activated control motivation orientation undermines positive automatic self-associations.

Study 2 lends further support for sex differences in defensiveness. In both studies, men showed more defensive SE by having higher self-reported than implicit SE. Although the Prime × Threat × Sex interaction on defensive SE from Study 1 was not observed in Study 2, other Study 2 patterns concur with Study 1 in suggesting that men's higher defense might occur because of their greater reactivity to threat situations. Specifically, Study 2 showed a marginally significant trend for the effect of prime on implicit SE to be moderated by sex, so that the undermining of implicit SE by control priming tended to be stronger among men. Additionally, and in contrast to Study 1, threat lowered implicit SE, an effect moderated by sex and seen only among men. Together, the sex differences suggest the intriguing possibility that the greater defensiveness of men might be related to their greater loss of implicit self-esteem under conditions of threat and control motivation. Nonetheless, in some critical ways, men and women responded similarly to primed control motivation, which attests to the importance of motivation orientation for implicit SE and defensiveness across men and women.

General Discussion

SDT views control motivation as being associated with contingent SE, requiring that continual attention be paid to maintaining a sense of self-worth (e.g., Deci & Ryan, 1995). More recently, Ryan and Brown (2003) observed that when individuals start "esteeming" (i.e., asking if they are worthy), SE is already in trouble, implying an inevitable connection between *contingent* SE and experiencing decreased SE *level*. In accord with this reasoning, we predicted that primed autonomy and control motivations would, respectively, increase and decrease SE level. Our results using implicit SE confirmed that primed control motivation led to a decrease in positive automatic self-associations in two studies, a finding that has not been demonstrated before. In Study 1, control motivation lowered implicit SE relative to autonomy motivation, and in Study 2 it also lowered implicit SE relative to a control condition. Motivation priming also showed a tendency to influence defensive SE in Study 2, in the direction of control priming causing greater defense and autonomy priming causing less defense, relative to the neutral comparison group. The effect was marginally significant, however, and not found in Study 1, so should be interpreted cautiously. The most robust finding for defensive SE was men's significantly higher defensive SE in both studies. Although sex differences in defensive SE have not been previously reported, the finding is consistent with men's greater defense using a different paradigm (Hodgins & Liebeskind, 2003; Hodgins et al., 1996b), an effect the authors suggested is due to men's lower threshold for threat.

The current findings support this speculation. Specifically, men in both studies showed lower implicit SE under threat, suggesting they were more reactive to threat than women. Moreover, men in Study 1 showed more defensive SE under a two-pronged threat (control manipulation and devaluing their in-group). Although this effect was unreliable in Study 2, the overall pattern in both studies consistently shows that men were more defensive than women by compensating on the explicit SE measure when their implicit SE was low, particularly under threat. Nonetheless, both men and women supported our focal hypothesis that priming control motivation would decrease implicit SE and showed that control motivated individuals experienced more negative automatic self-associations. This has not been demonstrated previously, but is an important aspect of the Hodgins and Knee (2002) model, which proposes that control motivation undermines SE, and that insecure SE subsequently causes individuals to continually defend against events that do not support SE, in an attempt to maintain self-worth. Past research supports the link between motivation and defensiveness in correlational data (Hodgins & Liebeskind, 2003; Hodgins et al., 1996a, 1996b; Knee, Neighbors, & Vietor, 2001; Knee & Zuckerman, 1996, 1998) and, more recently, with experimental data (Hodgins, Yacko, & Gottlieb, in press). However, the current studies provide the first causal evidence for the link between motivation and SE, which specifies that control motivation causes significantly lower implicit SE. It will be important for future research to test other aspects of the model by including motivation, SE, and defensive behavior in a single study. In the meantime, the current research provides further confirmation of the importance of seeking out and creating contexts that support autonomy and minimize control motivation: Our implicit, automatic evaluations of self-worth are affected by the cues around us.

Implications of the Research for the Subliminal Priming Measure

To date, the Spalding and Hardin (1999) measure has been used infrequently compared to the IAT and name letter tasks. Although one article has been published in Chinese (Shi, 2003), the only English language one that we know of (beyond Spalding & Hardin's original) is Bosson et al. (2000), a comprehensive investigation of implicit SE measures. The authors reported low test–retest reliability for the Spalding and Hardin measure, and concluded that tests with higher reliability, such as the IAT, should be used, which may have dampened enthusiasm for the Spalding and Hardin measure (see Dijksterhuis, 2004, p. 347). However, as noted earlier, test–retest reliability is not necessarily an advantage for state measures of implicit SE, and therefore not a disadvantage of the Spalding and Hardin measure.

Furthermore, and oddly, Bosson et al. (2000) reported low internal consistency ($\alpha = .49$) compared to what we found, αs = .90 and .93 (Spalding & Hardin, 1999, did not report internal consistency coefficients). This difference raises the question of whether Bosson et al.'s use of the Spalding and Harding measure differed in some way from ours, which followed the validation article precisely. We were unable to resolve the reason for the discrepancy (J. Bosson, personal communication, January 2006); thus, it remains a question for future research. Our studies, however, provide a compelling basis for researchers to use the underappreciated Spalding and Hardin measure, which intuitively seems to capture so well the spirit of implicit self-evaluation by measuring latencies following subliminal primes.

Limitations and Future Directions

Why does control motivation lower implicit SE? Our studies did not address the specific mechanism from among several that can explain priming effects (e.g., Bargh et al., 1996; DeMarree, Wheeler, & Petty, 2005; Dijksterhuis, 2001; Kawakami, Dovidio, & Dijksterhuis, 2005), however, we speculate that the biased activation account of self-activation theory (DeMarree et al., 2005) makes the most sense in explaining our findings. According to this view, prime-relevant content that is already contained in the chronic self-concept is activated by a prime so that self-representations change in a prime-consistent direction. This would mean that control priming activated participants' belief that their self-worth is contingent, leading to a decrease in the level of implicit SE.

Although the opposite effect was predicted for autonomy priming, in Study 2 we found no differences between this condition and the neutral-priming condition. Why might this be the case? First, contextual cues of control motivation might interfere with SE more than autonomy cues enhance it, *or* control motivation cues might lower SE *more quickly* than autonomy motivation cues raise it, so that individuals require a longer time in an autonomy-supportive context before SE is raised or becomes secure. Alternatively, it is possible that our participants had durable tendencies toward control motivation and contingent (and therefore vulnerable) SE. In support of this, Crocker and Park (2004) have suggested that contingent SE is much more common than genuine SE, and Levesque and Pelletier (2003) found empirical evidence that a chronic heteronomous motivational orientation toward academics is more common in college students than a chronic autonomous orientation. If our participants were highly control motivated, with highly contingent SE, then they might have been more responsive to cues of control motivation than cues of autonomy.

Unexpectedly, we obtained sex differences on the explicit state SE measure in both studies. As noted in note 2, the sex difference was due to the appearance subscale in both studies, with women judging their own appearance more harshly than men did. Given the cultural tendency to objectify women (e.g., Daubenmier, 2005; Fredrickson, Roberts, Noll, Quinn, & Twenge, 1998), it is not difficult to imagine this happening; however, a sex difference on the SSES appearance subscale has not been documented in previous studies. Thus, there might be something unique to our samples that caused a sex difference on the appearance subscale; it remains for future research to investigate.

The explicit SE did not show the expected defensive increase following control priming and threat manipulation, suggesting that explicit SE scores did not tap defensiveness directly. Also, and as in past research, implicit and explicit measures were uncorrelated, suggesting yet again that SE is a domain where dissociation occurs between the automatic self-evaluations tapped by the implicit measure and the controlled self-evaluations assessed by the explicit measure. The dissociation is consistent with the position that automatic and controlled evaluations stem from different sources (Rudman, 2004). Although some researchers state that implicit measures do not tap more "genuine" SE than do explicit measures (e.g., Jordan et al., 2003b), the presence of priming effects on the implicit and not explicit measure in the current studies supports the position that implicit measures provide better access to associative knowledge than do self-report measures (Greenwald et al., 2002). It also suggests that implicit measures may be more sensitive to context than self-reports and thus, contain rich possibilities for furthering our understanding of the factors that influence human behavior.

Notes

1. The Spalding and Hardin (1999) measure combines the four types of latencies and log transforms them, thus, implicit SE scores do not reflect absolute implicit SE level.
2. Heatherton and Polivy (1991) did not report sex differences in their five studies validating the SSES, so we were surprised to find them here. Analyses of the three subscales revealed that in Study 1 men ($M = 3.99$, $SD = 0.46$) scored significantly higher than women ($M = 3.29$, $SD = 0.71$) only on the appearance subscale,

$F(1, 74) = 13.89$, $p < .0001$, $r = .40$, not on the performance subscale (men: $M = 4.13$, $SD = 0.52$, women: $M = 3.87$, $SD = 0.60$), $F(1, 74) = 2.53$ $p = .12$, $r = .18$, or the social subscale (men: $M = 3.94$, $SD = 0.74$, women: $M = 3.76$, $SD = 0.74$), $F(1, 74) = 1.08$, $p = .30$. Likewise, in Study 2, men ($M = 3.66$, $SD = 0.77$) scored significantly higher than women ($M = 3.04$, $SD = 0.80$) on the appearance subscale, $F(1, 103) = 14.52$, $p < .0001$, $r = .36$, but not on the performance subscale (men: $M = 3.89$, $SD = 0.73$, women: $M = 3.76$, $SD = 0.67$), $F(1, 103) = 1.13$, $p = .29$, $r = .11$, or the social subscale (men: $M = 3.69$, $SD = 0.85$, women: $M = 3.64$, $SD = 0.73$), $F(1, 103) < 1$, $p = .68$.

3. Results on the defensive SE measure are not a result of the sex difference on the SSES appearance scale: When the appearance subscale is omitted, and the defensiveness SE scores calculated with performance and social SSES subscales, results show very similar patterns to the three subscale scores.

4. Degrees of freedom differ for explicit and implicit SE in Study 2 because one female participant did not complete the SSES explicit measure.

References

Assor, A., Roth, G., & Deci, E. L. (2004). The emotional costs of parents' conditional regard: A self-determination theory analysis. *Journal of Personality, 72*, 47–88.

Baccus, J. R., Baldwin, M. W., & Packer, D. J. (2004). Increasing implicit self-esteem through classical conditioning. *Psychological Science, 15*, 498–502.

Bargh, J. A. (1992). Does subliminality matter to social psychology? Being aware of the stimulus versus aware of its influence. In R. F. Bornstein & T. Pittman (Eds.), *Perception without awareness* (pp. 236–255). New York: Guilford Press.

Bargh, J. A., Chen, M., & Burrows, L. (1996) Automaticity of social behavior: Direct effects of trait construct and stereotype activation on action. *Journal of Personality and Social Psychology, 71*, 230–244.

Bargh, J. A., Gollwitzer, P. M., Lee-Chai, A., Barndollar, K., & Trotschel, R. (2001). The automated will: Nonconscious activation and pursuit of behavior goals. *Journal of Personality and Social Psychology, 81*, 1014–1027.

Baumeister, R. F. (1982). Self-esteem, self-presentation, and future interaction: A dilemma of reputation. *Journal of Personality, 50*, 29–45.

Baumeister, R. F., Heatherton, T. F., & Tice, D. M. (1993). When ego threats lead to self-regulation failure: Negative consequences of high self-esteem. *Journal of Personality and Social Psychology, 64*, 141–156.

Bergstrom, R. L., Neighbors, C., & Lewis, M. A. (2004). Do men find "bony" women attractive? Consequences of misperceiving opposite sex perceptions of attractive body image. *Body Image, 2*, 183–191.

Blair, I. V. (2002). The malleability of automatic stereotypes and prejudice. *Personality and Social Psychology Review, 6*, 242–261.

Blustein, D. L. (1988). The relationship between motivational processes and career exploration. *Journal of Vocational Behavior, 32*, 345–357.

Bosson, J. K., Brown, R. P., Zeigler-Hill, V., & Swann, W. B., Jr. (2003). Self-enhancement tendencies among people with high explicit self-esteem: The moderating role of implicit self-esteem. *Self and Identity, 2*, 169–187.

Bosson, J. K., Swann, W. B., Jr., & Pennebaker, J. W. (2000). Stalking the perfect measure of implicit self-esteem: The blind men and the elephant revisited? *Journal of Personality and Social Psychology, 79*, 631–643.

Cohen, J., & Cohen, P. (1983). *Applied multiple regression/correlation analysis for the behavioral sciences*. Hillsdale, NJ: Lawrence Erlbaum Associates, Inc.

Crocker, J., & Park, L. E. (2004). The costly pursuit of self-esteem. *Psychological Bulletin, 130*, 392–414.

Daubenmier, J. J. (2005). The relationship of yoga, body awareness, and body responsiveness to self-objectification and disordered eating. *Psychology of Women Quarterly, 29,* 207–219.

Deci, E. L., & Ryan, R. M. (1985a). The General Causality Orientations Scale: Self-determination in personality. *Journal of Research in Personality, 19,* 109–134.

Deci, E. L., & Ryan, R. M. (1985b). *Intrinsic motivation and self-determination in human behavior.* New York: Plenum Press.

Deci, E. L., & Ryan, R. M. (1995). Human autonomy: The basis for true self-esteem. In M. H. Kernis (Ed.), *Efficacy, agency, and SE* (pp. 31–49). New York: Plenum Press.

Deci, E. L., & Ryan, R. M. (2000). The "what" and "why" of goal pursuits: Human needs and the self-determination of behavior. *Psychological Inquiry, 11,* 227–268.

DeMarree, K. G., Wheeler, S. C., & Petty, R. E. (2005). Priming a new identity: Self-monitoring moderates the effects of nonself primes on self-judgments and behavior. *Journal of Personality and Social Psychology, 89,* 657–671.

Dijksterhuis, A. (2001). Automatic social influence: The perception–behavior link as an explanatory mechanism for behavior matching. In J. Forgas & K. D. Williams (Eds.), *Social influence: Direct and indirect processes* (pp. 95–108). Philadelphia: Psychology Press.

Dijksterhuis, A. (2004). I like myself but I don't know why: Enhancing implicit self-esteem by subliminal evaluative conditioning. *Journal of Personality and Social Psychology, 86,* 345–355.

Dovidio, J. F., Kawakami, K., Johnson, C., Johnson, B., & Howard, A. (1997). On the nature of prejudice: Automatic and controlled processes. *Journal of Experimental Social Psychology, 33,* 510–540.

Farnham, S. D., Greenwald, A. G., & Banaji, M. R. (1999). Implicit self-esteem. In D. Abrams & M. A. Hogg (Eds.), *Social identity and social cognition* (pp. 230–248). Malden, MA: Blackwell Publishing.

Fazio, R. H., Sanbonmatsu, D. M., Powell, M. C., & Kardes, F. R. (1986). On the automatic activation of attitudes. *Journal of Personality and Social Psychology, 50,* 229–238.

Fredrickson, B. L., Roberts, T. A., Noll, S. M., Quinn, D. M., & Twenge, J. M. (1998). That swimsuit becomes you: Sex differences in self-objectification, restrained eating, and math performance. *Journal of Personality and Social Psychology, 75,* 269–284.

Greenwald, A. G., Banaji, M. R., Rudman, L. A., Farnham, S. D., Nosek, B. A., & Mellott, D. S. (2002). A unified theory of implicit attitudes, stereotypes, self-esteem, and self-concept. *Psychological Review, 109,* 3–25.

Gum, T. (1997). *PsychLab.* V1.0–103.2 (Software)

Heatherton, T. F., & Polivy, J. (1991). Development and validation of a scale for measuring state self-esteem. *Journal of Personality and Social Psychology, 60,* 895–910.

Hetts, J. J., Sakuma, M., & Pelham, B. W. (1999). Two roads to positive regard: Implicit and explicit self-evaluation and culture, *Journal of Experimental Social Psychology, 35,* 512–559.

Hewitt, J., & Goldman, M. (1974). Self-esteem, need for approval, and reactions to personal evaluations. *Journal of Experimental Social Psychology, 10,* 201–210.

Hodgins, H. S., & Knee, C. R. (2002). The integrating self and conscious experience. In E. L. Deci & R. M. Ryan (Eds.), *Handbook of self-determination research* (pp. 87–100). Rochester, NY: University of Rochester Press.

Hodgins, H. S., Koestner, R., & Duncan, N. (1996a). On the compatibility of autonomy and relatedness. *Personality and Social Psychology Bulletin, 22,* 227–237.

Hodgins, H. S., & Liebeskind, E. (2003). Apology versus defense: Antecedents and consequences. *Journal of Experimental Social Psychology, 39,* 297–316.

Hodgins, H. S., Liebeskind, E., & Schwartz, W. (1996b). Getting out of hot water: Facework in social predicaments. *Journal of Personality and Social Psychology, 71,* 300–314.

Hodgins, H. S., Yacko, H., & Gottlieb, E. (in press). Autonomy and nondefensiveness. *Motivation and Emotion.*

Jordan, C. H., Spencer, S. J., & Zanna, M. P. (2003a). "I love me... I love me not": Implicit self-esteem, explicit self-esteem, and defensiveness. In S. J. Spencer, S. Fein, M. P. Zanna, & J. M. Olson (Eds.), *Motivated social perception: The Ontario symposium* (Vol. 9, pp. 117–145). Mahwah, NJ: Lawrence Erlbaum Associates, Inc.

Jordan, C. H., Spencer, S. J., & Zanna, M. P. (2005). Types of high self-esteem and prejudice: How implicit self-esteem relates to ethnic discrimination among high explicit self-esteem individuals. *Personality and Social Psychology Bulletin, 31,* 693–702.

Jordan, C. H., Spencer, S. J., Zanna, M. P., Hoshino-Browne, E., & Correll, J. (2003b). Secure and defensive high self-esteem. *Journal of Personality and Social Psychology, 85,* 969–978.

Kawakami, K., Dovidio, J. F., & Dijksterhuis, A. (2005). Effects of social category priming on personal attitudes. *Psychological Science, 14,* 315–319.

Kernis, M. H., & Paradise, A. W. (2002). Distinguishing between secure and fragile forms of high self-esteem. In E. L. Deci & R. M. Ryan (Eds.), *Handbook of self-determination research* (pp. 339–360). Rochester, NY: University of Rochester Press.

Kernis, M. H., Paradise, A. W., Whitaker, D., Wheatman, S., & Goldman, B. (2000). Master of one's psychological domain? Not likely if one's self-esteem is unstable. *Personality and Social Psychology Bulletin, 26,* 1297–1305.

Knee, C. R., Neighbors, C., & Vietor, N. (2001). Self-determination theory as a framework for understanding road rage. *Journal of Applied Social Psychology, 31,* 889–904.

Knee, C. R., & Zuckerman, M. (1996). Causality orientations and the disappearance of the self-serving bias. *Journal of Research in Personality, 30,* 76–87.

Knee, C. R., & Zuckerman, M. (1998). A nondefensive personality: Autonomy and control as moderators of defensive coping and self-handicapping. *Journal of Research in Personality, 32,* 115–130.

Levesque, C., & Pelletier, L. G. (2003). On the investigation of primed and chronic autonomous and heteronomous motivational orientations. *Personality and Social Psychology Bulletin, 29,* 1570–1584.

McFarlin, D. B., Baumeister, R. F., & Blascovich, J. (1984). On knowing when to quit: Task failure, self-esteem, advice, and nonproductive persistence. *Journal of Personality, 52,* 138–155.

McGregor, I., Nail, P. R., Marigold, D. C., & Kang, S. J. (2005). Defensive pride and consensus: Strength in imaginary numbers. *Journal of Personality and Social Psychology, 89,* 978–996.

Mikulincer, M., & Shaver, P. R. (2001). Attachment theory and intergroup bias: Evidence that priming the secure base schema attenuates negative reactions to out-groups. *Journal of Personality and Social Psychology, 81,* 97–115.

Neighbors, C., Larimer, M. E., Geisner, I. M., & Knee, C. R. (2004). Feeling controlled and drinking motives among college students: Contingent self-esteem as a mediator. *Self and Identity, 3,* 207–224.

Nuttin, J. M. (1985). Narcissism beyond Gestalt and awareness: The name letter effect. *European Journal of Social Psychology, 15,* 353–361.

Nuttin, J. M. (1987). Affective consequences of mere ownership: The name letter effect in twelve European languages. *European Journal of Social Psychology, 17,* 381–402.

Patrick, H., Neighbors, C., & Knee, C. R. (2004). Appearance-related social comparisons: The role of contingent self-esteem and self-perceptions of attractiveness. *Personality and Social Psychology Bulletin, 30,* 501–514.

Pyszczynski, T., Greenberg, J., Solomon, S., Arndt, J., & Schimel, J. (2004). Why do people need self-esteem? A theoretical and empirical review. *Psychological Bulletin, 130,* 435–468.

Raskin, R., Novacek, J., & Hogan, R. (1991). Narcissism, self-esteem, and defensive self-enhancement. *Journal of Personality, 59,* 19–38.

Reis, H. T., Sheldon, K. M., Gable, S. L., Roscoe, J., & Ryan, R. M. (2000). Daily well-being: The role of autonomy, competence, and relatedness. *Personality and Social Psychology Bulletin, 26*, 419–435.

Rosenthal, R., & Rosnow, R. L. (1984). *Essentials of behavioral research: Methods and data analysis.* New York: McGraw-Hill.

Roth, D. L., Snyder, C. R., & Pace, L. M. (1986). Dimensions of favorable self-presentation. *Journal of Personality and Social Psychology, 51*, 867–874.

Rudman, L. A. (2004). Sources of implicit attitudes. *Current Directions in Psychological Science, 13*, 79–82.

Ryan, R. M. (1989). The revised 17-item General Causality Orientations Scale. Unpublished manuscript, University of Rochester, Rochester, NY.

Ryan, R. M., & Brown, K. W. (2003). Why we don't need self-esteem: On fundamental needs, contingent love, and mindfulness. *Psychological Inquiry, 14*, 71–77.

Ryan, R. M., & Deci, E. L. (2004). Avoiding death or engaging life as accounts of meaning and culture: Comment on Pyszczynski et al. (2004). *Psychological Bulletin, 130*, 473–477.

Schneider, D. J. (1969). Tactical self-presentation after success and failure. *Journal of Personality and Social Psychology, 13*, 262–268.

Schneider, D. J., & Turkat, D. (1975). Self-presentation following success or failure. *Journal of Personality, 43*, 127–135.

Shi, W. (2003). A review of research on implicit self-esteem. *Psychological Science (China), 26*, 684–686.

Spalding, L. R., & Hardin, C. D. (1999). Unconscious unease and self-handicapping: Behavioral consequences of individual differences in implicit and explicit SE. *Psychological Science, 10*, 535–539.

Strauss, J., & Ryan, R. M. (1987). Autonomy disturbances in subtypes of anorexia nervosa. *Journal of Abnormal Psychology, 96*, 254–258.

Tice, D. M. (1991). Esteem protection or enhancement? Self-handicapping motives and attributions differ by trait self-esteem. *Journal of Personality and Social Psychology, 60*, 711–725.

Tice, D. M., & Baumeister, R. F. (1990). Self-esteem self-handicapping, and self-presentation: The strategy of inadequate practice. *Journal of Personality, 58*, 443–464.

Vallerand, R. J., Blais, M. R., LaCouture, Y., & Deci, E. (1987). The General Causality Orientations Scale: The Canadian French version of the General Causality Orientations Scale. *Canadian Journal of Behavioural Science, 19*, 1–15.

Vallerand, R. J., & Ratelle, C. F. (2002). Intrinsic and extrinsic motivation: A hierarchical model. In E. L. Deci & R. M. Ryan (Eds.), *The handbook of self-determination research* (pp. 37–63). Rochester, NY: University of Rochester Press.

Waschull, S. B., & Kernis, M. H. (1996). Level and stability of self-esteem as predictors of children's intrinsic motivation and reasons for anger. *Personality and Social Psychology Bulletin, 22*, 4–13.

Zuckerman, M., Hodgins, H. S., Zuckerman, A., & Rosenthal, R. (1993). Contemporary issues in the analysis of data: A survey of 551 psychologists. *Psychological Science, 4*, 49–53.

Appendix

Motivation Priming Items

Control motivation items	Autonomy motivation items
1. do we to this must	1. options have I two and
2. do I should to homework	2. feel are choiceful I usually
3. to I smile ought and	3. is to this opportunity my
4. for required to I'm study	4. I to we choose so leave
5. work to with obligated I'm	5. enjoy I freedom my he
6. meet we on deadlines must	6. in we autonomous often are
7. for boss coerced my me	7. have by preference a we
8. was obey we're compelled to	8. to go and I decided
9. compulsory to attendance is our	9. to our we classes selected
10. giving in to necessary is	10. on choice we a have
11. manipulates my to me boss	11. we today unconstrained were our
12. so behavior my they restrict	12. can self-regulate to usually I
13. forced by to study I'm	13. actions and my are independent
14. the by limits constrained us	14. Now to I unrestricted am
15. very are we pressured that	15. am I still for self-determined
Filler items	*Neutral motivation items (Study 2)*
1. book we the read top	1. by people walk some
2. sale for by sweatshirts are	2. books they be often read
3. dollars salad on costs two	3. the shall brown was dog
4. often soda but drink I	4. fence they but saw the
5. on bookmark used the she	5. two was had he hats
6. tablecloth and blue	6. plant I like obvious that
7. bright is the yes lamp the is	7. was sign a there too
8. is to here served lunch	8. porch the she white was
9. is the now desk wooden	9. soft indirect is light to
10. apple was to the delicious	10. the walk fish swims slowly
11. here the by telephone is	11. tall is Julia quite but
12. the her to fits shoe	12. pictures is our good were
13. you coffee the is hot	13. I student am a how
14. at the new computer is	14. are pencils hers the it
15. he now are wears glasses	15. am citizen from a I

Self and Identity, 6: 209–222, 2007
http://www.psypress.com/sai
ISSN: 1529-8868 print/1529-8876 online
DOI: 10.1080/15298860601118819

Psychology Press
Taylor & Francis Group

When Apologies Fail: The Moderating Effect of Implicit and Explicit Self-esteem on Apology and Forgiveness

JUDY EATON

Wilfrid Laurier University, Brantford, Ontario, Canada

C. WARD STRUTHERS
ANAT SHOMRONY
ALEXANDER G. SANTELLI

York University, Toronto, Ontario, Canada

The purpose of this research was to explore whether self-esteem, defined as both an implicit and an explicit evaluation of the self, moderates the apology–forgiveness process. It was predicted that those with defensive or fragile self-esteem (i.e., high explicit and low implicit self-esteem) would focus on and respond to the aspects of the apology that confirmed the harm done by the transgressor, rather than the transgressor's remorse, and thus respond with less forgiveness and more avoidance and revenge than when the transgressor does not apologize. Participants experienced a transgression, after which the transgressor either apologized or not. As predicted, compared to those with secure self-esteem, those with defensive self-esteem were the least forgiving and the most vengeful and avoidant after receiving an apology. These findings suggest that apologies may not have their intended effect when offered to individuals with defensive self-esteem. Potential mechanisms of this relationship were also examined.

Interpersonal conflict is an inevitable consequence of living in a social world. Because interpersonal transgressions can make their victims feel devalued (Scobie & Scobie, 1998), uncertain (Eaton, Struthers, & Santelli, 2006a), and defensive (Maltby & Day, 2004), this can have negative implications for the victims' self-worth (Aquino & Douglas, 2003; Fincham, 2000). In addition, it can make resolution of the conflict less likely, because individuals who experience ego threat often resort to self-enhancement strategies in order to regulate their self-worth, including retaliation by seeking revenge or using avoidance strategies (Aquino & Douglas, 2003). These behaviors clearly are not conducive to forgiveness.

This research was supported in part by a Social Sciences and Humanities Research Council of Canada (SSHRC) Standard Research Grant awarded to the second author.

We would like to thank Bryan Balandowich for serving as the transgressor, and Careen Khoury, Boyko Chopov, and Alexandra Revezs for their assistance with data entry. We would also like to thank Steve Spencer and two anonymous reviewers for their helpful comments.

Correspondence should be addressed to: Judy Eaton, Wilfrid Laurier University, Brantford Campus, 73 George Street, Brantford, Ontario, Canada N3T 2Y3. E-mail: jeaton@wlu.ca

Fortunately, apologies have been shown to reduce the negative thoughts, feelings, and behaviors associated with not forgiving and to help restore damaged relationships (e.g., Darby & Schlenker, 1982; Exline & Baumeister, 2000; Weiner, Graham, Peter, & Zmuidinas, 1991). Apologies, in addition to improving the victim's impression of the transgressor (Goffman, 1971) and increasing empathy toward the transgressor (McCullough, Worthington, & Rachal, 1997; McCullough et al., 1998), provide both explicit and implicit information about the transgression. Offenders who take responsibility for their acts by expressing remorse, acknowledging the harm done, and accepting responsibility for the transgression are, in effect, telling their victims, "You were right: I did this bad thing. I'm at fault, not you." This information not only reduces the uncertainty that victims may have had about the cause of the transgression or the offender's motivations, but it also lets victims know that they were correct in their interpretation of the event and that they have a legitimate right to be angry. This perceptual validation, or social verification that one is correct about one's interpretation of an event, may reduce the threat associated with the transgression and help individuals become more forgiving and less vengeful. There is evidence that perceptual validation mediates the apology–forgiveness relationship (Eaton et al., 2006a). In other words, apologies can help reduce the ego threat caused by interpersonal transgressions, thus paving the way for forgiveness.

Apologies do not always result in increased forgiveness, however. Certain situational factors may make a victim less willing to forgive, such as when the transgression is perceived to be intentional (Struthers, Eaton, & Santelli, 2005) or when the offender is expected to commit similar transgressions in the future (Gold & Weiner, 2000). In addition, there may be certain dispositional factors that preclude some individuals from forgiving. If transgressions threaten the integrity of the self, then it follows that how individuals react to transgressions may be dependent, in part, on how they evaluate themselves. One particularly well-researched aspect of self-evaluation is self-esteem. Self-esteem has been defined as "how much value people place on themselves" (Baumeister, Campbell, Krueger, & Vohs, 2003, p. 2). Recently, researchers have begun to distinguish between different types of self-esteem, and to speculate on how these different types of self-esteem may affect behavior. One such distinction is between explicit and implicit self-esteem (Bosson, Brown, Zeigler-Hill, & Swann, 2003; Jordan, Spencer, Zanna, Hoshino-Browne, & Correll, 2003; Kernis et al., 2005). Explicit self-esteem refers to the conscious evaluations of the self measured by self-report scales. It is this type of self-esteem that traditionally has been linked with positive outcomes for the individual (for a recent review, see Pyszczynski, Greenberg, Solomon, Arndt, & Schimel, 2004). In contrast, implicit self-esteem refers to the nonconscious, automatic evaluations of the self that are not readily accessible to the individual, and hence not measurable through self-report scales. Implicit self-esteem has been measured by assessing how favorably individuals rate stimuli closely associated with the self, such as the initials in their name (name letter effect; Kitiyama & Karasawa, 1997), and also by the Implicit Association Test (IAT; Greenwald & Farnham, 2000), which uses reaction times to assess how quickly individuals associate positive and negative concepts with themselves.

Implicit self-esteem has been found to moderate the effects of explicit self-esteem, in that those with high explicit but low implicit self-esteem tend to be more defensive than those with other combinations of self-esteem (Bosson et al., 2003; Jordan et al., 2003). This pattern of self-esteem has been referred to as *defensive* or *fragile* self-esteem, whereas the nondefensive patterns are referred to as *secure* self-esteem (Bosson et al., 2003; Jordan et al., 2003; Kernis et al., 2005). Compared to those with secure self-esteem, individuals with defensive self-esteem have been found to be higher in narcissism (Jordan et al., 2003) and, when threatened, more likely to engage in self-enhancement and self-promotion (Bosson et al., 2003; Kernis et al., 2005), compensatory conviction (McGregor & Marigold, 2003), and discrimination (Jordan et al., 2003; Kernis et al., 2005).

Despite the ego-threatening nature of interpersonal transgressions, little research has been conducted on the moderating role self-esteem may play in the forgiveness process. Although more or less positive links between explicit self-esteem and both dispositional forgiveness (Brown & Phillips, 2005; Neto & Mullet, 2004) and situational forgiveness (Eaton, Struthers, & Santelli, 2006b) have been found, these studies only measured explicit self-esteem. To our knowledge, no studies have examined both explicit and implicit self-esteem and forgiveness. There is, however, a small amount of research on defensiveness and forgiveness that may inform our predictions about how defensive self-esteem may affect forgiveness. For example, narcissism, which has been found to be a product of defensive self-esteem (Jordan et al., 2003), has been linked with lack of forgiveness. Exline, Baumeister, Bushman, Campbell, and Finkel (2004) found strong evidence that narcissists were less likely than non-narcissists to forgive others for interpersonal offences. This effect was robust across both naturalistic and laboratory settings, and is in line with research that has found that narcissists are more aggressive following ego threat than are non-narcissists (Bushman & Baumeister, 1998). Eaton et al. (2006b), in addition to finding a negative correlation between narcissism and both dispositional and situational forgiveness, found a similar relationship between personal need for structure and forgiveness. They found that those who scored high on need for personal structure, which is an individual difference variable associated with a low tolerance for uncertainty and increased defensiveness (Neuberg & Newsom, 1993; Thompson, Naccarato, & Parker, 2001), were less forgiving in general and less likely than those who scored low on need for personal structure to forgive following an actual transgression. These findings, although preliminary, suggest that defensiveness, as a result of ego threat, can be a barrier to forgiveness.

It is likely that most individuals, regardless of their self-esteem, experience some ego threat following an interpersonal transgression. We propose that the primary difference between those with defensive self-esteem and those with secure self-esteem is in how they respond to these transgressions. Secure self-esteem is proposed to provide a buffer against ego threat (Bosson et al., 2003). Therefore, individuals with secure self-esteem should have less of a need to self-enhance following a transgression, and hence should respond positively to a sincere apology from the offender. If the offender acknowledges his or her role in the transgression, accepts responsibility for committing harm, and expresses remorse, this should eliminate the ego threat caused by the transgression and help nondefensive victims forgive. Once the ego threat is removed, or reduced, these individuals will no longer have a need to defend their self-image, and thus they should be able to let go of their right to punish the transgressor and instead respond prosocially.

For individuals with defensive self-esteem, we predict that apologies will be less effective at facilitating forgiveness. There are two reasons for this. First, because individuals with defensive self-esteem are already under threat, they do not enjoy the same protection against ego-threatening transgressions as do individuals with secure self-esteem. Thus, apologies may be less effective at promoting forgiveness in these individuals because they experience negative events more vividly, and have a more difficult time letting go of the negative feelings the transgressions cause. Indeed, McCullough, Emmons, Kilpatrick, and Mooney (2003) found that defensive individuals report a higher incidence of perceived interpersonal transgressions than nondefensive individuals, which suggests that they are more sensitive to the threat associated with negative events. Second, because individuals with defensive self-esteem have more of a general need to self-enhance than do those with secure self-esteem, they may misinterpret, either deliberately or not, the intent of the apology. When an offender admits to a transgression by accepting the blame and taking on the responsibility of making an error, rather than accepting it and letting go of their anger and resentment, defensive individuals may instead focus on the aspects of the apology that help them elevate their self-worth. They may place less emphasis on the offender's expressed remorse and more on the offender's admission of harm and acceptance of responsibility. If they interpret the offender's response as a confirmation of the offender's unfair treatment of them it may, ironically, make them more angry and vengeful and less willing to forgive than if they did not receive an apology.

This increased confirmation of the unfair treatment they have received may be manifested as an increase in certainty about the event. If defensive individuals focus more on the information that the apology provides, rather than its overall intent, then they should also report being more certain about the cause of the event. Because individuals often become more convicted in their beliefs as a defense against self-threat (McGregor, Zanna, Holmes, & Spencer, 2001), we predict that individuals with defensive self-esteem, but not those with secure self-esteem, will report more causal certainty when they receive an apology than when they do not.

Another potential outcome of focusing on the causal information in the apology rather than the remorse is a decrease in empathy for the transgressor. McCullough and colleagues (1997, 1998) suggest that empathy is a mediator of the apology–forgiveness process, in that apologies are effective in part because they make their recipients feel more empathic toward the transgressor. It is likely that the aspect of the apology that creates empathy is the transgressor's remorse, because the causal information in the apology would simply confirm the transgressor's role in the negative event. When the transgressor expresses remorse, however, it lets the victim know that the transgressor regrets his or her actions, thus enabling the victim to care more about restoring the relationship (McCullough et al., 1997). If individuals with defensive self-esteem pay more attention to the informational properties of the apology and less attention to the remorse aspect of the apology, then this should result in lower empathy for the transgressor. Thus, we predict that individuals with defensive self-esteem will report less empathy toward a transgressor when they receive an apology than when they do not.

The purpose of this research was to explore whether self-esteem, defined as both an implicit and an explicit evaluation of the self, moderates the forgiveness process. Specifically, we were interested in how different combinations of implicit and explicit self-esteem affect how individuals respond to transgressors both when the transgressors apologize and when they do not. We measured explicit and implicit self-esteem in pretesting sessions, and then exposed our participants to an actual transgression, after which the transgressor either apologized or not.

We predicted that those with secure self-esteem would respond positively to the transgressor's remorse and thus be more forgiving and less likely to avoid or seek revenge against the transgressor than when the transgressor does not apologize.

We also predicted that, conversely, those with defensive self-esteem would focus on and respond more to the aspect of the apology that confirmed the harm done by the transgressor, rather than the transgressor's remorse, and thus respond with less forgiveness and more avoidance and revenge than when the transgressor does not apologize. In other words, we expected that, after receiving an apology, those with secure self-esteem should become more forgiving and those with defensive self-esteem should, ironically, become less forgiving. In an attempt to understand the mechanisms behind this process, we also measured the victim's causal certainty about the event and his/her empathy toward the transgressor.

Method

Participants

Participants were 79 undergraduate students (23 male and 56 female) in an upper-level course in organizational psychology. The average age was 22.7 years ($SD = 4.06$). Participants were given course credit in return for their participation.

Measures

Explicit self-esteem. Explicit self-esteem was measured with Rosenberg's (1965) Self-Esteem scale. This 10-item scale includes items such as: "I feel that I'm a person of worth, at least on an equal plane with others" and "I feel that I have a number of good qualities." Responses were measured on a 7-point scale, where $1 = disagree$ *strongly* and $7 = agree$ *strongly*. This scale is widely used and has good psychometric properties. Internal reliability for the measure was acceptable, with Cronbach's alpha of .87.

Implicit self-esteem. Implicit self-esteem was measured with the Name Letter Test (NLT; Koole & Pelham, 2003). In this test, participants are presented with the 26 letters of the alphabet and asked to rate their attraction to each letter, rated on a 9-point scale where $1 = not$ *at all attractive* and $9 = extremely$ *attractive*, and their liking of each letter, rated on a 9-point scale where $1 = dislike$ *very much* and $9 = like$ *very much*. Following the procedures outlined by Koole and Pelham (2003), for each participant, we computed an average score for the initials in their first and last name and an average score on all the remaining letters of the alphabet. The average for the remaining letters was subtracted from the average for the initial letters, resulting in a difference score. This difference score is an indication of implicit self-esteem, whereby the larger the difference (in the positive direction) between individuals' attraction to and liking for the letters in their own names and the other letters of the alphabet, the higher their implicit self-esteem. We averaged participants' difference scores for their attraction to and liking of the letters to create one measure of implicit self-esteem. This technique has been found to have acceptable test – retest reliability (Bosson, Swann, & Pennebaker, 2000).

Forgiveness. Forgiveness was measured in terms of both the presence of positive motivations (benevolence), referred to as forgiveness, and the absence of negative motivations (i.e., avoidance and revenge), referred to as unforgiveness. Forgiveness was measured with a number of items measuring positive motivation toward the transgressor, including: "Do you forgive the target?" and "Do you think that you will be able to let go of this issue with the target?" There were nine items in total, measured on a 7-point scale where $1 = not\ at\ all$ and $7 = very\ much\ so$. Cronbach's alpha for the scale was .94.

Unforgiveness was measured with the Transgression-Related Interpersonal Motivations scale (TRIM-12; McCullough et al., 1998), which measures the degree to which the offended party was motivated to avoid and seek revenge against the transgressor following the negative event. It contains 12 items, measured on 7-point scales (where $1 = not\ at\ all$ and $7 = very\ much\ so$), such as: "To what extent would you keep as much distance between you and the target as possible?" and "To what extent do you feel like you want to make the target pay?" Past research has found that the TRIM-12 is highly reliable and valid (e.g., McCullough et al., 1998; Exline et al., 2004). Cronbach's alpha for the scale was .95.

Causal certainty. The degree to which participants were certain about the cause of the transgression was measured with an 8-item scale developed for this study. Items, measured on a 7-point scale where $1 = not\ at\ all$ and $7 = a\ great\ deal$, included: "How confident are you in your interpretation of this event?" and "To what extent has your interpretation of the event been confirmed by the target?" Internal reliability for the scale was acceptable, with a Cronbach's alpha of .71.

Empathy. The degree to which participants felt empathy toward the transgressor was measured with a 6-item scale based on a measure developed by Batson (1990, 1991). Items, measured on a 7-point scale where $1 = not\ at\ all$ and $7 = a\ great\ deal$, included: "How much sympathy do you have for the target?" and "To what extent do you feel softhearted toward the target?" Cronbach's alpha for the scale was .93.

Manipulation check. In order to determine whether participants correctly perceived whether they had received an apology from the transgressor, they were asked to rate their agreement, on a 7-point scale where $1 = not\ at\ all$ and $7 = very\ much\ so$, with the following item: "To what extent did the target say he was sorry?"

Procedure

Participants completed the explicit self-esteem measure at the beginning of the term, as part of a larger pretesting session. Later in the term, the confederate, who was introduced as Bryan, a senior-level student, came to class, ostensibly to collect data for his honor's thesis. Students were informed that they would receive a small amount of extra course credit in return for completing the study, although they were under no obligation to participate. They were given the opportunity to complete the study during class time. The study, described as an investigation of the relationship between motivation and performance, was set up as a projective test, in which participants looked at a picture of two people interacting at work and were asked to describe what they felt was happening in the picture (these data were not actually used). They also completed the measure of implicit self-esteem. Participants were given a ballot to fill out, which would enter them in a draw to win $50 cash at the conclusion of the study. These ballots were handed in with the research materials. The next time the class met, participants were informed by the course director that Bryan, the researcher, had lost the data, and that this may jeopardize the course credit they were to receive and their participation in the cash draw. The course director said he would look into the problem and let them know what had happened. Three days later everyone who participated in the study received an e-mail from Bryan explaining how the data had been lost (he said that they were stolen from his supervisor's lab, which Bryan had left unlocked), and in which he either apologized or not.

Under the auspices of trying to decide whether to continue to allow researchers to collect data in his class, the course director asked participants to complete a question-naire regarding their experience with the honor's student's study. This occurred one week after they first learned of the transgression and four days after they had received Bryan's e-mail. This questionnaire contained the measures of forgiveness, unforgive-ness, causal certainty about the event, empathy toward the transgressor, and the manipulation check item. Participants were then thanked, fully debriefed, and given the extra course credit. The $50 draw was held on the last day of class.

Results

Manipulation Check

A t-test for independent samples confirmed that our manipulation of apology was successful. Those in the apology group were significantly more likely to report that the transgressor had said sorry ($M = 5.03$, $SD = 2.31$) than those in the no apology group ($M = 3.90$, $SD = 2.01$), $t(76) = 2.30$, $p < .05$.

Regression analyses

We conducted multiple regression analyses to determine the extent to which explicit self-esteem, implicit self-esteem, apology, and their interactions were related to both forgiveness and unforgiveness. Using procedures outlined by Aiken and West (1991), we dummy-coded the measure of apology as $0 = $ no apology and $1 = $ apology, centered the self-esteem variables by subtracting the mean from each score, and multiplied these new variables to create interaction terms. Forgiveness and unforgiveness were then regressed onto these variables.

There was a significant main effect of apology on forgiveness, $t(75) = -2.36$, $p < .05$ ($\beta = -.27$), whereby forgiveness was lower with apology than without. As predicted, however, this effect was qualified by a significant three-way interaction between apology, implicit self-esteem, and explicit self-esteem, $t(75) = 2.24$, $p < .05$ ($\beta = .41$). We tested the simple slopes at one standard deviation above and below the mean. As shown in Figure 1, those with high explicit and low implicit self-esteem were less forgiving when they received an apology than when they did not. This slope was significantly different from the slope for high explicit and high implicit self-esteem, $t(75) = 2.63$, $p < .05$, and marginally different from the slope for low explicit and low implicit self-esteem, $t(75) = -1.84$, $p = .07$.

A similar pattern was found for the measure of unforgiveness. There was a significant main effect of apology, $t(75) = 2.97$, $p < .05$ ($\beta = .32$), whereby unfor-giveness was higher when participants received an apology than when they did not. There was also an interaction between apology and implicit self-esteem, $t(75) = -2.57$, $p < .05$ ($\beta = -.40$), whereby those with low implicit self-esteem were more unforgiving when they received an apology than when they did not. These effects were qualified by the predicted significant three-way interaction between

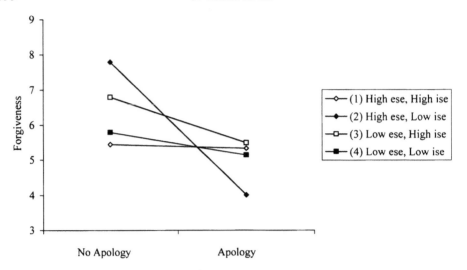

FIGURE 1 Forgiveness as a function of apology and explicit and implicit self-esteem. ESE = explicit self-esteem; ISE = implicit self-esteem. High ESE = +1 *SD*; low ESE = −1 *SD*; high ISE = +1 *SD*; low ISE = −1 *SD*.

apology, explicit self-esteem, and implicit self-esteem, $t(75) = -2.29$, $p < .05$ ($\beta = -.39$). Figure 2 shows the relationship between explicit and implicit self-esteem and forgiveness both when the participants received an apology and when they did not. As predicted, those with defensive self-esteem (i.e., low implicit self-esteem and high explicit self-esteem) were less forgiving when an apology was offered than when it was not. This slope was significantly different from the slope for high explicit and high implicit self-esteem, $t(75) = -3.17$, $p < .05$, and marginally different from the slope for low explicit and low implicit self-esteem, $t(75) = 1.93$, $p = .06$.

In an attempt to discover the underlying mechanisms of this relationship, we conducted similar analyses for participants' degree of causal certainty and empathy following the transgression. For causal certainty, there was a significant main effect of apology, $t(75) = 3.02$, $p < .05$ ($\beta = .33$), whereby causal certainty was higher when participants received an apology than when they did not. This main effect was qualified by a significant three-way interaction between apology, implicit self-esteem, and explicit self-esteem, $t(75) = -2.30$, $p < .05$ ($\beta = -.40$), whereby those with defensive self-esteem were more certain about the cause of the transgression when they received an apology as compared to when they did not receive an apology. As shown in Figure 3, this slope was significantly different from the slope for high explicit and high implicit self-esteem, $t(75) = -2.72$, $p < .05$, and the slope for low explicit and low implicit self-esteem, $t(75) = 2.34$, $p < .05$, and marginally different from the slope for low explicit and low implicit self-esteem, $t(75) = 1.86$, $p = .07$. This suggests that individuals with defensive self-esteem may withhold their initial judgments about transgressors because they are uncertain; however, when the transgressor apologizes, it reduces this uncertainty, which causes them to be less forgiving.

The reverse pattern was found for empathy. Although there was a significant interaction between apology and implicit self-esteem, $t(75) = 2.38$, $p < .05$ ($\beta = .40$), whereby those with low implicit self-esteem were more empathetic toward the transgressor when they received an apology as compared to when they did not, this

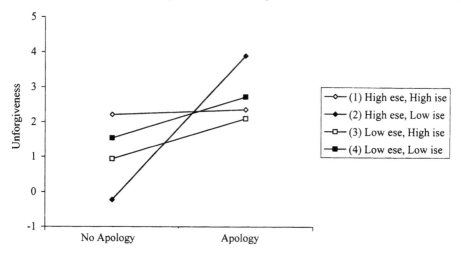

FIGURE 2 Unforgiveness (revenge and avoidance motivations) as a function of apology and explicit and implicit self-esteem. ESE = explicit self-esteem; ISE = implicit self-esteem. High ESE = +1 *SD*; low ESE = −1 *SD*; high ISE = +1 *SD*; low ISE = −1 *SD*.

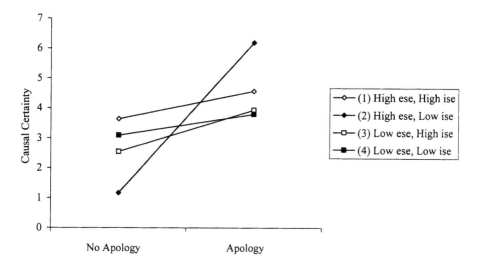

FIGURE 3 Causal certainty as a function of apology and explicit and implicit self-esteem. ESE = explicit self-esteem; ISE = implicit self-esteem. High ESE = +1 *SD*; low ESE = −1 *SD*; high ISE = +1 *SD*; low ISE = −1 *SD*.

was qualified by a significant three-way interaction between apology, explicit self-esteem, and implicit self-esteem, $t(75) = 2.00$, $p < .05$ ($\beta = .37$). Figure 4 shows that participants with high explicit and low implicit self-esteem were less empathic when they received an apology as compared to when they did not. This slope was significantly different from the slopes for high explicit and low implicit self-esteem, $t(75) = 2.85$, $p < .05$, low explicit and high implicit self-esteem, $t(75) = -2.17$, $p < .05$, and low explicit and low implicit self-esteem, $t(75) = -2.22$, $p < .05$.

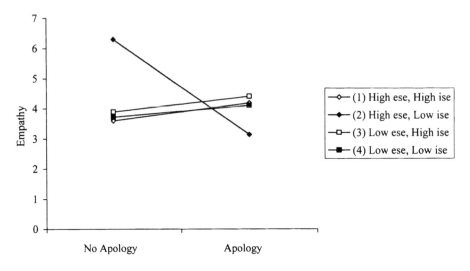

FIGURE 4 Empathy as a function of apology and explicit and implicit self-esteem. ESE = explicit self-esteem; ISE = implicit self-esteem. High ESE = +1 *SD*; low ESE = −1 *SD*; high ISE = +1 *SD*; low ISE = −1 *SD*.

Discussion

These findings suggest that apologies may not have their intended effect when offered to victims with defensive self-esteem. Ironically, apologies can actually make this group less forgiving and more likely to retaliate. We found that individuals with defensive self-esteem were less forgiving toward a transgressor and more motivated to respond with avoidance and revenge when they received an apology than when they did not. This counterproductive response may be due to differences in how the apology was perceived. Individuals with defensive self-esteem reported more causal certainty after an apology than did those with secure self-esteem, which suggests that, rather than interpreting the apology in the spirit in which it was intended (i.e., as an expression of remorse), the defensive individuals focused more on the causal information that the apology provided than on its expression of remorse. In addition, these same individuals were less empathic toward the transgressor when he apologized than when he did not.

Interestingly, although we did find main effects of apology on forgiveness and revenge and avoidance motivations, apology did not make much of a difference in how those with secure self-esteem responded to the transgressor. These participants were generally forgiving and non-vengeful regardless of whether they received an apology or not. In line with the theorizing of Bosson and colleagues (2003), this suggests that the individuals with secure self-esteem were sufficiently buffered against the ego-threatening properties of the transgression that they did not need an apology in order to forgive the transgressor. There is, however, another possible explanation for this finding. Our participants were faced with the possibility that they might not receive their bonus marks in spite of having participated in the study, a situation which, arguably, may have seemed fairly innocuous, especially when compared to interpersonal transgressions involving, for example, betrayal by loved ones. It is possible that our transgression did not provide enough of an ego threat to require an apology. In addition, it is possible that even though Bryan admitted to leaving the lab unlocked, they may not have held him completely responsible for the transgression. If they did not hold him responsible, there would be no need for him to apologize because there would be no need to forgive him (Struthers, Eaton, & Uchiyama, 2003).

We would argue that our participants, undergraduate students who likely had a large portion of their self-worth invested in their academic performance (Crocker, Luhtanen, Cooper, & Bouvrette, 2003), would have been threatened to some degree by the possibility of not receiving credit for work they had done. At the beginning of the questionnaire containing the forgiveness, causal certainty, and empathy measures, we asked participants to rate the severity of the event. The mean rating, out of 7, was 3.83 ($SD = 1.84$), with a median of 4, which suggests that participants found the transgression to be moderately severe.

We suggest that because our transgression was perceived as moderately severe, the participants with secure self-esteem were adequately buffered against ego threat, and thus did not require an apology. With a more severe transgression, involving a greater amount of ego threat, and possibly a greater degree of responsibility on the part of the transgressor, we would expect that this group would have been more forgiving and less vengeful when they received an apology than when they did not. We would also expect that the response of the group with defensive self-esteem would be amplified by a more severe transgression. Future research should address this issue, to explore whether it is the severity of the offense or the ego-threatening nature of the offense, or both, that moderates the effectiveness of apologies in facilitating forgiveness. Other possible moderators of the apology – forgiveness relationship that we are currently examining include the intentionality of the offense (Struthers et al., 2005) and the presence of sympathetic others during the transgression (Eaton, 2007). We are also examining a number of individual difference variables that may affect the relationship between apology and forgiveness, including the regulatory focus of the victim (Santelli, Struthers, & Eaton, 2006) and the extent to which the victim holds authoritarian values (Struthers, Santelli, Khoury, Marjanovic, & Rubin, 2007).

We also found that empathy ratings when the transgressor did not apologize were higher in the group with high explicit and low implicit self-esteem than in the other three groups. This is somewhat surprising, given that this group should be the most defensive of the three groups. It could be that, although they were aware that Bryan had lost the data, they may not have perceived it as a threat against themselves unless he apologized. The fact that they also reported lower causal certainty when Bryan did not apologize indicates that this group may have been processing the information differently from those who did receive an apology. Although a test of this is beyond the scope of this study, future studies should examine in more detail how individuals initially perceive transgressions and if there are differences in perceptions when an apology is offered and when it is not. A longitudinal design may be more effectively able to assess changes in empathy both before and after an apology is received.

The fact that those with defensive self-esteem also reported more causal certainty about the event and less empathy toward the transgressor when he apologized as compared to when he did not suggests that these variables mediate the apology – forgiveness relationship, and that this mediation is moderated by self-esteem. Our study design does not allow for this to be tested empirically because we measured forgiveness before causal certainty and empathy; however, future research should take this into consideration. Another potential mediator is narcissism. Jordan and his colleagues (2003) found that those individuals who are high in explicit self-esteem but low in implicit self-esteem are also high in narcissism. Although there is not enough research in this area to suggest that narcissism is a proxy for defensive self-esteem, we believe that it is worth testing with future research whether narcissism moderates or mediates the apology–forgiveness relationship.

The results of this study have implications for both conflict resolution and self research. Our findings suggest that an important consideration in research on interpersonal conflict and forgiveness is the extent to which transgressions threaten the self-worth of their recipients. If transgressions create ego threat, and there is growing evidence to suggest that they do (e.g., Eaton et al., 2006a; Maltby & Day, 2004; Scobie & Scobie, 1998), then how conflicts are resolved is at least in part dependent on how this ego threat is dealt with by the victims of the transgressions. Our findings show that some individuals are better able to deal with threats to their ego than others, and this can make them more or less responsive to attempts to resolve the conflict (i.e., apologies). Clearly, research on self-esteem, and on the self in general, can greatly inform forgiveness research.

Our findings also lend support to the conceptualization of self-esteem as a combination of both implicit and explicit self-evaluations. We found that individuals with defensive self-esteem were less forgiving when they received an apology than when they did not. This finding was in line with our predictions, and adds to recent research that has found those with incongruent implicit and explicit self-esteem to be generally less secure and more defensive than those with congruent self-esteem (Bosson et al., 2003; Jordan et al., 2003; Kernis et al., 2005).

The findings of this study suggest that certain individuals may have more difficulty than others forgiving because they lack the resources to deal with transgressions in a prosocial manner. It should be noted that, although we found that apologies made our defensive participants less forgiving, we do not suggest that apologies are always ineffective for this group. It may be that, in order for them to take the apology in the true spirit in which it was intended, measures first need to be taken to reduce their defensiveness. Perhaps if these individuals receive some type of validation or confirmation that they have a right to be angry (either from the transgressor or a third party) and then have some time to absorb this information before receiving an apology, this might provide the affirmation they need in order to be receptive to the remorse of the transgressor.

If defensiveness can prevent individuals from accepting an apology and forgiving a transgressor, then it is important to help the individual deal with this defensiveness in addition to helping restore the relationship. Future research should address the issue of how to help individuals with defensive self-esteem resolve interpersonal conflict.

References

Aiken, L. S., & West, S. G. (1991). *Multiple regression: Testing and interpreting interactions.* London: Sage.

Aquino, K., & Douglas, S. (2003). Identity threat and antisocial behavior in organizations: The moderating effects of individual differences, aggressive modeling, and hierarchical status. *Organizational Behavior and Human Decision Processes, 90,* 195–208.

Batson, C. D. (1990). How social an animal? The human capacity for caring. *American Psychologist, 45,* 336–346.

Batson, C. D. (1991). *The altruism question.* Hillsdale, NJ: Lawrence Erlbaum Associates, Inc.

Baumeister, R. F., Campbell, J. D., Krueger, J. I., & Vohs, K. D. (2003). Does high self-esteem cause better performance, interpersonal success, happiness, or healthier lifestyles? *Psychological Science in the Public Interest, 4*, 1–44.

Bosson, J. K., Brown, R. P., Zeigler-Hill, V., & Swann, W. B., Jr. (2003). Self-enhancement tendencies among people with high explicit self-esteem: The moderating role of implicit self-esteem. *Self and Identity, 2*, 169–187.

Bosson, J. K., Swann, W. B., Jr., & Pennebaker, J. (2000). Stalking the perfect measure of implicit self-esteem: The blind men and the elephant revisited? *Journal of Personality and Social Psychology, 79*, 631–643.

Brown, R. P., & Phillips, A. (2005). Letting bygones be bygones: Further evidence for the validity of the Tendency to Forgive scale. *Personality and Individual Differences, 38*, 627–638.

Bushman, B. J., & Baumeister, R. F. (1998). Threatened egotism, narcissism, self-esteem, and direct and displaced aggression: Does self-love or self-hate lead to violence? *Journal of Personality and Social Psychology, 75*, 219–229.

Crocker, J., Luhtanen, R. K., Cooper, M. L., & Bouvrette, A. (2003). Contingencies of self-worth in college students: Theory and measurement. *Journal of Personality and Social Psychology, 85*, 894–908.

Darby, B. W., & Schlenker, B. R. (1982). Children's reactions to apologies. *Journal of Personality and Social Psychology, 43*, 742–753.

Eaton, J. (2007, January). *You didn't deserve that! The effects of validation from a third party on interpersonal forgiveness.* Poster presented at the Society for Personality and Social Psychology Eighth Annual Meeting, Memphis, TN, USA.

Eaton, J., Struthers, C. W., & Santelli, A. G. (2006a). The mediating role of perceptual validation in the repentance–forgiveness process. *Personality and Social Psychology Bulletin, 32*, 1389–1401.

Eaton, J., Struthers, C. W., & Santelli, A. G. (2006b). Dispositional and state forgiveness: The role of self-esteem, need for structure, and narcissism. *Personality and Individual Differences, 41*, 371–380.

Exline, J. J., & Baumeister, R. F. (2000). Expressing forgiveness and repentance: Benefits and barriers. In M. E. McCullough, K. I. Pargament, & C. E. Thoresen (Eds.), *The psychology of forgiveness* (pp. 133–155). New York: Guilford.

Exline, J. J., Baumeister, R. F., Bushman, B. J., Campbell, W. K., & Finkel, E. J. (2004). Too proud to let go: Narcissistic entitlement as a barrier to forgiveness. *Journal of Personality and Social Psychology, 87*, 894–912.

Fincham, F. D. (2000). The kiss of the porcupines: From attributing responsibility to forgiving. *Personal Relationships, 7*, 1–23.

Goffman, E. (1971). *Relations in public: Microstudies of the public order.* New York: Basic.

Gold, G. J., & Weiner, B. (2000). Remorse, confession, group identity, and expectancies about repeating a transgression. *Basic and Applied Social Psychology, 22*, 291–300.

Greenwald, A. G., & Farnham, S. D. (2000). Using the Implicit Association Test to measure self-esteem and self-concept. *Journal of Personality and Social Psychology, 79*, 1022–1038.

Jordan, C. H., Spencer, S. J., Zanna, M. P., Hoshino-Browne, E., & Correll, J. (2003). Secure and defensive high self-esteem. *Journal of Personality and Social Psychology, 85*, 969–978.

Kernis, M. H., Abend, T. A., Goldman, B. M., Shrira, I., Paradise, A. N., & Hampton, C. (2005). Self-serving responses arising from discrepancies between explicit and implicit self-esteem. *Self and Identity, 4*, 311–330.

Kitiyama, S., & Karasawa, M. (1997). Implicit self-esteem in Japan: Name-letters and birthday numbers. *Personality and Social Psychology Bulletin, 23*, 736–742.

Koole, S. L., & Pelham, B. W. (2003). On the nature of implicit self-esteem: The case of the name letter effect. In S. Fein & S. J. Spencer (Eds.), *Motivated social perception: The Ontario symposium* (Vol. 9, pp. 93–116). Mahwah, NJ: Lawrence Erlbaum Associates, Inc.

Maltby, J., & Day, L. (2004). Forgiveness and defense style. *Journal of Genetic Psychology*, *165*, 99–110.

McCullough, M. E., Emmons, R. A., Kilpatrick, S. D., & Mooney, C. N. (2003). Narcissists as "victims": The role of narcissism in the perception of transgressions. *Personality and Social Psychology Bulletin*, *29*, 885–893.

McCullough, M. E., Rachal, K. C., Sandage, S. J., Worthington, E. L., Jr., Brown, S. W., & Hight, T. L. (1998). Interpersonal forgiving in close relationships: II. Theoretical elaboration and measurement. *Journal of Personality and Social Psychology*, *76*, 1586–1603.

McCullough, M. E., Worthington, E. L. J., & Rachal, K. C. (1997). Interpersonal forgiving in close relationships. *Journal of Personality and Social Psychology*, *73*, 321–336.

McGregor, I., & Marigold, D. C. (2003). Defensive zeal and the uncertain self: What makes you so sure? *Journal of Personality and Social Psychology*, *85*, 838–852.

McGregor, I., Zanna, M. P., Holmes, J. G., & Spencer, S. J. (2001). Compensatory conviction in the face of personal uncertainty: Going to extremes and being oneself. *Journal of Personality and Social Psychology*, *80*, 472–488.

Neto, F., & Mullet, E. (2004). Personality, self-esteem, and self-construal as correlates of forgivingness. *European Journal of Personality*, *18*, 15–30.

Neuberg, S. L., & Newsom, J. T. (1993). Personal need for structure: Individual differences in the desire for simple structure. *Journal of Personality and Social Psychology*, *65*, 113–131.

Pyszczynski, T., Greenberg, J., Solomon, S., Arndt, J., & Schimel, J. (2004). Why do people need self-esteem? A theoretical and empirical review. *Psychological Bulletin*, *130*, 435–468.

Rosenberg, M. (1965). *Society and the adolescent self-image*. Princeton, NJ: Princeton University Press.

Santelli, A. G., Struthers, C. W., & Eaton, J. (2006). *Fit to forgive: Exploring the interaction between regulatory focus, repentance, and forgiveness*. Manuscript submitted for publication.

Scobie, E. D., & Scobie, G. E. W. (1998). Damaging events: The perceived need for forgiveness. *Journal for the Theory of Social Behaviour*, *28*, 373–401.

Struthers, C. W., Eaton, J., & Santelli, A. (2005, January). *The effects of control, intent, and repentance on responsibility attributions and forgiveness*. Poster presented at the Society for Personality and Social Psychology Sixth Annual Meeting, New Orleans, LA, USA.

Struthers, C. W., Eaton, J., & Uchiyama, M. (2003, February). *Saying sorry is only half of the story: The reason matters too*. Poster presented at the Society for Personality and Social Psychology Fourth Annual Meeting, Los Angeles, CA.

Struthers, C. W., Santelli, A. G., Khoury, C., Marjanovic, Z., & Rubin, H. (2007, January). *The effect of authoritarianism and repentance on the forgiveness process*. Poster presented at the Society for Personality and Social Psychology Seventh Annual Meeting, Memphis, TN, USA.

Thompson, M. M., Naccarato, M. E., & Parker, K. H. (2001). The personal need for structure and personal fear of invalidity scales: Historical perspectives, current applications and future directions. In G. B. Moskowitz (Ed.), *Cognitive social psychology* (pp. 19–39). Mahwah, NJ: Lawrence Erlbaum Associates, Inc.

Weiner, B., Graham, S., Peter, O., & Zmuidinas, M. (1991). Public confession and forgiveness. *Journal of Personality*, *59*, 281–312.

Self and Identity, 6: 223–237, 2007
http://www.psypress.com/sai
ISSN: 1529-8868 print/1529-8876 online
DOI: 10.1080/15298860601115351

The Mask of Zeal: Low Implicit Self-esteem, Threat, and Defensive Extremism

IAN MCGREGOR

York University, Toronto, Ontario, Canada

CHRISTIAN H. JORDAN

Wilfrid Laurier University, Waterloo, Ontario, Canada

Theorists have long proposed that vulnerable people turn to zeal in the face of perceived self-threats because doing so somehow masks the threats. The present study supports this idea, and suggests that low implicit self-esteem may be a key vulnerability that predisposes individuals toward defensive zeal. Undergraduate participants with low implicit self-esteem, as assessed by an Internet version of the Implicit Association Test, reacted to an experimentally manipulated academic threat with zeal about their opinions toward capital punishment, the US invasion of Iraq, and suicide bombing. Significant effects were found for two aspects of zeal— extremism and exaggerated estimates of social consensus for personal opinions. Results for each issue were independent of whether participants were in favor of, or against the issue.

The uncompromising attitude is more indicative of an inner uncertainty than of deep conviction. (Eric Hoffer, 1954, p. 41)

Crusades and inquisitions may be what first come to mind when one thinks about the dark side of zeal, but even today zeal seems to fuel wars and massacres with grim regularity. This article investigates the idea that expressing zeal helps people with low implicit self-esteem cope with inner troubles. We use the term zeal to refer to extremism and exaggerated conviction and consensus estimates for personal opinions.

Pioneering theorists promoted the idea that vulnerable people use zeal to mask disturbing thoughts. William James (1902/1958) concluded that for sick souls, "religious rapture, moral enthusiasm, ontological wonder, and cosmic emotion, are all unifying states of mind, in which the sand and grit of self-hood incline to disappear" (p. 240). Three years later, Freud claimed that neurotic individuals mask disturbing thoughts by seizing on "supervalent," "reactive" thoughts with a "surplus

The present research was funded by separate grants to both authors from the Social Sciences and Humanities Research Council of Canada.

We thank Denise Marigold for helpful comments; and Steve Spencer and Christine Logel for their materials and program for computing implicit self-esteem scores.

Correspondence should be addressed to: Ian McGregor, Department of Psychology, York University, 4700 Keele Street, Toronto, Ontario, Canada. E-mail: ianmc@yorku.ca of intensity" (Gay, 1989, p. 200). He went on to say that such extreme thoughts form "mental dams" to keep unwanted thoughts at bay (pp. 261–262). Consistent with these seminal ideas, Pavlov (1927) and Lewin (1933, 1935) observed that aversive conflicts caused extreme and obdurate reactions in dogs and toddlers, respectively. Lewin argued that when reality is intolerable, flight to single-minded and fantastical ideas can help exclude disturbing thoughts from the mental field. This theme of zealous escapism was foundational for early explanations of the origins of the zealous worldviews and prejudices that were prevalent during World War II Specifically, Adorno, Frenkel-Brunswik, Levinson, and Sanford (1950) and Fromm (1941) concluded that internalized childhood experiences of shame and uncertainty grow into closed-minded authoritarianism and fascism (cf. Jost, Glaser, Kruglanski, & Sulloway, 2003, for recent evidence of the link between vulnerability and closed-mindedness). The themes shared by these psychodynamically rooted ideas are that: (a) situational threats cause zeal; (b) zeal helps mask self-threatening information; and (c) threat is most likely to induce zeal among people with vulnerable self-concepts. In the following sections, we review research that probes these three ideas, and present the results of an experiment that investigates the role of low implicit self-esteem as a key risk factor for zeal.

Do Self-threats Cause Compensatory Zeal?

McGregor and his colleagues have repeatedly found that self-threats cause individuals to exaggerate aspects of zeal. In one study, being reminded of troubling personal dilemmas caused participants to exaggerate conviction for their value-laden opinions (McGregor et al., 2001, Study 1). Specifically, participants who were randomly assigned to grapple with their personal uncertainties about relationships or career paths reacted by claiming exaggerated conviction and social consensus for their attitudes about capital punishment and abortion. Personal uncertainty in one domain thus seemed to motivate exaggerated certainty and zeal in unrelated domains.

In a related study, the same dilemma-uncertainty manipulation caused participants to bolster zeal for their life values and passion for their current goals (McGregor, Zanna, Holmes, & Spencer, 2001, Study 2). After being reminded of their personal dilemmas, participants heightened the importance of their core value priorities and the meaningfulness of their top ten personal projects. For example, they rated projects like, "be nicer to my mother," "get As in all my courses," and even "walk the dog every day" as higher in value congruence and importance to their self-identity. In other studies the same dilemma-uncertainty manipulation has also caused some Canadians to become less tolerant of Islam (Haji & McGregor, 2002), and to answer questions about their own character more decisively (i.e., they made faster me-not-me decisions about character traits; McGregor & Marigold, 2003, Study 1). Together, these studies demonstrate that thinking about personal problems can motivate compensatory zeal about opinions, values, goals, and identity.

Other forms of psychological distress have had similar effects. In one study a classic, induced-compliance cognitive dissonance manipulation caused some participants to become zealous about unrelated opinions (McGregor & Crippen, 2003). Specifically, after being subtly coerced to write in support of an offensive academic policy, some undergraduates reacted by exaggerating their estimates of social consensus for their personal opinions on capital punishment and abortion. Even after seeing a list of ten diverse, common opinions across the ideological spectrum for each issue, dissonance-threatened participants still lunged toward consensus and estimated that 66% of all people would agree with their opinions.

Similar compensatory zeal reactions have also followed threats to system-justice beliefs and personal meanings. In one study, participants in the Southern USA were exposed to information about the Enron corporate scandal that took place in Texas, where corporate executives swindled average investors out of millions of dollars, with seemingly minimal repercussions. This threat to participants' faith in the American corporate and justice systems caused them to react with exaggerated preference for an author who praised broad American values over one who criticized them (McGregor, Nail, Marigold, & Kang, 2005, Study 3). In another study, reflecting on the transience of cherished personal memories caused individuals to heighten their desire to find meaning in their lives. It also caused zeal about personal values, exaggerated personal project meaningfulness, and exaggerated preference for an author who upheld their lifestyle norms over an author who criticized their lifestyle norms (McGregor et al., 2001).

There is thus substantial evidence that epistemic threats related to personal dilemmas, cognitive inconsistency, and disruptions in meaning can motivate compensatory zeal. Zeal in response to threat, however, is not limited to such epistemic threats. Experiences that reflect negatively on self-worth also seem to motivate zeal. One study recently found that failure on a difficult statistics exercise caused exaggerated zeal (McGregor et al., 2005, Study 1). Undergraduate psychology majors in the threat condition were required to summarize a passage about structural equation modeling from a graduate statistics text. The passage was loaded with Greek symbols and bewildering mathematical formulae. This statistics-failure manipulation not only decreased implicit self-esteem on a shortened version of the Implicit Association Test (IAT; adapted from Greenwald & Farnham, 2000), it also caused exaggerated consensus estimates for opinions about capital punishment and abortion. Another study found that even just reflecting on past failures can cause zealous reactions. In this study, Haji and McGregor (2002) found that writing about past academic or vocational failures amplified disdain for Islam.

There is also evidence that, like epistemic and esteem threats, relationship threats can cause the same kinds of zeal reactions. An imagery exercise that required participants to imagine moving to an inhospitable foreign country, cut off from contact with loved ones, caused some participants to claim exaggerated consensus for their opinions about capital punishment and abortion (McGregor et al., 2005, Study 2). Reflecting on real-life relationship problems also caused zeal reactions in another study. Some participants wrote about a personal relationship that was not going well, and was at risk of dissolution. Compared to participants who instead wrote about someone else's relationship problems, those who described their own distressed relationships reacted with exaggerated conviction for their views on capital punishment and abortion (McGregor & Marigold, 2003, Study 3).

Finally, reflecting on one's own mortality can motivate personal zeal. In two studies, instructions to write about the disturbing topic of personal death and body decay caused some participants to exaggerate perceptions of the meaningfulness of their personal projects and self-identifications (McGregor & Gailliot, 2006, Study 2; McGregor et al., 2001, Study 4). Together, these results provide solid evidence for the conclusion that self-threats—whether epistemic, esteem, relationship, or mortality related—can motivate reactive zeal.

Does Zeal Mask Self-threats?

Why do people react to threats with zeal? One possibility is that focusing on exaggerated conviction can somehow make threats in other domains seem less urgent. In other words, zealous thoughts might help insulate people from concern with threatening thoughts. This possibility is consistent with the previously mentioned claims of James and Freud, who proposed that zeal helps mask troubling thoughts. To test this idea, McGregor and his colleagues conducted five experiments to assess the effects of zeal on the subjective salience of participants' unrelated personal uncertainties. Subjective salience refers to the extent to which participants rate threatening experiences as feeling big, urgent, pressing, significant, and difficult to ignore. In all five experiments, participants first wrote about threatening personal uncertainties (which have caused distress and defensiveness in past research; e.g., McGregor et al., 2001). Some participants were then given the opportunity to express personal zeal about specified unrelated topics. In all five experiments, expressing zeal related to opinions, values, successes, loves, or group-identifications significantly decreased the subjective salience of threatening personal uncertainties that had been written about at the beginning of the experimental session (McGregor, 2004a; McGregor, 2006; McGregor & Marigold, 2003, Study 4; McGregor et al., 2005, Study 4). Moreover, in another study, after a threat, the intensity of participants' spontaneous zeal correlated negatively with subsequently assessed subjective salience of the threat topic (McGregor, 2004b). In five of the six studies, the apparent threat-masking effects of zeal emerged only among participants with defensive personality tendencies, and were not apparent in no-threat control conditions. These results converge on the conclusion that motivated, reactive zeal can mask unrelated self-threats.

How does zeal mask threat? Intriguingly, counter to early speculation (McGregor, Newby-Clark, & Zanna, 1999) distraction does *not* seem to be the mechanism. Evidence from several studies now indicates that even after repeated reminders of the threatening information, the salience reducing effect of zeal persists (McGregor, 2006; McGregor & Crippen, 2003). An alternative possibility is that the benefits of zeal derive from the principles of "regulatory fit." Higgins and colleagues have shown that when information matches an individual's regulatory focus, it looms larger than when it mis-matches (Higgins, 2005). For example, messages that emphasize threat resonate particularly strongly for individuals with a state or trait tendency to focus on vigilant prevention of undesirable outcomes. In contrast, individuals who tend to focus on eager promotion of desirable outcomes are relatively oblivious to threat-framed messages. They are more motivationally focused on approaching ideals than avoiding threats. Accordingly, we are currently investigating the idea that, in the face of threat, people turn to eager preoccupation with zealous ideals because doing so initiates a promotion-focused state that down-regulates vigilant prevention-focus on threats. This possibility seems promising because zeal is idealistic and ideals are central to promotion focus (Higgins, Roney, Crowe, & Hymes, 1994). Moreover, recent evidence suggests that there is a reciprocal inhibition of activity in brain regions that specialize in promotion and prevention focus (Amodio, Shah, Sigelman, Brazy, & Harmon-Jones, 2004; see McGregor, in press, for a more in-depth account of the regulatory mis-fit idea and for a review of literature related to possible neuropsychological substrates). Thus, zeal may render threats less subjectively salient by shifting motivational emphasis toward eager promotion of the zealous ideal, and away from vigilant preoccupation with the threat.

Low Implicit Self-esteem and Zeal

Evidence reviewed to this point indicates that threats do cause zeal and that zeal does mask threats. But the classic theorists also suggested that "sick souls" with vulnerable selves should be particularly inclined to seek solace in defensive zeal. Low implicit self-esteem may be a particularly relevant vulnerability in the face of self-threat because it specifically reflects *experiential* associations of the self with negative affect (Conner & Barrett, 2005; Robinson & Meier, 2005; Rudman, 2004). Moreover, these negative associations are especially prominent under conditions of self-focus (Cheng, Govorun, & Chartrand, 2006), which is induced by self-threat and negative affect (Greenberg & Pyszczynski, 1986; Mor & Winquist, 2002; Wood, Saltzberg, Neale, Stone, & Rachmiel, 1990). Accordingly, in two of the studies reported above, in which implicit self-esteem was assessed, significant two-way interactions revealed highest zeal about opinions among *low* implicit self-esteem participants in the threat conditions (McGregor & Marigold, 2003, Study 3; McGregor et al., 2005, Study 1). Implicit self-esteem in those studies was assessed with a version of the IAT, which assesses the relative strength of associations between the self and positive versus negative affect (following Greenwald & Farnham, 2000; Jordan, Spencer, Zanna, Hoshino-Browne, & Correll, 2003b). As such, this implicit measure was particularly well suited for assessing vulnerabilities relating to negative experiential self-associations, which may not be foremost in conscious awareness (and thus, which map onto classic psychodynamic theories).

Indeed, in both of the studies described above, in which significant implicit self-esteem by threat interaction effects on zeal were found, conventional questionnaire measures of explicit self-esteem were not correlated with implicit self-esteem. Moreover, whereas in both studies, threats caused the most zeal among participants with *low implicit* self-esteem, equally significant two-way interactions also showed that threats caused most zeal among participants with *high explicit* self-esteem. In those studies, the three-way interaction was also significant, with highest zeal observed among threatened participants possessing both low implicit and high explicit self-esteem. Ongoing theory and research is currently probing how various measures of implicit self-esteem interact with explicit self-esteem to produce different types of defensiveness (e.g., Bosson, Brown, Zeigler-Hill, & Swann, 2003; Jordan, Spencer, & Zanna, 2003a; Jordan, Spencer, & Zanna, 2005; McGregor & Marigold, 2003; McGregor et al., 2005; Ziegler-Hill, 2006). What is clear so far and of particular relevance to the present research, however, is that experimentally manipulated self-threats have reliably caused exaggerated zeal about value-laden opinions among individuals with low implicit (but not explicit) self-esteem.

The Present Experiment

The present research extends these past findings in two ways. First, it investigates whether the defensive zeal of threatened participants with low implicit self-esteem will extend to opinions about incendiary topics, such as suicide bombing and the US invasion of Iraq. Second, it provides an important extension of past defensive zeal by assessing defensive extremism for the first time. Extremism is assessed along with exaggerated consensus, which is a well-established facet of defensive zeal. One might expect that as opinion extremity increases, consensus estimates should decrease as the opinion-holder recognizes that he or she is on the fringe of credibility. Classic theorizing on defensiveness and everyday observation seem to indicate, however, that extremism and delusional confidence sometimes co-occur. The present study probes this frightening co-occurrence, and is the first to assess defensive extremism and exaggerated consensus estimates for opinions together in the same study.

After completing the implicit self-esteem measure, participants were randomly assigned to a self-threat or a control condition. For the dependent measures, participants viewed a list of diverse statements about capital punishment, the recent war in Iraq, and suicide bombing, that varied in extremity for or against each issue. After circling the one statement about each issue that came closest to their own opinion, they estimated social consensus for that statement. We expected that participants with low implicit self-esteem in the self-threat condition would endorse the most extreme opinions and also provide the most exaggerated estimates of social consensus for them.

Method

Participants and Procedure

Data were collected over the Internet from 23 undergraduate students (15 female, 3 male, 5 unspecified) who participated in exchange for course credit. Participants completed the materials at their convenience, with no laboratory personnel present. The study was described to participants in an on-line consent form, but participants did not record their names or any other identifying information at any time. To indicate their consent, they simply pressed a button to continue with the study, with the understanding that they could quit at any time. As in past compensatory zeal research, the assessment of implicit self-esteem was embedded in a packet of questionnaires at the beginning of the study. After the threat manipulation, participants completed a few additional questionnaires and then the dependent variable that assessed extremity and consensus estimates for their opinions about social issues.

Implicit Self-esteem

We used a modified version of the IAT to assess implicit self-esteem (following Jordan et al., 2003b; Jordan et al., 2005; McGregor & Marigold, 2003; McGregor et al., 2005). To streamline the IAT for web administration, we shortened the number of trials from 40 to 36 in each block, and eliminated two of the practice trial blocks. As in our past research, a neutral category (i.e., "object") was used to oppose the "self" category in this IAT, rather than the category of "other" (see Jordan et al., 2003b; Jordan et al., 2005). This was done to remove the influence of attitudes toward others in the IAT measurement and ensure it is strictly a measure of implicit self-esteem (see Karpinski, 2004, for further discussion of this issue). Also, to avoid using a negated category, the labels "self" and "object" were used, rather than the "self" and "not-self" labels that we have used in some of our past research. Sample stimuli for the pleasant and unpleasant words were sunshine, gift, smile, joy, garbage, vomit, cockroach, and evil. Stimuli for the self and object words were me, myself, it, and that. In the "consistent" critical block of trials, participants categorized 36 stimulus words as either self/pleasant or object/unpleasant. In the "inconsistent" critical block of trials, participants categorized the same stimulus words as either self/unpleasant or object/pleasant. We computed implicit self-esteem scores by subtracting the average response latency to the consistent categorizations from the average response latency to the inconsistent categorizations. Thus, as usual, the implicit self-esteem scores reflected how much more easily participants could work with the pairing of self/pleasant categories than self/unpleasant categories. Following Greenwald and Farnham (2000), we recoded response latencies longer than 3000 ms as 3000 ms and those shorter than 300 ms as 300 ms. The latencies of incorrect responses were not included in the average latency scores. No participant had more than a 20% error rate and so all data were retained for analyses.[1]

Threat Manipulation

Participants in the threat condition read and summarized an extremely difficult statistics passage about LISREL that was taken (out of context) from a graduate statistics textbook. The instructions were as follows:

> The passage below is from an introduction to a statistical procedure called Linear Structural Relations, or LISREL. LISREL is a tool for analyzing causal relations among psychological variables. We are interested in assessing how understandable it is to you. Please take five minutes to read the passage below, and then summarize it as best you can.

The passage (taken from Pedhazur, 1982, pp. 639–640) read:

> The measurement model specifies the relations between unobserved and observed, or latent and manifest, variables. Two equations describe this model: $y = \Lambda_y n + \epsilon$ Where y is a p by 1 vector of measures of dependent variables; Λ (lambda) is a p by m matrix of coefficients, or loadings, of y on the unobserved dependent variables (n); ϵ (epsilon) is a p by 1 vector of errors of measurement of $y \cdot x = \Lambda_r \xi + \delta$ Where x is a q by 1 vector of measures of independent variables; Λ (lambda) is a q by n matrix of coefficients, or loadings, of $\times$ on the unobserved independent variables (ξ); and δ (delta) is a q by 1 vector of errors of measurement of x. . . .

In previous research, this manipulation decreased implicit self-esteem[2] and caused exaggerated consensus estimates for opinions about capital punishment and abortion among individuals with low implicit self-esteem (McGregor, et al., 2005, Study 1). In this previous work, participants in the control condition summarized a simple and easy passage about the usefulness of statistics. In the present study, instead, they completed a more clearly negative exercise that involved writing about the experience of dental pain (which is frequently used as a control condition exercise in research on reactions to mortality salience; Greenberg, Solomon, & Pyszczynski, 1997). We did not expect the dental pain materials to cause zeal, because although dental pain is aversive it does not pose any obvious threat to the self-concept and writing about it has not caused self-righteous zeal in past research (McGregor, in press).

Zeal: Extremism and Exaggerated Consensus Estimates

Past compensatory conviction research has relied on assessing opinions about capital punishment and abortion issues (McGregor & Marigold, 2003; McGregor et al., 2001, 2005). We kept the capital punishment issue in the present research, but to expand generalizability we replaced the abortion issue with two highly charged social issues of current international relevance. Participants thus read lists of eleven diverse opinions about capital punishment, the recent invasion of Iraq by the United States, and suicide bombing.

The opinion statements that participants could choose from ranged evenly across the ideological spectrum, covering opinions that were mildly to extremely in favor of each topic and mildly to extremely against each topic. Across the three topics, 16 of the statements were critical, and 17 favorable. Extremity was also balanced, with 10 of the statements expressing mild opinions, 12 expressing moderate opinions, and 11 expressing extreme opinions. Two independent raters also rated the favorability of each of the 33 provided opinions from − 3 (*extremely unfavorable*) to − 1 (*mildly unfavorable*) or + 3 (*extremely favorable*) to + 1 (*mildly favorable*). The two sets of ratings correlated at $r = .95$, and were averaged to yield a favorability rating for each opinion statement. Each opinion statement was then translated into an extremity rating (from 1 to 3), by taking the absolute value of the favorability rating. Participants' overall extremity scores were computed by averaging the extremity ratings of the opinions they endorsed for the three issues (capital punishment, Iraq, and suicide bombing). Among the statements that we coded as extreme were: "A murderer deserves to die"; "Capital punishment is absolutely never justified"; "The US did the right thing. Iraq was a menace and had it coming"; "George Bush is a dangerous maniac"; "Suicide bombing is one of the most horrible and despicable acts imaginable"; and "Suicide bombers' courage and willingness to die for what they believe shows a lot of integrity."

For each issue, participants selected the one opinion they most agreed with from the list of eleven, and then: (a) rated the percentage of people who they thought would *agree* with their selected opinion; and (b) rated the percentage who they thought would *agree most* with their selected opinion. We averaged participants' six consensus ratings across the three issues to create an overall measure of perceived social consensus for social issue opinions.

Finally, we standardized and averaged participants' overall consensus and extremity scores to create an overall index of zeal, which served as our main dependent variable (alpha = .62).

Results

As shown in Table 1, participants endorsed opinions that were, on average, mildly critical of capital punishment, the US invasion of Iraq, and suicide bombing. The same table shows that, on average, participants endorsed moderately extreme positions, for which they estimated around 60% social consensus. Overall extremity and consensus scores were significantly correlated, $r(22) = .45, p < .05$.

For the main analysis, we regressed participants' overall zeal scores onto implicit self-esteem (centered), threat (effect coded) and the implicit self-esteem × threat interaction. Results of this analysis revealed a significant interaction between implicit self-esteem and threat, $t(19) = 2.89, p < .01$. As show in Figure 1, highest zeal was expressed by participants with relatively low implicit self-esteem in the threat condition (high and low implicit self-esteem correspond to values one standard deviation above and below the mean of implicit self-esteem; see Aiken & West, 1991). Importantly, at low implicit self-esteem the simple effect of threat on overall zeal was significant, $t(19) = 2.70, p < .01$, but at high implicit self-esteem it was marginally significant in the opposite direction, $t(19) = − 1.81, p = .09$. Further, the simple slope of implicit self-esteem was significant in the threat condition, $t(19) = 3.20, p < .005$, but not in the control condition, $t(19) = 0.16, p < .87$. This pattern of results reveals that the academic threat manipulation caused people with low implicit self-esteem to exaggerate their zeal about highly charged social issues.

TABLE 1 Means (Standard Deviations) of Participants' Endorsed Opinion Favorability, Extremity, and Consensus Estimates

	Capital punishment	US invasion of Iraq	Suicide bombing
Favorability (from -3 to $+3$)	$-.20$ (1.76)	-1.24 (1.36)	-1.17 (1.22)
Extremity (from $1-3$)	1.59 (.72)	1.72 (.62)	2.39 (.64)
% Consensus estimate	57 (20)	60 (28)	63 (21)

The positive correlation between the extremity and consensus facets of the zeal index, reported above, might seem surprising because, for each issue, participants had seen an array of eleven diverse opinion statements before selecting their own. Thus, they had just been reminded of how socially contentious each issue really was. One might expect, therefore, that they should have felt *less* supported, and out on a precarious limb to the extent that they took the more extreme positions. The positive correlation between extremity and exaggerated consensus suggests the defensive, motivational nature of both constructs.

Indeed, as shown in Figure 1, the implicit self-esteem × threat interaction pattern of results was similarly significant for both opinion extremity, $t(19) = 2.08$, $p < .05$, and consensus, $t(19) = 2.68$, $p < .05$. Threatened participants with low implicit self-esteem endorsed opinions that were over a full standard deviation more extreme than those endorsed by the control condition participants with low implicit self-esteem, and they also hiked their estimates of social consensus for their opinions to a seemingly fanatical level of over 84%.

Moreover, the motivated zeal response appears to be systemic. As summarized in Table 2, the betas (βs; between .38 and .53) for the implicit self-esteem × threat interaction effects on zeal about each individual issue were substantial and similarly significant. The only exception was suicide bombing, which may have shown a weaker effect ($p < .11$) because it was the third issue (i.e., the threat may have been partially dissipated or masked by zeal about the previous two issues). Future research with more power should use within-subject analyses across counterbalanced issues to assess this possibility.

It is important to note that the present results reflect general zeal, and not a normative shift toward a directional bias in favor of, or against, each topic. When the regression analyses were repeated for zeal about each topic, with topic favorability statistically controlled as a covariate, the results did not change. With

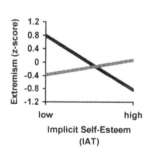

FIGURE 1 Overall zeal, extremism, and social consensus estimates as a function of implicit self-esteem and threat.

TABLE 2 Betas and *P*-values for the Implicit Self-Esteem × Threat Interaction Effect on Overall Zeal and Facets of Zeal

Dependent variable	Interaction effect β and *p*-value
Overall zeal across issues	.62, $p < .009$
Zeal about capital punishment	.51, $p < .05$
Zeal about Iraq	.53, $p < .04$
Zeal about suicide bombing	.38, $p < .11$
Zealous consensus across issues	.55, $p < .02$
Zealous extremism across issues	.51, $p < .05$

opinion favorability as a covariate, the βs for the implicit self-esteem × threat interaction effects on zeal about each issue increased by .01 for two issues, and decreased by .01 for the other issue. (Indeed, with opinion favorability as a covariate, the β for the interaction effect on zeal about suicide bombing shifted from being a trend to being marginal in significance, $p < .09$.) Moreover, with overall zeal across all three issues as the dependent variable, the β and significance of the interaction effect increased from $\beta = .62$, $p < .009$ to $\beta = .68$, $p < .004$ when all three favorability ratings were included as covariates in the main regression analysis. Thus, the defensive zeal reactions of participants with low implicit self-esteem clearly do not reflect a normative shift in any particular ideological direction. Rather, they reflect exaggerated moral enthusiasm for idiosyncratic personal opinions.

Discussion

The present results extend past research on defensive zeal in several ways. First, they show that threats cause zeal even about highly charged, international topics such as suicide bombing and the US invasion of Iraq. Second, the present results provide a replication of previous observations that experimentally manipulated threats cause zeal among individuals with low implicit self-esteem but not high implicit self-esteem (McGregor & Marigold, 2003; McGregor et al., 2005). That the present study was powerful enough to yield significant results with a small sample responding over the Internet attests to the robustness of the defensive zeal phenomenon. Finally, the most important new contribution of the present study was that it demonstrated defensive *extremism* among threatened individuals with low implicit self-esteem. Previous findings have found that the same individuals react to threats with defensive certainty and consensus about their opinions (McGregor & Marigold, 2003; McGregor et al., 2005) but this is the first study to demonstrate defensive extremism. Accordingly, the present findings provide support for classic theorists' claims that vulnerable individuals use excessively intense, supervalent forms of moral enthusiasm to defend against self-threats. Together, the available evidence now indicates that individuals with low implicit self-esteem react to self-threats with wide-ranging zeal about diverse opinions. That ordinary undergraduates can be so easily induced to endorse the potent combination of delusional consensus and extremism about such highly charged social issues is disturbing.

Remaining Questions and Future Directions

The present, sobering results are consistent with the classic view that vulnerable individuals, that is, those with low implicit self-esteem, use malignant zeal for protection from self-threats. They are also consistent with recent findings indicating that people with low implicit self-esteem are especially likely to use alcohol to mask distressing thoughts (McGregor, 2005, 2006). Evidence for the full pathways from threat, to zealous/alcoholic defenses, to decreased salience of threat for individuals with low implicit self-esteem remains to be demonstrated in a single study.

Future research should also be designed to more clearly assess the joint roles of implicit and explicit self-esteem, and other explicitly assessed personality variables that have been associated with defensive zeal such as high personal need for structure (Kang, Haji, & McGregor, 2006; McGregor & Gailliot, 2006; McGregor & Marigold, 2003; McGregor et al., 2005; Neuberg & Newsom, 1993). Whereas low implicit self-esteem may signal a special *vulnerability* to self-threats, explicit need for structure and explicit self-esteem may be *gating variables* that determine whether zeal will seem like an appealing response to those threats in certain circumstances. Individuals with high personal need for structure scores are especially attracted to self-serving and simplistic social judgments (Kang et al., 2006; Neuberg & Newsom, 1991), especially when in challenging situations (Kruglanski & Webster, 1996), and individuals with high explicit self-esteem scores are not shy about zealously wielding defenses that involve public self-promotion. Individuals with low explicit self-esteem, on the other hand, seem to more humbly lean toward less risky, interdependence-based responses to threats (Baumeister, Tice, & Hutton, 1989; Vohs & Heatherton, 2001). Indeed, this may help account for why, in the two previously published studies that assessed both implicit self-esteem and explicit self-esteem, and then zeal after a manipulated self-threat, the most zealous reactions were among threatened participants with low implicit and high explicit self-esteem. In those studies, in addition to the threat × implicit self-esteem and threat × explicit self-esteem 2-way interaction effects, the 3-way interaction effects were also significant.

A differential willingness of participants with high versus low explicit self-esteem to publicly self-promote might explain a curious auxiliary finding in the present study. Explicit self-esteem was one of the questionnaires assessed in the battery of questionnaires at the beginning of our study, and supplementary analyses showed no interaction effect at all for the explicit self-esteem × threat effect in the present study, $F < 1$. This null effect is puzzling, because high explicit self-esteem has been a reliable moderator of zeal after self-threats in past research—in the two previous studies just described, which assessed both implicit and explicit self-esteem, high explicit self-esteem interacted just as strongly with threat as low implicit self-esteem did (McGregor & Marigold, 2003; McGregor et al., 2005). It is interesting to speculate that the unusual null role of explicit self-esteem in the present study may have been due to the fact that the study was conducted anonymously, over the Internet. As such, self-presentation concerns were likely minimized (Bargh, Fitzimmons, & McKenna, 2003), which may have opened the normally closed gate to expression of zeal for individuals with low explicit self-esteem. This interpretation should be carefully assessed with a larger experiment that measures implicit and explicit self-esteem and manipulates public versus private zeal after self-threats.

If the gating role of explicit self-esteem is correct, then other kinds of self-protective defenses to threats that do not involve public self-promotion should be moderated by implicit self-esteem alone and not by explicit self-esteem. Accordingly, only implicit self-esteem, and not explicit self-esteem ($F < 1$) has been found to moderate defensive alcohol consumption after a self-threat (McGregor, 2005, 2006). Similarly, in other research implicit self-esteem alone, and not explicit self-esteem, moderated defensive self-handicapping after threat (Spalding & Hardin, 1999). Neither alcohol consumption nor self-handicapping requires risky self-promotion. Thus, these findings are consistent with the view that low implicit self-esteem is a key vulnerability to self-threats, and that high explicit self-esteem may be a gating variable that moderates the use of publicly self-promoting, defensive reactions.

One final promising avenue for future research is the neuropsychological basis of the interaction effect of implicit self-esteem and threat on zeal. In a preliminary study using the IAT, we found that this interaction significantly predicted cerebral hemisphericity (Jordan & McGregor, 2006). Specifically, results revealed that, in the control condition, low implicit self-esteem was associated with relative right hemisphere activation (which is associated with avoidance motivation; Sutton & Davidson, 1997). Importantly, however, threatened individuals with low implicit self-esteem shifted towards relatively more left-hemisphere activation, which is related to promotion focus, approach-motivation, defensiveness, and insulation from threat (Amodio et al., 2004; Harmon-Jones & Allen, 1997; Jackson et al., 2003; Martin & Shrira, 2004; see McGregor, in press, for a review of related literature). In contrast, individuals with high implicit self-esteem shifted towards relative right-hemisphere activation (which is associated with threat processing; Martin & Shrira, 2004; Nitschke, Heller, Palmieri, & Miller, 1999), which may reflect their lack of defensiveness and willingness to openly process the threat as opposed to masking it with zeal. Although preliminary, these intriguing results are consistent with a motivated cerebral hemisphericity account of low implicit self-esteem individuals' tendency to react to threats with zeal. Seizing on zealous thoughts may provide approach-motivated hemispheric insulation against concern with threats.

Concluding Comments

One conclusion that can be confidently drawn from the available evidence, including the present study, is that low implicit self-esteem predisposes people toward zealous reactions to self-threats. Three experiments have now demonstrated that low implicit self-esteem (IAT assessed), whether measured in a lab or over the Internet, interacted with experimentally manipulated self-threats to cause zeal about social issues. The present results extend past findings, and show that defensive zeal reactions involve extremism, as well as exaggerated conviction and consensus estimates for a broad range of vital social issues. Taken together, the research reviewed and presented here supports all three claims made by the classic theorists discussed in the introduction: threats cause zeal; zeal masks threats; and vulnerable people (i.e., those with low implicit self-esteem) are most inclined to use zeal to mask threats. Disturbingly, the present results demonstrate how easily individuals with low implicit self-esteem can be induced to confidently endorse zealous extremes, even on explosive topics.

Notes

1. We opted against relying on the new D statistic scoring procedure advocated by Greenwald, Nosek, and Banaji (2003) for practical and theoretical reasons. The practical reason was that our streamlined IAT measure used only 5 blocks instead of 7 (we dropped two of the practice blocks); included only 36 trials per block instead of 40; and did not give performance feedback. Each of these changes would have required adjustments to the D statistic scoring procedure, with unknown effects. The theoretical reason for not adopting the new scoring procedure is that it was empirically derived to maximize correlations between implicit and explicit measures. For self-attitudes,

especially, this seems like a questionable criterion, given how motivationally sensitive implicit and explicit self-assessments can be (e.g., Baumeister & Vohs, 2001; McGregor et al., 2005, Study 1; Pyszczynski, Greenberg, Solomon, Arndt, & Schimel, 2004). Indeed, implicit and explicit self-esteem have produced opposite moderating effects in the two published studies that have compared moderating roles of both implicit and explicit self-esteem on zealous reactions to manipulated self-threats (McGregor & Marigold, 2003, Study 3; McGregor et al., 2005, Study 5). For comparison purposes, however, we did compute the D statistic measure of implicit self-esteem (following the Greenwald, Nosek, & Banaji, 2003, algorithm as closely as possible given our modifications). It correlated at $r(22) = .91$ with our simpler index.
2. Participants are extensively debriefed and affirmed after this manipulation.

References

Adorno, T. W., Frenkel-Brunswik, E., Levinson, D. J., & Sanford, R. N. (1950). *The authoritarian personality.* New York: Harper.

Aiken, L. S., & West, S. G. (1991). *Multiple regression: Testing and interpreting interactions.* Newbury Park, CA: Sage.

Amodio, D. M., Shah, J. Y., Sigelman, H., Brazy, P. C., & Harmon-Jones, E. (2004). Implicit regulatory focus associated with asymmetrical frontal cortical activity. *Journal of Experimental Social Psychology, 40,* 225–232.

Bargh, J. A., Fitzsimons, G. M., & McKenna, K. Y. A. (2003). The self, online. In S. J. Spencer, S. Fein, M. P. Zanna, & J. M. Olson (Eds.), *Motivated social perception: The Ontario symposium* (Vol. 9, pp. 195–213). Mahwah, NJ: Lawrence Erlbaum Associates.

Baumeister, R. F., Tice, D. M., & Hutton, D. G. (1989). Self-presentational motivations and personality differences in self-esteem. *Journal of Personality, 57,* 547–579.

Baumeister, R. F., & Vohs, K. D. (2001). Narcissism as an addiction to esteem. *Psychological Inquiry, 12,* 206–210.

Bosson, J. K., Brown, R. P., Zeigler-Hill, V., & Swann, W. B., Jr. (2003). Self-enhancement tendencies among people with high explicit self-esteem: The moderating role of implicit self-esteem. *Self and Identity, 2,* 169–187.

Cheng, C. M., Govorun, O., & Chartrand, T. L. (2006). *Mirror, mirror on the wall . . . : Implicit self-esteem predicts mood following self-awareness.* Paper presented at the annual meeting of the Society for Personality and Social Psychology, Palm Springs, CA, USA.

Conner, T., & Barrett, L. F. (2005). Implicit self-attitudes predict spontaneous affect in daily life. *Emotion, 5,* 476–488.

Fromm, E. (1941). *Escape from freedom.* New York: Holt, Rinehart, & Winston.

Gay, P. (1989). *The Freud reader.* New York: Norton.

Greenberg, J., & Pyszczynski, T. (1986). Persistent high self-focus after failure and low self-focus after success: The depressive self-focusing style. *Journal of Personality and Social Psychology, 50,* 1039–1044.

Greenberg, J., Solomon, S., & Pyszczynski, T. (1997). Terror management theory of self-esteem and cultural worldviews: Empirical assessments and conceptual refinements. In M. P. Zanna (Ed.), *Advances in experimental social psychology* (pp. 61–139). San Diego, CA: Academic Press.

Greenwald, A. G., & Farnham, S. D. (2000). Using the implicit association test to measure self-esteem and self-concept. *Journal of Personality and Social Psychology, 79,* 1022–1038.

Greenwald, A. G., Nosek, B. A., & Banaji, M. R. (2003). Understanding and using the Implicit Association Test: I. An improved scoring algorithm. *Journal of Personality and Social Psychology, 85,* 197–216.

Haji, R., & McGregor, I. (2002). *Compensatory zeal and extremism about Canada and Islam: Responses to uncertainty and self-worth threats.* Poster presented at the meeting of the Society for the Psychological Study of Social Issues, Toronto, Canada.

Harmon-Jones, E., & Allen, J. B. (1997). Behavioral activation sensitivity and resting frontal EEG asymmetry: Covariation of putative indicators related to risk for mood disorders. *Journal of Abnormal Psychology, 106,* 159–163.

Higgins, E. T. (2005). Value from regulatory fit. *Current Directions in Psychological Science, 14,* 209–213.

Higgins, E. T., Roney, C. J. R., Crowe, E., & Hymes, C. (1994). Ideal versus ought predilections for approach and avoidance distinct self-regulatory systems. *Journal of Personality and Social Psychology, 66,* 276–286.

Hoffer, E. (1954). *The passionate state of mind.* New York: Harper & Row.

Jackson, D. C., Mueller, C. J., Dolski, I., Dalton, K. M., Nitschke, J. B., Urry, H. L., et al. (2003). Now you feel it, now you don't: Frontal brain electrical asymmetry and individual differences in emotion regulation. *Psychological Science, 14,* 612–616.

James, W. (1958). *The varieties of religious experience.* New York: Mentor. (Original work published 1902).

Jordan, C. H. & McGregor, I. (2006). *Implicit self-esteem, self-threat, and cerebral hemisphericity.* Raw data. Wilfrid Laurier University, Waterloo, Canada.

Jordan, C. H., Spencer, S. J., & Zanna, M. P. (2003a). I love me, I love me not: Implicit self-esteem, explicit self-esteem, and defensiveness. In S. J. Spencer, S. Fein, & M. P. Zanna (Eds.), *Motivated social perception: The Ontario symposium* (Vol. 9, pp. 117–146). Mahwah, NJ: Lawrence Erlbaum Associates, Inc.

Jordan, C. H., Spencer, S. J., & Zanna, M. P. (2005). Types of high self-esteem and prejudice: How implicit self-esteem relates to ethnic discrimination among high explicit self-esteem individuals. *Personality and Social Psychology Bulletin, 31,* 693–702.

Jordan, C. H., Spencer, S. J., Zanna, M. P., Hoshino-Browne, E., & Correll, J. (2003b). Secure and defensive self-esteem. *Journal of Personality and Social Psychology, 85,* 969–978.

Jost, J. T., Glaser, J., Kruglanski, A. W., & Sulloway, F. J. (2003). Political conservatism as motivated social cognition. *Psychological Bulletin, 129,* 339–375.

Kang, S.-J., Haji, R., & McGregor, I. (2006). *If my group's ok your group's ok, too: Meaningful in-group identification can promote openness to outgroups.* Unpublished manuscript. York University, Toronto, Canada.

Karpinski, A. (2004). Measuring self-esteem using the Implicit Association Test: The role of the other. *Personality and Social Psychology Bulletin, 30,* 22–34.

Kruglanski, A. W., & Webster, D. M. (1996). Motivated closing of the mind: "Seizing" and "freezing". *Psychological Review, 103,* 263–283.

Lewin, K. (1933). Environmental forces. In C. Murchison (Ed.), *A handbook of child psychology* (2nd ed., pp. 590–625). Worcester, MA: Clark University Press.

Lewin, K. (1935). *A dynamic theory of personality* (D. K. Adams & K. E. Zaner, Trans.). New York: McGraw-Hill.

Martin, L. L., & Shrira, I. (2004). *The cerebral hemispheres as a framework for social psychology theorizing.* Unpublished Manuscript, University of Georgia, GA, USA.

McGregor, I. (2004a). Zeal, identity, and meaning: Going to extremes to be one self. In J. Greenberg, S. L. Koole, & T. Pyszczynski (Eds.), *Handbook of experimental existential psychology* (pp. 182–199). New York: Guilford.

McGregor, I. (2004b). Raw data. York University, Toronto, Canada.

McGregor, I. (2005, January). *Myopic solutions for bewildered selves: Beer, zeal, and implicit self-esteem.* Paper presented at the Self and Identity Pre-Conference of the annual meeting of the Society for Personality and Social Psychology, New Orleans, LA, USA.

McGregor, I. (in press). Offensive defensiveness: Toward an integrative neuroscience of compensatory zeal after mortality salience, personal uncertainty, and other poignant self-threats. *Psychological Inquiry.*

McGregor, I. (2006). Zeal appeal: The allure of moral extremes. *Basic and Applied Social Psychology, 28,* 343–348.

McGregor, I. (2006). Personal projects as compensatory convictions: Passionate pursuit and the fugitive self. To appear in B. R. Little, K. Salmela-Aro, J. Nurmi, & S. D. Phillips (Eds.), *Personal project pursuit: Goals, action, and human flourishing*. Thousand Oaks, CA: Sage.

McGregor, I., & Crippen, M. (2003). Raw data. York University, Toronto, Canada.

McGregor, I., & Gailliot, M. T. (2006). *Defensive zeal after mortality salience: Clarifying the role of dispositional self-esteem*. Unpublished manuscript. York University, Toronto, Canada.

McGregor, I., & Marigold, D. C. (2003). Defensive zeal and the uncertain self: What makes you so sure? *Journal of Personality and Social Psychology, 85*, 338–852.

McGregor, I., Nail, P. R., Marigold, D. C., & Kang, S.-J. (2005). Defensive pride and consensus: Strength in imaginary numbers. *Journal of Personality and Social Psychology, 89*, 978–996.

McGregor, I., Newby-Clark, I. R., & Zanna, M. P. (1999). "Remembering" dissonance: Simultaneous accessibility of inconsistent cognitive elements moderates epistemic discomfort. In E. Harmon-Jones & J. Mills (Eds.), *Cognitive dissonance: Progress on a pivotal theory in social psychology* (pp. 325–353). Washington, DC: American Psychological Association.

McGregor, I., Zanna, M. P., Holmes, J. G., & Spencer, S. J. (2001). Compensatory conviction in the face of personal uncertainty: Going to extremes and being oneself. *Journal of Personality and Social Psychology, 80*, 472–488.

Mor, N., & Winquist, J. (2002). Self-focused attention and negative affect: A meta-analysis. *Psychological Bulletin, 128*, 638–662.

Neuberg, S. L., & Newsom, J. T. (1993). Personal need for structure: Individual differences in the desire for simple structure. *Journal of Personality and Social Psychology, 65*, 113–131.

Nitschke, J. B., Heller, W., Palmieri, P. A., & Miller, G. A. (1999). Contrasting patterns of brain activity in anxious apprehension and anxious arousal. *Psychophysiology, 36*, 628–637.

Pavlov, I. P. (1927). Conditioned reflexes: An investigation of the physiological activity of the cerebral cortex. (G. V. Anrep, Trans.). (Available at: http://psychclassics.yorku.ca/Pavlov/lecture17.htm).

Pedhazur, E. J. (1982). *Multiple regression in behavioral research: Explanation and prediction* (2nd ed.). Fort Worth, TX: Holt, Rinehart & Winston.

Pyszczynski, T., Greenberg, J., Solomon, S., Arndt, J., & Schimel, J. (2004). Why do people need self-esteem? A theoretical and empirical review. *Psychological Bulletin, 130*, 435–468.

Robinson, M. D., & Meier, B. P. (2005). Rotten to the core: Neuroticism and implicit evaluations of the self. *Self and Identity, 4*, 361–372.

Rudman, L. A. (2004). Sources of implicit attitudes. *Current Directions in Psychological Science, 13*, 79–82.

Spalding, L. R., & Hardin, C. D. (1999). Unconscious unease and self-handicapping: Behavioral consequences of individual differences in implicit and explicit self-esteem. *Psychological Science, 10*, 535–539.

Sutton, S. K., & Davidson, R. J. (1997). Prefrontal brain asymmetry: A biological substrate of the behavioral approach and inhibition systems. *Psychological Science, 8*, 204–210.

Vohs, K. D., & Heatherton, T. F. (2001). Self-esteem and threats to self: Implications for self-construals and interpersonal perceptions. *Journal of Personality and Social Psychology, 81*, 1103–1118.

Wood, J. V., Saltzberg, J. A., Neale, J. M., Stone, A. A., & Rachmiel, T. B. (1990). Self-focused attention, coping responses, and distressed mood in everyday life. *Journal of Personality and Social Psychology, 58*, 1027–1036.

Zeigler-Hill, V. (2006). Discrepancies between implicit and explicit self-esteem: Implications for narcissism and self-esteem instability. *Journal of Personality, 74*, 119–143.

Self and Identity, 6: 238–255, 2007
http://www.psypress.com/sai
ISSN: 1529-8868 print/1529-8876 online
DOI: 10.1080/15298860601115344

Psychology Press
Taylor & Francis Group

Children and Social Groups: A Developmental Analysis of Implicit Consistency in Hispanic Americans

YARROW DUNHAM

Harvard Graduate School of Education, Cambridge, Massachusetts, USA

ANDREW SCOTT BARON
MAHZARIN R. BANAJI

Harvard University, Cambridge, Massachusetts, USA

We investigated the development of three aspects of implicit social cognition (self-esteem, group identity, and group attitude) and their interrelationships in Hispanic American children (ages 5 to 12) and adults. Hispanic children and adults showed positive implicit self-esteem and a preference for and identification with their in-group when the comparison group was another disadvantaged minority group (African American). However, challenging the long-held view that children's early intergroup attitudes are primarily egocentric, young Hispanic children do not show implicit preference for or identification with their in-group when the comparison was the more advantaged White majority. Results also supported predictions of cognitive-affective balance in the youngest children. Strikingly, balance was absent in adults, suggesting that in disadvantaged minority groups, cognitive-affective consistency may actually decline with age.

Attitudes about the self serve as primary organizers of social cognition, including preferences and beliefs that drive action. For example, attitudes about oneself and one's social group are often closely interrelated, showing how group membership and group status in the larger society shape the individual (Aberson, Healy, & Romero, 2000; Greenwald et al., 2002; Jackson, 2002; Valk, 2000).

One of the most striking results from the past five decades of research on the person–group relationship is the idea of in-group favoritism (e.g., Plous, 2002). From the random assignment of a person to a group by birthplace or family, to the more self-selected affiliations with politics, sports, or profession, belonging to a group regularly produces favoring of one's own group—a fact so commonplace as to seem natural and even warranted. However, this form of in-group favoritism may not be so robust when one's in-group is viewed in a less favorable light by

This research was supported by grants from the 3rd Millennium Foundation, the Wallace Foundation, and the National Institute of Mental Health to MRB.

Correspondence should be addressed to: Yarrow Dunham, Department of Psychology, 15th Floor, William James Hall, 33 Kirkland Street, Cambridge, MA 02138, USA. E-mail: dunhamya@gse.harvard.edu the larger society (e.g., see Jost & Banaji, 1994). In these cases, members of socially disadvantaged groups often do not reveal a preference for their own group, at least when implicit, less conscious measures of such preferences are utilized to test attitudes (Nosek, Banaji, & Greenwald, 2002; Jost, Banaji, & Nosek, 2004).

Does the absence of in-group preference have consequences for self-esteem and group identification? This question was placed in the context of theories of cognitive-affective consistency by Greenwald and colleagues (Greenwald et al., 2002). They posited that the self occupies a central position in mental life, and from this basic assumption generated a set of predictions about expected interrelationships among self-esteem, group identity and group attitudes (see also Heider, 1958). These expectations took the form of interactions. To the extent that the self was associated with an in-group and the in-group was favorable, the self was also expected to be favorable, at least when these constructs were measured at the implicit level. For example, Whites high on both implicit self-esteem and identification with Whites tend to show strong implicit preference for Whites.

However, being a member of a disadvantaged group may pose a threat to cognitive-affective balance. If members of a socially disadvantaged group internalize culturally prevalent negative associations of their in-group, then forming positive associations with the group might threaten other aspects of self-esteem and self-identity. Protecting self-esteem might require the inhibition of positive attitudes towards the in-group, or even the avoidance of balance all together. These possibilities dovetail with the findings that implicit in-group preference is absent in disadvantaged minorities at the population level (for adults, Nosek et al., 2002; for adolescents, Baron, Shusterman, Bordeaux, & Banaji, 2004), but implicit self-esteem is not markedly lower in these groups (Baron et al., 2004; Nosek et al., 2002; Pelham & Hetts, 1999; Verkuyten, 2005; see Crocker & Major, 1989, for a similar pattern of findings for explicit self-esteem). What is more, preliminary examinations of cognitive-affective balance in non-majority or non-privileged populations also support this possibility. Balance among African Americans was the weakest of the tests presented by Greenwald and colleagues in their initial formulation of the balanced identity model (Greenwald et al., 2002), and balance was considerably weaker for students at relatively less-valued compared to more-valued university residential colleges (Lane, Mitchell, & Banaji, 2005). This pattern of findings can be explained by the idea that when the in-group is disparaged, this particular form of cognitive-affective consistency is avoided, possibly as a means of protecting self-esteem. If correct, it challenges the ubiquity of in-group favoritism and raises questions about inequities in person – group identity imposed on members of the minority.

In the research to be presented here, we turned our attention to Hispanic Americans, a minority group that has been largely ignored in research on implicit social cognition (but see Weyant, 2005). We examined the implicit attitudes among this group toward their in-group when the in-group was compared to another disadvantaged minority (African Americans) as well as an advantaged majority (White Americans). We also measured their implicit identifications with each group and their implicit self-esteem. Finally, we examined the interrelationships among these components of implicit social cognition to observe the degree of consistency among these components, allowing a test of the central predictions, and possible limitations, of the balanced identity framework.

Attitudes and other social psychological constructs do not emerge for the first time, fully formed, at age 18; we know that these mental structures have antecedents in early childhood. Indeed, children devote much energy to attempting to understand their own place in the world, including the impressions that others have of them and the groups to which they belong (Eisenberg, Losoya, & Guthrie, 1997). However, little empirical attention has been devoted to examining *implicit* social processes from a developmental perspective, perhaps because of the practical challenges of working with children and the methodological hurdles that need to be cleared in adapting existing implicit methodologies for use with them (but see McGlothlin, Killen, & Edmonds, 2005, who investigated implicit processes using children's interpretations of ambiguous situations). These hurdles have now been overcome (Baron & Banaji, 2006; Dunham, Baron, & Banaji, 2006; Rutland, Cameron, Milne, & McGeorge, 2005), and we argue that a developmental focus is particularly critical when investigating components of social cognition that are as basic as attitudes toward self and group; in these cases, the developmental processes that give rise to stable attitudes may reveal much about the nature of the adult "end state."

Do young children from a disadvantaged group initially exhibit positive attitudes towards their in-group that are then gradually undone? If so, what are the consequences for group identification and self-esteem? Most broadly, there is now considerable evidence that childhood experiences do affect adult implicit attitudes in multiple domains (for a review, see Rudman, 2004), and that parent–child implicit attitudes do relate, especially for children who identify strongly with their parents (Sinclair, Dunn, & Lowery, 2005). Furthermore, Rutland and colleagues (Rutland et al., 2005) found that, like adults, 6-year-old children's self-reported group attitudes are affected by self-presentational demands, while their implicit attitudes are not, suggesting that the implicit constructs function similarly in children and adults. In our own research, we found that implicit race attitudes in majority populations both in the USA and Japan are present in adult-like magnitude as early as we can successfully measure them (by age 5–6), and that the strength of these attitudes shows little change over the course of development (Baron & Banaji, 2006; Dunham et al., 2006).

These developmental studies of implicit social cognition have all focused on members of the advantaged majority in the USA, Europe, and Japan. There are reasons to believe that being a member of a minority group may predispose children to be particularly sensitive to social status cues (e.g., Aboud, 1988; Tropp & Wright, 2003), perhaps because in this case social status information about the in-group conflicts with a tendency towards in-group favoritism and egocentrism more broadly (e.g., Jost & Burgess, 2000). Thus minority children's implicit attitudes may be the result of a more dynamic psychological management, one that includes balancing egocentrism with socially learned values and potentially yielding a different developmental pattern. Studying their emergence is an important step towards understanding the mental life of minority children and hence the influence of social hierarchies on associated mental structures. It may also be a place to expect limits on the expected balance among affective-cognitive components that have been studied under the label of cognitive consistency (Greenwald et al., 2002).

Method

Participants

In total, 234 elementary school students and 71 adults participated in the study. Elementary school students were recruited from summer programs affiliated with two elementary schools in Houston, TX, and adults were recruited from public locations in the surrounding community. All participants were of Latin American descent and were predominately Spanish – English bilinguals living in Hispanic communities in the Houston area. The children were between ages 5 years 6 months and 12 years 2 months ($M = 8$ years 7 months, $SD = 1$ year 7 months), with roughly equal number of children between the ages of 6 and 11. Adults were between 18 and 24 years of age. Figure 1 presents the overall age breakdown of all participants.

Parental consent for child participants was secured in advance of all testing, and compensation was limited to a small toy. Adults were compensated with $5 in exchange for their participation.

Implicit Materials

Measures of implicit social cognition consisted of the child friendly version of the Implicit Association Test (IAT; Greenwald, McGhee, & Schwartz, 1998), the child IAT, developed by Baron and Banaji (2006; see also Dunham et al., 2006). The IAT is a speeded dichotomous categorization task that estimates the relative strength of association between pairs of concepts. The speed and accuracy with which a social group concept such as Hispanic can be paired with attributes such as Good or Bad, versus the speed and accuracy with which the concept White can be paired with the same attributes of Good and Bad, is taken as a measure of the relative implicit attitude toward these social groups. The greater the speed and accuracy of pairing Hispanic + Good/White + Bad versus Hispanic + Bad/White + Good, the greater the assumed implicit positive attitude toward the group Hispanic relative to White.

The IAT has received extensive empirical validation, and demonstrates acceptable levels of reliability (Cunningham, Preacher, & Banaji, 2001), construct validity (Banaji, 2001; Greenwald & Nosek, 2001), and predictive validity (Poehlman, Uhlmann, Greenwald, & Banaji, 2005). The child IAT involves two major changes to

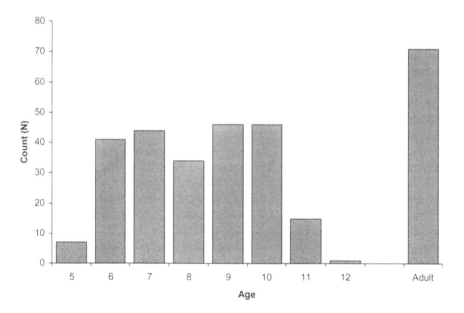

FIGURE 1   Histogram of participant ages.

the traditional procedure. First, to avoid reliance on reading ability, written stimuli are not used. Social groups are presented via consensually identifiably faces of group members (as is often the case with the adult IAT, although the faces used here were faces of children) and Good and Bad words are presented auditorily via headphones. Second, to reduce reliance on fine motor ability that may disadvantage the youngest children faced with using a traditional computer keyboard, we replaced the keyboard with two large response buttons for left and right responses. Several studies have now used this method and have found that children as young as age 5 are readily able to complete the procedure and produce analyzable data in multiple domains (Baron & Banaji, 2006; Baron, Dunham, & Banaji, 2005; Dunham et al., 2006).

Participants in this study, both children and adults, completed three child IATs. These were: a self-esteem IAT, in which self-relevant and other-relevant words were paired with positive and negative adjectives (see Appendix for a list of all stimulus words used across all child IATs); a Hispanic attitude IAT (pairing photographs of Hispanic and Black or White children with positive and negative adjectives); and a Hispanic identity IAT (pairing photographs of Hispanic and Black or White children with self-relevant and other-relevant words). In other words, while all participants completed three tests (self-esteem, group identity, group attitude), half the participants paired the Hispanic in-group with a White out-group, and half paired the Hispanic in-group with an African American out-group.

Auditory stimuli for this experiment were recorded by native English and Spanish speakers (to provide participants' dominant language; see procedure) as high-fidelity digital recordings, and were back translated by different native speakers to ensure accuracy and ease of comprehension. To ensure that self-relevant stimuli would not cross any salient social category boundaries, male participants heard a male voice for all self-relevant or other-relevant words and a female voice for all pleasant and unpleasant adjectives, while female participants received the opposite voice pairings.

Explicit Materials

Explicit measures were included but they were not of primary interest in this investigation, as past investigations of cognitive consistency have not found balance at the explicit level (Greenwald et al., 2002). As such, they appeared at the end because of concern that the youngest children may not be able to complete all measures in a single session (although almost all children were able to complete the entire experiment). For self-esteem, 5-point Likert-type items assessed self-liking, perception of being liked by others, and ability at school and games (see Appendix for all scale items). These four items were then averaged to produce a single self-esteem measure. The group attitude measure consisted of forced choice options of dichotomous preferences for one of two children, presented via photographs and matched on gender, who differed along racial/ethnic lines. Pairs included Hispanic and White, Hispanic and African American, and White and African American. The trials with Hispanic in-group photos were analyzed, and for each contrast the percentage of trials on which the Hispanic in-group was selected was computed. The group identification measure was similar, but instead of seeking a report of preference, for each pair the participant stated who they thought they were most similar to; here too we produced a single measure for each contrast, indicating the percent of trials on which the Hispanic in-group member was selected as more similar to self.

In designing these explicit measures, we sought a format that was comparable to the IAT (e.g., involving a dichotomous judgment of preference, as compared to the IAT's dichotomous categorization as good or bad). However, it was not clear how to achieve this for a self-esteem measure. For example, the overall tendency towards a positivity bias in children (see Stipek & MacIver, 1989, for a review) makes it unlikely that we would *ever* get explicit pairings of the self with bad in a dichotomous choice task. This led us to the scalar measure discussed above, which was able to produce some variability despite its structural divergence from the IAT.[1] Unfortunately, our explicit self-esteem measure exhibited low reliability (Cronbach's $\alpha = .41$), pointing to the need to develop a better assessment tool for this construct.

Procedure

Child participants completed the experiment in a private room at their school. Adults participated in field settings in the community. All participants completed the study on a laptop computer and were tested one-on-one with an experimenter present to instruct and answer questions. Data collection was conducted by both White and Hispanic experimenters. Children completed the procedure in the dominant language, Spanish or English, while adults completed the procedure in Spanish. Otherwise, the experimental protocol and all measurement items were identical for adults and children.

All participants completed three child IATs including measures of self-esteem, group attitude, and group identification. For the latter two measures, participants were randomly placed in one of two conditions. In both conditions, the in-group was consistently Hispanic but the comparison out-group—White or African American—was varied as a between-subjects factor (thus the sample sizes for these measures are always approximately half that of the self-esteem IAT).

Results and Discussion

The race of experimenter (White or Hispanic), the test language (English or Spanish), and participant gender did not significantly affect our results, and so we collapsed across these variables for our principal analyses.

Scoring Procedure for the Child IAT

Child IATs were scored using the scoring algorithm prescribed by Greenwald, Nosek, and Banaji (2003), based on its superior performance in analyses of large web-based data collections. The method produces an effect size estimate (the IAT D effect, a variant of Cohen's d) for each participant on each IAT test, as well as exclusion criteria for individual trials and individual participants, which were used here. We made one deviation from the procedure outlined in the scoring algorithm, a change necessitated by the mixed modality presentations of stimuli (see Baron & Banaji, 2006, for more detailed discussion). While pictures generally produce more rapid responses than words, this difference is magnified in the child IAT because of the auditory presentation of evaluative words. This essentially created two independent but interspersed distributions, one for visual and one for auditory stimuli. Failing to account for this difference would lead to underestimation of actual effect sizes because of the artificial inflation of response latency variance caused by the two overlapping distributions. To correct for this, we computed two IAT

D measures for each participant, one corresponding to the auditory stimuli and one to the visual stimuli, and then averaged these two D scores to determine that participant's final score.[2]

Results for Implicit and Explicit Measures

All participants completed three child IATs including measures of self-esteem, group attitude, and group identification. Table 1 summarizes the overall child IAT results for children and adults.

Self-esteem.   Child IAT data from five child participants were eliminated due to prescribed exclusion criteria in Greenwald et al. (2003). On average, child participants were faster to respond to the self + good pairing, compared to the reverse pairing of self + bad, revealing a relative positive association between self and good attributes, $D = .11$, $t(228) = 5.19$, $p < .0001$. Submitting self-esteem scores to a regression analysis with participant age as a predictor revealed no effect of age, $F(1, 228) = 0.93$, $p > .33$, allowing us to collapse across age in subsequent analyses.

Turning to adults, the mean effect of implicit self-esteem was also significantly positive, $D = .09$, $t(70) = 2.21$, $p < .04$, and no significant difference between adult and child self-esteem emerged, $t(298) = 0.38$, $p > .70$. This finding replicates several previous reports of positive implicit self-esteem in non-majority samples (Baron et al., 2004; Nosek et al., 2002; Pelham & Hetts, 1999; Verkuyten, 2005), and is the first to directly compare children's and adult's implicit self-esteem. Of course, it is still possible that minorities who live in integrated settings with members of the majority (as opposed to our participants, who lived in a predominately Hispanic community) might show lower self-esteem (see Gray-Little & Hafdahl, 2000; Verukyten & Thijs, 2002, for some evidence to support this possibility). However, it should also be noted that other populations theorized to be lower in self-esteem (e.g., Japanese) turn out to have equivalent, high levels of self-esteem when measurements are made at the implicit level (Yamaguchi et al., 2006).

Nonetheless, the effect sizes we observe here are notably smaller than those found in other studies using the IAT. For example, three representative studies all found average implicit self-esteem effect sizes equivalent to $D > .92$ in predominately majority samples (Greenwald & Farnham, 2000; Lane et al., 2005; Rudman, Greenwald, & McGhee, 2001).[3] By contrast, the mean effect size here, collapsing across adults and children, is $D = .11$. Of course, our measure, the child IAT, is different from the traditional IAT in several respects. Until we use this procedure

TABLE 1   Mean IAT Effect Size (D) and Standard Deviation (SD) for Each IAT

	Children		Adults	
Test type	Effect (D)	SD	Effect (D)	SD
Self-esteem	.11***	.33	.10*	.36
Hispanic over African American preference	.19***	.38	.18**	.33
Hispanic over White preference	.00	.47	.06	.38
Hispanic over African American identification	.12***	.26	.17*	.17
Hispanic over White identification	.06	.41	.14*	.14

Note: *$p < .05$; **$p < .01$; ***$p < .0001$.

with majority children and adults, we will not be able to definitively settle this issue; however, see note 2 for some reasons to think differences in measures cannot account for this discrepancy. We tentatively conclude that implicit self-esteem, while still positive, is low in this population.

Explicit self-esteem scores could range between 1 (low self-esteem) and 5 (high self-esteem); the mean self-esteem for children was towards the high end of this range, $M = 4.3$, $SD = 0.59$, while that of adults was somewhat lower, $M = 3.9$, $SD = 0.69$. This group difference was reliable, $F(1, 299) = 22.69$, $p < .0001$. Regression analysis to examine the effect of age within children also revealed a pronounced trend towards lower self-esteem in older children, $F(1, 231) = 19.01$, $p < .0001$. Broadly, this result replicates other developmental work reporting a decline in self-reported self-esteem over these ages that is generally assumed to be driven by more realistic self-assessments and increasing social pressures associated with body image, popularity, and related concerns that rise to prominence as adolescence is approached (e.g., Harter, 2001).

Group attitude. Exclusion criteria led to the elimination of 1 child and 6 adult participants from analyses involving the attitude IAT. In children, we found a positive Hispanic + good association when the comparison out-group was African American ($D = .19$) but not when the out-group was White ($D = .00$). We turned to regression analyses to examine effects of age and comparison out-group (White or African American) within the same model. This analysis showed that the IAT effect was significantly stronger when the out-group was African American rather than when the out-group was White, $F(1, 230) = 11.68$, $p < .001$. No effect of age, $F(1, 230) = 0.01$, $p > .81$, and no interaction between age and out-group, $F(1, 230) = 1.55$, $p > .21$, was observed. Simple effects tests revealed that the Hispanic over African American preference was significantly different from 0, $t(116) = 5.55$, $p < .0001$, but, of course, the Hispanic over White preference was not. That is, our participants failed to manifest a positive Hispanic + good association when comparing themselves to the White American out-group. This failure to find in-group pre-ference is a first in research on implicit social cognition in young children, and it implicates the effect of early internalization of cultural knowledge about the status of social groups on children's own positive association with their group.

In the adult sample the pattern was similar. Adults showed a positive Hispanic + good association when the out-group was African American ($D = .18$) but not when the out-group was White ($D = .06$). The simple effect was greater than 0 in the case of the African American out-group, $t(32) = 3.20$, $p < .01$, but not when the out-group was White Americans, $t(31) = 0.90$, $p > .37$, although the difference between the two was not significant, $t(63) = 1.38$, $p > .17$. As we noted, adult and adolescent African American populations also show no mean-level in-group preference when comparing themselves to Whites, the majority group (Baron et al., 2004; Nosek et al., 2002). Our replication of this basic finding is particularly interesting given that nearly all our participants lived in an overwhelmingly Hispanic local environment, suggesting the influence of the culture-at-large above and beyond the local milieu.

Given the lack of age effects in the child data, we collapsed across age and compared children directly to adults. For both tests, there were no significant differences between children and adults' implicit attitudes, both $ts < .74$, $ps > .46$.

Explicit group attitude results are summarized in Figure 2. Similar in pattern to the implicit data, children showed robust preference for the in-group as compared

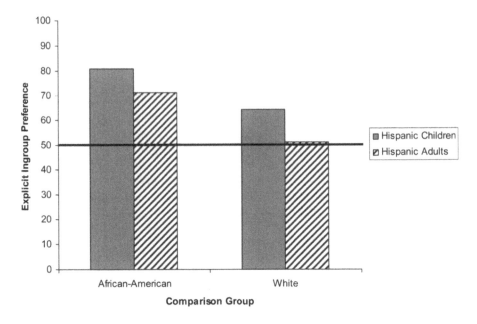

FIGURE 2 Self-reported (explicit) preference for Hispanic over African American and White (chance responding = 50%).

to both out-groups, but especially when the out-group was African American. In the case of the African American out-group, children preferred their Hispanic in-group 81% of the time, a figure which differed strongly from chance performance, $t(233) = 20.09$, $p < .0001$. In the case of the White out-group, children preferred their in-group 65% of the time, which also differed from chance, $t(233) = 8.19$, $p < .0001$. To determine whether there were any effects of age, overall preference was submitted to a regression analysis with two predictors, out-group (African American or White) and age. This analysis revealed a main effect of out-group, with preference for Hispanic stronger when the out-group was African American than when it was White, $F(1, 465) = 50.07$, $p < .0001$. However, neither the effect of age nor the Age × Out-group interaction approached significance (both $ps > .74$); subsequent analyses were collapsed across age for the child participants. Thus self-reported preference for Hispanic over White contrasts sharply with their implicit attitude, which showed no in-group preference for Hispanic over White.

Adults showed less consistency in their self-reported in-group bias. When comparing themselves to African Americans, they preferred their in-group 71% of the time, a figure which still differed from chance, $t(68) = 6.42$, $p < .0001$. However, when the comparison group was White, adult participants did not show in-group preference, preferring the Hispanic in-group only 51% of the time, a figure which did not differ from chance, $t(68) = 0.26$, $p > .79$; in-group preference was stronger when the out-group was African American, $F(1, 134) = 18.96$, $p < .0001$. As these data suggest, self-reported in-group preference was substantially weaker in adults than in children, $F(1, 600) = 23.79$, $p < .0001$, but this difference did not differ as a function of the out-group, $F(1, 600) = 0.35$, $p > .55$. In other words, both Hispanic adults and children explicitly and implicitly revealed less in-group preference when comparing their group to the advantaged White majority, rather than the disadvantaged African American minority.

This overall pattern of results is quite different from what we have repeatedly found in majority children, both in the USA and Japan, where young children show equal and robust in-group preference whether comparing themselves to a high- or low-status out-group (Dunham et al., 2006). Instead, our Hispanic participants *do not* show in-group preference when comparing themselves to the White majority. We interpret this as evidence for the more rapid internalization of social group information in minority children, something that has previously been suggested by self-report data (e.g., Aboud, 1988).

Consistent with earlier findings on the development of implicit intergroup attitudes, these results reveal an early dissociation between implicit and explicit group attitudes. At the explicit level, children showed strong preference for their in-group over either out-group, but at the implicit level, in-group preference appeared only when comparing to African Americans. This is an interesting contrast with the majority populations we have studied, where implicit attitudes reveal substantially *more* in-group favoritism than do self-report measures; in this case, implicit attitudes show substantially *less* favoritism than do self-report measures. However, in both these cases it was the *explicit* form of attitude that showed the more pronounced developmental shift, while implicit attitude remained stable across the age groups tested here.

Group identity. Exclusion criteria led to the elimination of 15 child and 12 adult participants from analyses involving the group identity IAT. Children showed a tendency to associate self + Hispanic compared to self + African American ($D = .12$) or self + White ($D = .06$). Simple effects testing revealed that children implicitly identified with Hispanic when the comparison group was African American, $t(111) = 4.71$, $p < .0001$, but not when the comparison group was White, $t(106) = 1.62$, $p < .11$. However, a regression analysis showed no significant effects of out-group, $F(1, 215) = 1.88$, $p > .17$, age, $F(1, 215) = 2.44$, $p > .11$, or their interaction, $F(1, 215) = 1.31$, $p > .25$.

Adults showed a clear association of self with Hispanic compared to African American ($D = .18$) and White ($D = .14$). Both effects were statistically significant— African American contrast $t(28) = 2.55$, $p < .02$; White contrast $t(29) = 2.05$, $p < .05$—and the two did not differ from each other, $t(57) = 0.39$, $p > .69$. Adults and children did not differ from each other on either test, both $ts < 0.96$, $ps > .36$, indicating no age-related differences in implicit group identity.

One child and one adult failed to complete the self-report identity measure. Explicitly, children robustly identified with their in-group over the African American out-group, $M = 87\%$, $t(232) = 21.36$, $p < .0001$, as well as the White out-group, $M = 62\%$, $t(232) = 4.41$, $p < .0001$. We used regression analysis to directly compare these effects while also examining the effect of age. This analysis revealed main effects of out-group and age, qualified by their interaction, $F(1, 462) = 6.09$, $p < .03$. Predicted values of in-group identification, as a function of out-group and age, are presented in Figure 3. The age-related increase in the strength of Hispanic identi-fication is clearly visible when the out-group was White, but not when the out-group was African American. By comparison, adults showed in-group identification both with respect to the African American out-group, $M = 74\%$, $t(67) = 5.82$, $p < .0001$, and the White out-group, $M = 62\%$, $t(67) = 2.38$, $p < .03$, with the former value marginally greater in strength than the latter, paired $t(67) = 1.82$, $p < .08$. That is,

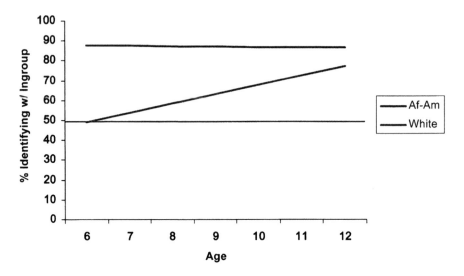

FIGURE 3 Self-reported (explicit) identification with the Hispanic in-group as a function of children's age and comparison out-group, predicted from OLS regression model (chance responding = 50%).

young children are not clearly differentiating themselves from the White majority, although identification with the in-group does occur by middle childhood and remains present in adults.

In summary, on a measure of implicit identity, children associated themselves with their in-group (Hispanic) when the comparison was African Americans but *not* when the comparison was White Americans. By adulthood, however, implicit identification was present regardless of the comparison out-group. At the explicit level, the pattern was quite similar, with young children identifying with Hispanic over African American but not Hispanic over White. The identification with Hispanic over White showed a gradual, age-related increase in strength, while the identification with Hispanic over African American remained stable and high. The lack of identification with the in-group at both the implicit and explicit level, as well as the lack of in-group preference when the out-group is the White majority, is reminiscent of the classic finding from Clark and Clark (1933), which showed a tendency towards out-group identification in young African American children. Given the strong tendency to identify with the in-group when comparing oneself to the African American minority, this finding suggests a similar interpretation: Minority children may not strongly identify with their own in-group because they are already aware of the status differences between their in-group and the dominant majority; indeed, in a separate study, Hispanic adolescents implicitly identified with the White majority over the African American minority when these two out-groups were directly pitted against each other (Baron et al., 2004).

Bivariate relationships between measures. At the implicit level, only one correlation reached significance. This was the correlation between in-group attitude and identity when the contrast group was African Americans, $r(140) = .22$, $p < .01$. At the explicit level, several correlations emerged, which are shown in Table 2.

TABLE 2 Correlations Between Explicit Measures (Pearson's *r*)

	2	3	4	5
1. Self-Esteem	.16**	.09	.07	−.04
2. Hispanic over African American preference	–	.31***	.32***	.10
3. Hispanic over White preference		–	.14*	.35***
4. Hispanic over African American identification			–	−.05
5. Hispanic over White identification				–

Note: *p < .05; **p < .01; ***p < .001.

As can be seen, moderate correlations emerged between measures of attitude and identification within out-group conditions, and between the two measures of attitude. There was also a modestly positive correlation between self-esteem and attitude when the contrast group was African Americans. While we do not want to over-interpret this modest correlation, positive differentiation from a disadvantaged minority could be a means to bolster self-esteem, a possibility consistent with social identity theory (Tajfel & Turner, 1979, 1986). We will return to this possibility below.

Balanced Identity Analyses

To examine the interrelationships between these measures, we investigated the higher-order relationships using a balanced identity design suggested by Greenwald et al. (2002). The assumption underlying the balanced identity approach is that any one of the three core constructs of self-esteem, identification, and attitude can be predicted from the relationship between the values of the other two. That is, if one shows a strong association of self + good (high positive self-esteem) and between self + in-group (strong group identity), then in-group + good (positive attitude) is expected to result, because this is the only outcome that produces affective-cognitive balance in implicit social cognition. Statistically, this logic suggests the use of the two-way interaction term between any two constructs as the predictor of the third construct.

The balanced identity procedure involves first predicting each outcome with this interaction term (Step 1), and then adding the main effect terms to test whether additional variance is accounted for above and beyond the interaction term (Step 2). More precisely, the following results are predicted: The regression coefficient of the interaction term (hereafter b_1) should account for substantial variance in the outcome and should be numerically positive at Step 1; b_1 should remain positive in Step 2; the increment in variance explained from Step 1 to Step 2 should not be statistically significant; and neither regression coefficient corresponding to the simple effects of the two predictors (hereafter b_2 and b_3) should be statistically different from zero in Step 2 (see Greenwald et al., 2002, for further details of the statistical procedure). We followed this procedure, conducting separate analyses for each out-group and concentrating on the IAT because past research has not shown balance for explicit cognitions (Greenwald et al., 2002; Rudman & Goodwin, 2004). Because these analyses require three IATs per participant, participants who were excluded from any individual IAT, above, were also excluded from these analyses.

African American contrast set.   A total of 110 children and 28 adults contributed to these analyses. For the analyses involving children, preliminary tests showed that age did not emerge as a statistically significant simple effect or interaction; the strength of balance did not appear to vary across the age ranges tested here. Following the logic outlined in the analysis section above, we first entered each construct (self-esteem, group attitude, and group identity) into a regression equation with a single predictor composed of the two-way interaction of the other two constructs (Step 1). For children, the three models provided validation of the balance predictions; one model was marginally significant, $F(1, 109) = 3.21, p < .08$, and the other two were statistically significant (both $Fs > 6.70, ps < .02$). In each model, the standardized values of b_1 revealed moderate effect sizes (mean standardized $b_1 = .24$) and all were numerically positive. In Step 2, we entered each main effect term corresponding to our two predictors into each of the regression models from Step 1. These regressions again largely bore out the predictions of the balanced identity model; b_1 remained positive across all models at near-identical levels to Step 1 (mean $b_1 = .22$), and none of the increases in variance explained or the main effects b_2 or b_3 reached the $p < .05$ level of significance. However, in two of the three models the increase in variance explained was of marginal significance ($p = .06$ and $p = .08$, respectively), and in one model one main effect term was also of marginal significance, $F(1, 107) = 3.22, p < .08$. While suggesting a confirmation of the balance model in children, these results also suggest that balance is somewhat less robust than has been found in prior research.

For adults, the picture was remarkably different. None of the three models approached significance (all $Fs < 0.08, ps > .77$), only two of the three estimates of b_1 were numerically positive, and the values of b_1 were quite small (mean standardized $b_1 = .01$). Thus, Step 1 failed to confirm balance predictions in adults. Given this, Step 2 becomes superfluous and results will not be presented here.

White contrast set.   A total of 105 children and 29 adults contributed to these analyses. In this case, for children, the predictions of the balance model were not born out at Step 1; none of the three models explained a statistically significant proportion of variance in the outcome (all $Fs < 0.75, ps > .39$). While the values of b_1 were numerically positive, they were quite small (mean standardized $b_1 = .053$); again, no effect of age emerged in these analyses. For adults, predictions were also not born out at Step 1 (all $Fs < 0.11, ps > .75$, mean standardized $b_1 < .01$). Given the manifest failure at Step 1, we will not report results from Step 2 here. In short, no evidence of balance emerged in either adults or children when the comparison group was White.

These data suggest that degree of balance differs as a function of the contrast set (whether the comparison group was African American or White). In the former case (African American contrast), children did show balance between the three constructs. For the White American contrast, there was no evidence of balance in children or adults.

The differences between the two contrast sets is interesting; our considerations at the outset suggested that balance might be problematic for minorities because of internalized negativity associated with the in-group. Consistent with this interpretation, we found no evidence of balance when comparisons were with the White majority. However, children did show some evidence of balance when comparing themselves to African Americans, suggesting that positive differentiation from another disadvantaged minority might play an important role in early affective-cognitive development.

Conclusion

A developmental test of implicit social cognition in a disadvantaged minority led to several broad conclusions and generated new questions for further study. First, the in-group preference seen so robustly in adult members of a wide range of groups is absent in adult Hispanic Americans when they compare their group to White Americans. This finding replicates past results reported with African American adults, suggesting that the result is not particular to African Americans but may be the norm for disadvantaged racial or ethnic groups. What is more, this pattern has its genesis in early childhood; 5- and 6-year-old Hispanic children also showed no overall preference for their in-group as compared to the White majority. We regard these data as showing that the internalization of societal knowledge and attitudes about the relative status of social groups happens quite early in minority children, working to moderate in-group bias. This is an important difference from our findings with majority populations, in which young children as well as adults show strong preference for their racial in-group (Baron & Banaji, 2006; Dunham et al., 2006). That said, when comparing themselves to another disadvantaged minority, both children and adults showed strong preference for their in-group. Thus, while the minority in-group is not viewed more positively than the majority out-group, it *is* considerably more positive than at least one other minority out-group. Thus, the social status of the comparison group appears to play a central role.

Similarly, young Hispanic children implicitly identified equally with their in-group and the White majority, but identified more strongly with their in-group than the other minority group, again evidencing early internalization of social status information. Interestingly, older children and adults *do* begin to identify more with their own group even when compared to the White majority. That is, despite not developing more positive *attitudes* towards their own group, patterns of *identification* gradually shift, a trend that could be the result of the more integrated ethnic identity that develops in adolescence (e.g., see Phinney, 1989). An anonymous reviewer also suggests the intriguing possibility that, for our younger participants, ethnic categorization might rely primarily on skin color, in which case White and Hispanic might not always be distinct, given both a potential assimilative motive to identify with the dominant group, and the fact that some of our participants were relatively light-skinned. In older children, the social and political aspects of ethnicity may become more prominent, increasing the motivation to identify with the ethnic in-group over and above the White majority. If so, Hispanic subgroups of African heritage might display a quite different pattern of early identifications.

Broadly speaking, our pattern of results is interpretable via social identity theory (SIT; Tajfel & Turner, 1979, 1986). SIT argues that we seek to emphasize positive aspects of the social groups to which we belong so as to then benefit from those memberships in terms of increased self-esteem. In the case of disadvantaged minorities, prevailing social negativity (or prevailing positivity towards the majority) may disrupt the formation of positive attitudes towards the in-group. This could make the process described by SIT of much less utility, because in the absence of positive in-group attitude, self-esteem cannot be bolstered via identification with that group. In other words, SIT provides a complimentary model to balanced identity, explaining why we might often see integration of self-esteem and group attitudes and affiliations; it may also explain why we don't see cognitive balance in members of the minority.

While it may be tempting to suggest that the lack of balance should be interpreted as a negative, this conclusion would not be warranted. First, the conditions under which balance does and does not form are not yet fully understood. For example, men, who have higher status than women, do not show balance with respect to gender attitudes (whereas women do; Rudman & Goodwin, 2004). Second, given that our participants maintained positive self-esteem, it is equally possible that this "lack" of balance is an optimal strategy for children growing up in a setting in which their group identity is disparaged. In other words, the self-esteem of members of the minority may be protected, in part, precisely because it is not contingent on the positive distinctiveness of an ethnic in-group identity. The notion that children actively seek adaptive pathways to optimal development is an exciting direction in developmental psychology (e.g., Fischer, Ayoub, & Singh, 1997), and could be further explored in this context.

Our results suggest that understanding the complex interplay of implicit self constructs will require considerable work with non-majority populations, who may represent an important test case for the generality of theoretical models (e.g., the factors influencing cognitive balance may be more complex in minority, compared with majority, populations, and the principles underlying social identity theory may be less applicable). We would also argue that further developmental work is required to tease apart the ramifications of declining balance in childhood and adulthood for minority populations, and to investigate the onset and prevalence of assimilation of cultural information. A better understanding of these processes can contribute to both our theoretical understanding of the role of implicit social constructs across the lifespan and our practical knowledge of when and how change occurs in children's cognitive representations of themselves and their world.

Notes

1. It is possible that the lack of parallel structure across our implicit and explicit measures could limit our ability to detect correlations between them (Hofmann, Gawronski, & Gschwendner, 2005). Developing a more parallel measure of explicit self-esteem may be an important task for future research.

2. We have conducted extensive pilot testing, including several independent data collections comparing the child IAT to the standard IAT, to confirm that this scoring method is appropriate and the child IAT is closely related to the adult IAT. The method described here produces effect size estimates in adults that are of equivalent magnitude and highly correlated with effect sizes from the standard adult IAT.

3. Greenwald and Farnham (2000) and Rudman et al. (2001) were conducted prior to the development of the revised IAT scoring algorithm, and thus results reported in those papers were based on Cohen's d rather than the revised IAT effect size measure D. To allow rough comparisons with our analyses, which employed the revised algorithm, we converted Cohen's d to the IAT D measure using the formula provided in Nosek and Sriram (in press).

References

Aberson, C. L., Healy, M., & Romero, V. (2000). In-group bias and self-esteem: A meta-analysis. *Personality and Social Psychology Review, 4*(2), 157–173.

Aboud, F. (1988). *Children and prejudice.* New York: Basil Blackwell.

Banaji, M. R. (2001). Implicit attitudes can be measured. In H. L. Roediger, III, J. S. Nairne, I. Neath, & A. M. Surprenant (Eds.), *The nature of remembering: Essays in honor of Robert G. Crowder* (pp. 117–150). Washington, DC: APA.

Baron, A. S., & Banaji, M. R. (2006). The development of implicit attitudes: Evidence of race evaluations from ages 6, 10 & adulthood. *Psychological Science, 17*(1), 53–58.

Baron, A. S., Dunham, Y., & Banaji, M. R. (2005, April). *The development of implicit gender attitudes.* Poster presented at the Biennial Conference of the Society for Research in Child Development, Atlanta, GA, USA.

Baron, A. S., Shusterman, A., Bordeaux, A., & Banaji, M. R. (2004). *Implicit race attitudes in African American and Hispanic children.* Poster presented at the 5th Annual Meeting of the Society for Personality and Social Psychology, Austin, TX, USA.

Clark, K. B., & Clark, M. K. (1939). The development of consciousness of self and the emergence of racial identification of Negro preschool children. *Journal of Social Psychology, 10,* 591–599.

Crocker, J., & Major, B. (1989). Social stigma and self-esteem: The self-protective properties of stigma. *Psychological Review, 96*(4), 608–630.

Cunningham, W. A., Preacher, K. J., & Banaji, M. R. (2001). Implicit attitude measures: Consistency, stability, and convergent validity. *Psychological Science, 12*(2), 163–170.

Dunham, Y., Baron, A. S., & Banaji, M. R. (2006). From American city to Japanese village: A cross-cultural investigation of implicit race attitudes. *Child Development, 77,* 1268–1281.

Eisenberg, N., Losoya, S., & Guthrie, I. K. (1997). Social cognition and prosocial development. In S. Hala (Ed.), *The development of social cognition.* Hove, UK: Psychology Press.

Fischer, K. W., Ayoub, C., & Singh, I. (1997). Psychopathology as adaptive development along distinctive pathways. *Development and Psychopathology, 9*(4), 729–748.

Gray-Little, B., & Hafdahl, A. R. (2000). Factors influencing racial comparisons of self-esteem: A quantitative review. *Psychological Bulletin, 126,* 26–54.

Greenwald, A. G., & Banaji, M. R. (1995). Implicit social cognition: Attitudes, self-esteem, and stereotypes. *Psychological Review, 102*(1), 4–27.

Greenwald, A. G., Banaji, M. R., Rudman, L. A., Farnham, S. D., Nosek, B. A., & Mellott, D. S. (2002). A unified theory of implicit attitudes, stereotypes, self-esteem, and self-concept. *Psychological Review, 109*(1), 3–25.

Greenwald, A. G., & Farnham, S. D. (2000). Using the Implicit Association Test to measure self-esteem and self-concept. *Journal of Personality and Social Psychology, 79*(6), 1022–1038.

Greenwald, A. G., McGhee, D. E., & Schwartz, J. L. K. (1998). Measuring individual differences in implicit cognition: The Implicit Association Test. *Journal of Personality and Social Psychology, 74*(6), 1464–1480.

Greenwald, A. G., & Nosek, B. A. (2001). Health of the Implicit Association Test at age 3. *Zeitschrift Für Experimentelle Psychologie, 48*(2), 85–93.

Greenwald, A. G., Nosek, B. A., & Banaji, M. R. (2003). Understanding and using the Implicit Association Test: I. An improved scoring algorithm. *Journal of Personality & Social Psychology, 85*(2), 197–216.

Heider, F. (1958). *The psychology of interpersonal relations.* New York: Wiley.

Jackson, J. W. (2002). Intergroup attitudes as a function of different dimensions of group identification and perceived intergroup conflict. *Self and Identity, 1*(1), 11–33.

Jost, J. T., & Banaji, M. R. (1994). The role of stereotyping in system-justification and the production of false consciousness. *British Journal of Social Psychology, 33,* 1–27.

Jost, J. T., Banaji, M. R., & Nosek, B. A. (2004). A decade of system justification theory: Accumulated evidence of conscious and unconscious bolstering of the status quo. *Political Psychology, 25,* 881–919.

Jost, J. T., & Burgess, D. (2000). Attitudinal ambivalence and the conflict between group and system justification motives in low status groups. *Personality and Social Psychology Bulletin, 26*, 293–305.

Harter, S. (2001). *The construction of the self: A developmental perspective.* New York: Guilford Press.

Hofmann, W., Gawronski, B., & Gschwendner, T. (2005). A meta-analysis on the correlation between the Implicit Association Test and explicit self-report measures. *Personality and Social Psychology Bulletin, 31*(10), 1369–1385.

Lane, K. A., Mitchell, J. P., & Banaji, M. R. (2005). Me and my group: Cultural status can disrupt cognitive consistency. *Social Cognition, 23*(4), 353–386.

McGlothlin, H., Killen, M., & Edmonds, C. (2005). European American children's intergroup attitudes about peer relationships. *British Journal of Developmental Psychology, 23*(2), 227–249.

Nosek, B. A., Banaji, M. R., & Greenwald, A. G. (2002). Harvesting implicit group attitudes and beliefs from a demonstration web site. *Group Dynamics: Theory, Research, & Practice, 6*(1), 101–115.

Nosek, B. A., & Sriram, N. (in press). Criticizing others for one's own faulty assumptions: A comment on Blanton, Jaccard, Gonzales, and Christie (2006). *Journal of Experimental Social Psychology.*

Pelham, B. W., & Hetts, J. J. (1999). Implicit and explicit personal and social identity: Toward a more complete understanding of the social self. In T. R. Tyler, R. M. Kramer, & O. P. John (Eds.), *The psychology of the social self* (pp. 115–143). Mahwah, NJ: Lawrence Erlbaum Associates, Inc.

Phinney, J. S. (1989). Stages of ethnic identity development in minority group adolescents. *Journal of Early Adolescence, 9*(1–2), 34–49.

Plous, S. (2002). *Understanding prejudice and discrimination.* New York: McGraw-Hill.

Poehlman, T. A., Uhlmann, E., Greenwald, A. G., & Banaji, M. R. (2005). *Understanding and using the Implicit Association Test: III. Meta-analysis of predictive validity.* Unpublished manuscript, Yale University, New Haven, CT, USA.

Rudman, L. A. (2004). Sources of implicit attitudes. *Current Directions in Psychological Science, 13*(2), 79–82.

Rudman, L. A., & Goodwin, S. A. (2004). Gender differences in automatic in-group bias: Why do women like women more than men like men? *Journal of Personality and Social Psychology, 87*(4), 494–509.

Rudman, L. A., Greenwald, A. G., & McGhee, D. E. (2001). Implicit self-concept and evaluative implicit gender stereotypes: Self and in-group share desirable traits. *Personality and Social Psychology Bulletin, 27*(9), 1164–1178.

Rutland, A., Cameron, L., Milne, A., & McGeorge, P. (2005). Social norms and self-presentation: Children's implicit and explicit intergroup attitudes. *Child Development, 76*(2), 451–466.

Sinclair, S., Dunn, E., & Lowery, B. S. (2005). The relationship between parental racial attitudes and children's implicit prejudice. *Journal of Experimental Social Psychology, 41*(3), 283–289.

Stipek, D. J., & MacIver, D. (1989). Developmental change in children's assessment of intellectual competence. *Child Development, 60*, 521–538.

Tajfel, H., & Turner, J. C. (1979). An integrative theory of intergroup conflict. In W. G. Austin & S. Worchel (Eds.), *The social psychology of intergroup relations.* Monterey, CA: Brooks/Cole.

Tajfel, H., & Turner, J. C. (1986). The social identity theory of intergroup behavior. In S. Worchel & W. G. Austin (Eds.), *The psychology of intergroup relations.* Chicago: Nelson/Hall.

Tropp, L. R., & Wright, S. C. (2003). Evaluations and perceptions of self, in-group, and out-group: Comparisons between Mexican American and European American children. *Self and Identity, 2*, 203–221.

Valk, A. (2000). Ethnic identity, ethnic attitudes, self-esteem and esteem toward others among Estonian and Russian adolescents. *Journal of Adolescent Research, 15*(6), 637–651.

Verkuyten, M. (2005). The puzzle of high self-esteem among ethnic minorities: Comparing explicit and implicit self-esteem. *Self and Identity, 4,* 177–192.

Verkuyten, M., & Thijs, J. (2002). Racist victimization among children in the Netherlands: The effect of ethnic group and school. *Ethnic and Racial Studies, 25,* 310–331.

Weyant, J. M. (2005). Implicit stereotyping of Hispanics: Development and validity of a Hispanic version of the Implicit Association Test. *Hispanic Journal of Behavioral Sciences, 27*(3), 355–363.

Yamaguchi, S., Greenwald, A. G., Banaji, M. R., Murakami, F., Chen, D., Shiomura, K., et al. (2006). *Comparisons of implicit and explicit self-esteem among Chinese, Japanese, and North American university students.* Unpublished manuscript, University of Tokyo, Japan.

Appendix

Experimental stimuli

Child IAT Category Stimuli

Category	Stimuli
Positive traits	good (bueno/a), happy (feliz), nice (simpático/a), fun (divertido/a)
Negative traits	bad (malo/a), mad (enojado/a), mean (antipático/a), yucky (fuchi)
Self words	me (mi), I (yo), myself (mimismo/a), my (mía)
Other words	them (sus), they (ellos/as), themselves (ellos/as mismos/as), their (suyos/as)
Hispanic	Color facial photographs
African American	Color facial photographs
White	Color facial photographs

Explicit Self-esteem Questions

1. How much do you like yourself? (¿Cuánto te quieres a tí mismo?)
2. How much do other people like you? (¿Qué tan bien le caes a otras personas?)
3. How good are you at games? (¿Qué tan bueno eres para los juegos?)
4. How good are you at school? (¿Qué tan bueno eres para la escuela?)

Self and Identity, 6: 256–277, 2007
http://www.psypress.com/sai
ISSN: 1529-8868 print/1529-8876 online
DOI: 10.1080/15298860601118710

College Education and Motherhood as Components of Self-concept: Discrepancies between Implicit and Explicit Assessments

THIERRY DEVOS
PRISCILA DIAZ
ERIN VIERA
ROGER DUNN

San Diego State University, San Diego, California, USA

Three studies examined the explicit and implicit self-concepts of college women. Participants completed self-report measures and implicit association tests measuring identification with the concepts "college education" and "motherhood." Explicitly, participants identified more with college education than with motherhood. Implicitly, however, participants identified more with motherhood than with college education. The dissociation between mean levels of explicit and implicit identifications was more pronounced for students without children than for mothers (Study 2). In line with principles of affective – cognitive consistencies, the more motherhood was linked to the self, the stronger the correlation between attitude toward motherhood and self-esteem (Study 3). The findings show a clear discrepancy between explicit and implicit self-knowledge and reveal that motherhood plays a more important role in the self-concept of undergraduate women than self-reports would suggest.

Decades of social and political effort have increased the access to career pathways for women. These expanded opportunities have been additions to, not substitutions for, plans for motherhood. Women who pursue a college education face what has been termed the "motherhood mandate," "superwoman syndrome," and the "do-both syndrome" (Baber & Monaghan, 1988; Herrera & DelCampo, 1995; Vasquez, 1982). A flurry of research in the 1980s explored the potential burden of widening horizons for young women. University-aged women reported some apprehension about balancing dual roles but they hoped to make it possible by delaying childbirth for a few years after starting a career, taking time off from work for childbirth, and sharing the parenting duties with their husbands (Baber & Monaghan, 1988; cf. Spade & Reese, 1991). Motherhood, while no longer perceived as prerequisite for

This research was supported in part by National Institute of Mental Health Grant 5T34MH 65183. Portions of this research were presented at the 6th Annual Meeting of the Society for Personality and Social Psychology, New Orleans, Louisiana, January 2005; at the 84th Annual Convention of the Western Psychological Association, Phoenix, Arizona, April 2004; and at the 7th Annual Meeting of the Society for Personality and Social Psychology, Palm Springs, California, January 2006.

Correspondence should be addressed to: Thierry Devos, Department of Psychology, San Diego State University, 5500 Campanile Drive, San Diego, CA 92182–4611, USA. E-mail: tdevos@sciences.sdsu.edu happiness, was still a treasured adult role (Hare-Mustin, Bennett, & Broderick, 1983; Knaub, Eversoll, & Voss, 1983).

Having it all—motherhood and a career—has not become notably easier in the years since these assessments. Childbirth is now delayed and family leave is longer and more readily available (Kamerman & Gatenio, 2003), but parenting is still regarded as a gendered talent and a gendered obligation. Young women continue to struggle to achieve their career goals without sacrificing fulfillment of a mothering role (Gorman & Fritzsche, 2002; Hoffnung, 2004). Undergraduate women still plan to focus on educational and career goals for the immediate future with long-term plans to be mothers. The difference is that young women today report less concern about combining motherhood and career; the goal of "superwoman" has become the norm (Hoffnung, 2004). In the United States of America, women's undergraduate enrollment has increased more than twice as rapidly as men's in the last 30 years and the trend is expected to continue (US Department of Education, National Center for Education Statistics, 2005).

The present research examined the extent to which academic and family aspirations were incorporated into the self-concept of college women. Since at least the 1970s, the self has been profitably conceptualized as a structure of social knowledge (Kihlstrom & Cantor, 1984; Kihlstrom & Klein, 1994). An important portion of self-knowledge can be represented as a network of associations. From this theoretical vantage point, a self-concept is the association of the self with one or more attribute concepts. Pioneer investigations have revealed that some of these associative links are not necessarily available to consciousness or under volitional control (Bargh, 1982; Bargh & Tota, 1988; Higgins, Van Hook, & Dorfman, 1988; Markus, 1977; Rogers, Kuiper, & Kirker, 1977; Strauman & Higgins, 1987). Advances in the study of implicit social cognition have provided new paradigms to study these facets of the self-concept that are marked by a lack of conscious awareness, control, intention, or self-reflection (see Devos & Banaji, 2003; Greenwald & Banaji, 1995, for reviews). Recently developed techniques allow researchers to assess the direction and the strength of implicit associations between concepts such as self, social groups, or attributes (Greenwald & Farnham, 2000; Greenwald et al., 2002; Nosek, Banaji, & Greenwald, 2002b).

Implicit measures are particularly informative when they reveal a reality different than evident in the responses based on more deliberative processes. Evidence for reduced sexism, eroding gender roles and stereotypes, and increased acceptance of traditionally masculine traits in women's self-concepts are based to a large extent on self-report data (Diekman & Eagly, 2000; Diekman, Eagly, Mladinic, & Ferreira, 2005; Harris & Firestone, 1998; Spence & Hahn, 1997; Twenge, 1997a, 1997b). In contrast, implicit assessments of gender stereotypes show the pervasive influences of traditional gender roles (Banaji & Hardin, 1996; Blair & Banaji, 1996; Blair, Ma, & Lenton, 2001; Rudman, Greenwald, & McGhee, 2001). For example, although women elicit overall a more positive attitude than do men (Rudman & Goodwin, 2004), female authority figures elicit negative implicit attitudes from both men and women (Rudman & Kilianski, 2000). Even outside the realm of gender relations, beliefs and attitudes bolstering the status quo are more readily observable at the implicit level (Devos & Banaji, 2005; Jost, Banaji, & Nosek, 2004; Jost, Pelham, & Carvallo, 2002; Nosek, Banaji, & Greenwald, 2002a; Rudman, Feinberg, & Fairchild, 2002).

The present research attempts to provide information about these elements of self-concept that may not be documented using self-report measures. In the literature, the term *implicit* is often used to imply unconsciousness or lack of awareness. A review of the available evidence regarding unconscious features of indirect measures suggests that this meaning is adequate with regard to a lack of impact awareness, but it should not be interpreted as a lack of content or source awareness (Gawronski, Hofmann, & Wilbur, 2006). In the present line of research, the term *implicit* is used in reference to associations that cannot be consciously manipulated. The Implicit Association Test (IAT; Greenwald, McGhee, & Schwartz, 1998) was used in the series of studies presented here to assess implicit identification with the concepts "college education" and "motherhood" in undergraduate women. This technique is based on the assumption that the strength of associations between various concepts can be revealed by the ease with which participants discriminate (or pair) stimuli representing these concepts under different conditions. For example, if it is easier for someone to combine self-related words with pictures representing the concept "college education" than to pair the same self-related words with pictures linked to the concept "motherhood," it would suggest that this person identifies more strongly with college education than with motherhood. In line with a substantial body of research (Banaji, 2001; Devos & Banaji, 2003; Fazio & Olson, 2003), we capitalized on the fact that this technique, by definition, does not require introspective access and minimizes the role of conscious control. There is ample evidence that: (1) participants have much less control over their responses on the IAT than on self-report measures, and (2) the controllability of their responses on this task is minimal when they have limited experience with the technique and are not provided specific instructions on how to modify their IAT score (Greenwald & Nosek, 2001; Nosek, Greenwald, & Banaji, in press).

In responses reflecting deliberate processes, college women may not stress the importance of motherhood because they are committed to their academic goals or because they feel pressured to live up to contemporary expectations of women. Revealing their aspirations to become mothers would not be consistent with their conscious values and beliefs. Their aspiration to become mothers may, however, become evident on measures tapping self-knowledge that is less consciously controllable. Measures that do not require introspective access are particularly suitable to reveal cultural or environmental influences that contrast with principles of equality or social justice and justify existing social arrangements (Devos & Banaji, 2005; Jost et al., 2004). Directly relevant to the present research, Nosek et al. (2002a) found robust implicit associations of male with career and female with family. Self-report measures revealed slightly weaker links between gender categories and these concepts. Moreover, women showed a stronger effect than men on the IAT, but a weaker effect than men on the explicit measure. In sum, women endorsed a less gender-stereotypic definition of social roles than men at the explicit level, but they displayed stronger deviations from their convictions at the implicit level.

Given the changing role expectations of men in our society, discrepancies between explicit and implicit self-knowledge might also be revealed among men pursuing a college degree. This being said, the pressure to balance parental and academic aspirations remains greater for women than for men. At this stage of the research process, we deemed it more important to document discrepancies between explicit and implicit self-concepts in college women rather than to investigate potential gender differences in the identification with "college education" and "parenthood." This deliberate decision does not imply that issues tackled in this research do not affect men.

Study 1: Discrepancies between Explicit and Implicit Self-Concepts

Study 1 investigated potential discrepancies between the explicit and implicit self-concepts of women who were attending a large, ethnically diverse southwestern university. On explicit assessments, we predicted that women currently pursuing a college degree would express a stronger identification with college education than with motherhood. Thus, responses based on deliberative processes should reflect that college women define themselves as academically oriented rather than aspiring to become mothers. A variety of self-report measures were used to assess the extent to which these concepts were incorporated in the explicit self-concept of college women. The potential contributions of college education and motherhood in the implicit self-concept were assessed using the IAT. The contrast between college education and motherhood framed these representations as competing self-definitions in order to provide a direct test of the relative strength of these identifications. We predicted that undergraduate women would demonstrate a difficulty associating the self with the concept "college education" when this concept is contrasted with the concept "motherhood." In other words, implicit responses were expected to deviate from explicit responses such that a more traditional self-definition would be produced when conscious control is relatively unavailable.

Method

Participants

Participants were 77 college undergraduate women at San Diego State University attending the main campus located in San Diego.[1] Participants received partial course credit for their participation. The sample included 45 European Americans, 10 Latinas, 6 African Americans, 5 Asian Americans, 4 Filipinas, and 7 individuals of multiethnic background. Participants' ages ranged from 18 to 32 years old; the median age was 20 years old. Only two participants were married. Participants were asked to indicate the number of years until they planned to have children. Estimates ranged from 2 to 19 years, with a median value of 6 years. Only 6 participants considered having children within the next 4 years.

Stimuli

A preliminary study was conducted to select pictorial stimuli representing the concepts "college education" and "motherhood." A large set of potential stimuli was submitted to a sample of 24 female college students (15 Latinas and 9 European Americans). Participants were asked to rate the extent to which each image was associated with the concepts "college education" or "motherhood" on 7-point scales ranging from "*not at all*" to "*very much.*" Participants were also asked to indicate, as quickly as possible, whether they associated these pictures with the two target concepts. Based on these data, we created two sets of pictures that could be categorized easily and unambiguously. The first set included eight pictures strongly linked to the concept "college education" ($M = 6.56$, $SD = 0.60$) and weakly linked to the concept "motherhood" ($M = 2.13$, $SD = 1.54$): a backpack, binders, a computer lab, a student studying, and four graduation pictures (e.g., cap and gown ceremony). The second set included eight pictures strongly linked to the concept "motherhood" ($M = 6.65$, $SD = 0.48$) and weakly linked to the concept "college education" ($M = 1.24$, $SD = 0.59$): a crib, a baby bottle, a hand of a baby, a mother pushing a carriage, and four pictures of a mother with her child. In line with previous research (Bosson, Swann, & Pennebaker, 2000; Greenwald & Farnham, 2000), five pronouns or terms that were self-relevant (I, me, mine, my, self) and five pronouns or terms that designate other people (they, them, their, it, people) were used to represent, respectively, the concepts "me" and "not-me."

Procedure

Participants were seated individually in front of a desktop computer in a small room with four computers. The computers were separated by partitions to ensure privacy. After giving their informed consent, participants completed implicit and explicit measures administered on PCs running Inquisit (Draine, 1998). Although it is possible that the order in which implicit and explicit measures are completed could influence participants' responses to the IAT or to the questionnaire portion of the study, previous research indicates that such order effects in most circumstances are minimal. A systematic manipulation of task order produced little to no effect in large web-based studies (Nosek, Greenwald, & Banaji, 2005). A similar conclusion can be drawn based on a recent meta-analysis of IAT studies (Hofmann, Gawronski, Gschwendner, Le, & Schmidt, 2005).

Initial presentation of pictorial stimuli. First, to acquaint participants with the pictorial stimuli used to represent the concepts "college education" and "motherhood," each stimulus was presented in the center of the screen for 2000 ms under the appropriate label. Participants were instructed to watch the stimuli carefully. The order of presentation of the eight stimuli within each category was randomized across participants.

Implicit self-concept. Participants completed an IAT assessing the strength of identification with the concepts "college education" and "motherhood." Stimuli were presented sequentially at the center of the computer screen. Participants were asked to categorize, as quickly as possible, each stimulus by pressing a key that was either toward the left or the right of the keyboard. Response times were recorded from the onset of a stimulus to its correct classification. Correct responses terminated a trial and the inter-trial interval was 400 ms. Labels for the concepts were positioned at the top left and top right of the screen to indicate the requested pairing. If a stimulus was incorrectly classified, a red "X" appeared below the stimulus. Participants then had to provide the correct answer to move on to the next trial. The single categorization blocks included 20 trials. Each double categorization block included 20 practice trials and 40 test trials. In one of the double categorization blocks, participants were asked to categorize "me" words and "college education" pictures on one side and "not-me" words and "motherhood" pictures on the other side. The opposite pairing was presented in the other double categorization block. This time, "me" words would be combined with "motherhood" images and "not-me" words would share the same response option as "college education" images. Stimuli were selected alternately from each pair of concepts. The order of the critical blocks was counterbalanced across participants.[2]

Explicit self-concept. Next, participants completed a series of explicit measures. First, the extent to which participants explicitly identified with college education and motherhood was assessed using four comparative statements. Participants were asked to indicate on 7-point scales: (1) To what extent college education or motherhood was more important to them; (2) Whether they valued college education or motherhood more; (3) To what extent getting a college degree or becoming a mother was more important to them; and (4) Whether they valued attending college or raising a family more. The two end-points of the scales expressed the idea that one alternative was *much more* important to them than the other or that they value one option *much more* than the other. The mid-point of the scale expressed the idea that both alternatives were equally important or valued (e.g., "College education and motherhood are *equally* important to me").

Participants also completed two scales assessing independently their identification with college education and motherhood. Given the lack of instruments allowing us to compare the strength of these identifications, scales were developed specifically for this research. Many items were adapted from a scale assessing aspirations to attend graduate school (Battle & Wigfield, 2003). Sample items for the scale measuring identification with college education included: "When I think about getting a college degree I feel good about myself"; "I would be very upset if I did not graduate from college"; "I find the idea of being a college graduate to be very appealing"; and "I don't need a college degree to fulfill my potential" (reversed item). Symmetric items for the scale assessing identification with motherhood were: "When I think about wanting to raise a family I feel good about myself"; "I would be very upset if I did not start a family of my own"; "I find the idea of being a mother to be very appealing"; and "I don't need to be a mother to fulfill my potential" (reversed item). Responses were provided on 7-point scales ranging from "*strongly disagree*" to "*strongly agree.*" Each scale included 15 items. The order of the 30 items was randomized across participants.

In addition, participants were asked to indicate to what extent they identified with the pictorial stimuli used in the IAT. They were told that we were interested in the extent to which certain images are important to them or represent who they are. The 16 stimuli were presented, one by one, in the middle of the screen. The question: "To what extent does this image represent an aspect of your self-concept?" appeared below the stimuli and responses were provided on 7-point scales ranging from "*not at all*" to "*completely.*" The order of presentation of the stimuli was randomized across participants.

Demographic information. Participants completed a short demographic questionnaire that included items such as ethnicity, gender, and age. Finally, participants were debriefed and thanked for their participation.

Results and Discussion

Explicit Self-concept

First, we examined the extent to which participants explicitly identified with college education and motherhood. The four comparative statements were aggregated ($\alpha = .84$). A one-sample t-test revealed that the mean was significantly below the mid-point of the scale, $M = 3.53$, $SD = 1.21$, $t(75) = -3.37$, $p < .002$, $d = 0.39$, suggesting that participants identified more strongly with college education than with motherhood. Responses on the multi-item scales were also aggregated ($\alpha = .86$ for college education and $\alpha = .91$ for motherhood). A paired samples t-test indicated that participants identified more with college education ($M = 4.22$, $SD = 0.54$) than with motherhood ($M = 3.45$, $SD = 0.72$), $t(75) = 7.68$, $p < .001$, $d = 0.88$. Finally, the extent to which participants considered that the pictorial stimuli represented an important aspect of their self-concept was examined. The ratings were aggregated for each set of eight pictures ($\alpha = .90$ for college education and $\alpha = .96$ for motherhood). A paired samples *t*-test indicated that participants identified more strongly with pictorial stimuli representing college education ($M = 5.84$, $SD = 1.05$) than with images associated with motherhood ($M = 3.84$, $SD = 1.79$), $t(75) = 8.79$, $p < .001$, $d = 1.01$.

Implicit Self-concept

IAT data were analyzed following the algorithm recommended by Greenwald, Nosek, and Banaji (2003). Data from one participant were discarded because she responded at a rate faster than 300 ms on more than 10% of the trials, leaving 76 participants for analysis.[3] The difference between the mean response latency for the two double categorization blocks, divided by the associated pooled standard deviation, was computed. This quotient was computed separately for the practice and test trials; the two values were then averaged. In the present case, this index (IAT *D*) reflects the direction and the strength of identification with college education relative to motherhood. As recommended by Greenwald et al. (2003), statistical analyses were performed on this index. A one sample *t*-test showed that the self + motherhood association was stronger than the self + college education association, $M = -0.15$, $SD = 0.40$, $t(75) = -3.38$, $p < .002$, $d = 0.39$. In other words, participants categorized "me" words significantly faster with "motherhood" stimuli than with "college education" stimuli.

On all the explicit measures, participants reported that college education was clearly more important to them than motherhood. In contrast to these reports, participants implicitly identified more with motherhood than with college education. This pattern of results revealed a clear dissociation between mean levels of explicit and implicit identifications. Academic aspirations were a more central aspect of college women's explicit self-concept. Family aspirations, however, prevailed in the assessment of self-knowledge operating outside of conscious control. It should be noted that comparing the direction of effects obtained on the IAT and on self-reports assumes that the metric of these measures is meaningful (see Greenwald, Nosek, & Sriram, 2006a; Greenwald, Rudman, Nosek, & Zayas, 2006b; cf. Blanton & Jaccard, 2006a, 2006b). On the IAT developed for the present research, zero values were taken to indicate the absence of a difference in strength of the me + college education vs. not-me + motherhood associations and the me + motherhood vs. not-me + college education associations. Similarly, responses located on the mid-point of the scale on the comparative statements or difference scores of zero for the other explicit measures were taken as evidence for the absence of a difference in strength of identification with college education and motherhood.

Correlations between implicit and explicit measures were significant, but relatively weak. The IAT was positively correlated with the comparative statements ($r = +.30$, $p < .02$), with the multi-item scales ($r = +.28$, $p < .02$), and with the ratings of the stimuli ($r = +.26$, $p < .03$).[4] These relatively weak correlations suggest that implicit and explicit measures were tapping distinct constructs, but they should be interpreted with caution because the small sample size prevented us from correcting for measurement error (Cunningham, Preacher, & Banaji, 2001).

The concepts and the stimuli used to represent the concepts are not independent of the feminine – masculine distinction. Obviously, the concept "motherhood" is linked to the category "women" to a greater extent than the concept "college education." However, this observation does not account for discrepancies between explicit and implicit self-concepts. The important conclusion that can be drawn from this study is that traditional gender roles may have shaped self-definitions to a greater extent than self-reports would suggest. A gendered role (motherhood) was strongly linked to the self at the implicit level, but its importance was less apparent in assessments based on more deliberative processes.

Study 2: Aspiring to Motherhood versus Being a Mother

The second study focused on potential discrepancies between implicit and explicit self-definitions in women attending a two-year upper-division university campus in a rural area along the US – Mexico border. Many of the students on this campus are mothers, affording us the opportunity to compare the self-concepts of students with and without children. Students who have children are currently and constantly balancing the identities and responsibilities of students and mothers, whereas motherhood may be viewed as only a long-term goal for students with no children. As a result, students who have children should be more likely to report that motherhood is an important aspect of their self-concept than students for whom motherhood is a more distant prospect. The saliency and accessibility of this role should facilitate an explicit self-concept aligned with motherhood.

The setting for this study also allowed us to investigate the generality of the findings from Study 1. Unlike the predominantly European American sample in the first study, most of the students on this campus are Mexican American. This difference in ethnicity, combined with the rural setting for Study 2, suggests that these women are likely to feel greater pressure to marry and focus on the role of being a wife, mother, and daughter regardless of other goals (Niemann, Romero, & Arbona, 2000). From this perspective, Mexican American women are more likely to define themselves along traditional gender roles rather than based on professional or career goals. On the other hand, the pressures on Mexican American women appear to be changing, at least overtly, with more emphasis on equity in the home driven by the need to work outside the home to maintain an adequate family income (Herrera & DelCampo, 1995). The fact that these women are currently pursuing their education beyond the community college level means that they, like the students in the first study, may display discrepancies between implicit and explicit identification with the concepts "college education" and "motherhood."

Employing the procedures used in the first study, this second study assessed explicit and implicit self-knowledge about college education and motherhood. Students who were mothers were expected to be more cognizant of and willing to report the importance of motherhood in their self-concept, reducing the difference between the results of explicit and implicit measures. Students who were not mothers were expected to show the pattern of results obtained in the first study, i.e., explicit alignment with college education and implicit alignment with motherhood.

Method

Participants

Participants were 59 college undergraduate women at San Diego State University attending a small (900 students) satellite campus located in Calexico, approximately 120 miles east of San Diego and a few blocks from the international border. Participants received partial course credit for their participation. The sample included 50 Latinas, 6 European Americans, 1 Filipina, and 2 individuals of multi-ethnic background. Participants' ages ranged from 18 to 46 years old; the median age was 23 years old. Of the participants, 21 were mothers and 18 were married. Participants who had no children were asked to indicate the number of years until they planned to have children. Estimates ranged from 1 to 15 years, with a median value of 4 years. For the purpose of analysis, participants were compared as a function of whether they were mothers ($n = 21$), planned on having children within 4 years or less ($n = 20$), or within more than 4 years ($n = 18$). We will refer to this variable as participants' motherhood status.

Procedure

The procedure was identical to that of Study 1 with the exceptions that sessions were run in a classroom equipped with 24 computers and the data were gathered in three sessions.

Results and Discussion

Data were aggregated and analyzed following the steps described for Study 1, but the main focus of Study 2 was to examine the impact of participants' motherhood status on their explicit and implicit self-concepts. Not surprisingly, students who had children were older than students who had no children, $F(2, 56) = 20.92, p < .001$, $\eta^2 = .43$. Participants' age was introduced as a covariate in analyses of variance because it could be argued that the impact of age on women's biology is likely to strengthen identification with motherhood. Means and standard deviations as a function of participants' motherhood status are reported for each measure in Table 1.

Explicit Self-concept

On the explicit measure assessing the relative identification with college education and motherhood ($\alpha = .90$), an analysis of variance (ANOVA) revealed a highly significant effect of participants' motherhood status, $F(2, 55) = 6.25, p < .005, \eta^2 = .19$ (see Comparative statements in Table 1). Pairwise comparisons[5] indicated that students who had children identified more strongly with motherhood than with college education, $t(20) = 4.36, p < .001, d = 0.95$, whereas students who planned on having children in more than four years identified more strongly with college

TABLE 1 Means and Standard Deviations for Explicit and Implicit Self-Concepts, Study 2

	Participants' motherhood status					
	Mothers > 4 years ($n = 18$)		Mothers 0–4 years ($n = 20$)		Mothers ($n = 21$)	
Measure	M	SD	M	SD	M	SD
Comparative statements	2.74a	1.66	3.74	1.19	4.82b	0.86
Ratings of college education stimuli	6.62	0.39	6.16	0.95	6.14	0.83
Ratings of motherhood stimuli	3.63a	2.24	4.37a	2.40	6.47b	0.77
Implicit Association Test	−0.16a	0.26	−0.07a	0.32	−0.34b	0.38

Note: For each measure, means in the same row with different subscripts are reliably different ($p < .05$) using the Bonferroni adjustment procedure.

education than with motherhood, $t(17) = -3.23$, $p < .006$, $d = 0.76$. Students who considered having children within the next four years indicated that both identities were equally important to them, $t(19) = -0.99$, $p > .30$, $d = 0.22$, but they differed significantly from students who had children.[6]

An ANOVA performed on the ratings of the pictorial stimuli ($\alpha = .84$ for college education and $\alpha = .98$ for motherhood) revealed a highly significant interaction between participants' motherhood status and target concepts, $F(2, 55) = 8.24$, $p < .002$, $\eta^2 = .23$ (see Ratings of stimuli in Table 1). Simple effects tests indicated that the three groups differed reliably in the extent to which participants identified with pictures representing the concept "motherhood," $F(2, 55) = 6.81$, $p < .003$, $\eta^2 = .20$, but not in the extent to which they identified with pictures representing the concept "college education," $F(2, 55) = 2.04$, $p > .14$, $\eta^2 = .07$. Students with children considered that pictures representing the concept "motherhood" reflected an important aspect of their self-concept to a greater extent than students who had no children. Students who planned on having children in more than four years, $F(1, 55) = 30.51$, $p < .001$, $\eta^2 = .36$, or within four years, $F(1, 55) = 15.66$, $p < .001$, $\eta^2 = .22$, reported a stronger identification with "college education" than with "motherhood" stimuli, while students who were mothers identified strongly and equally with both sets of stimuli, $F < 1$.

Implicit Self-concept

Once again, the self + motherhood association was stronger than the self + college education association ($M = -0.19$, $SD = 0.34$), $t(58) = -4.37$, $p < .001$, $d = 0.57$. This IAT D effect varied as a function of participants' motherhood status, $F(2, 55) = 5.62$, $p < .007$, $\eta^2 = .17$ (see Implicit Association Test in Table 1). Identification with motherhood was stronger among female college students who had children, $t(20) = -4.07$, $p < .002$, $d = 0.89$, than among female college students who planned to have children in more than four years, $t(17) = -2.62$, $p < .02$, $d = 0.62$, or within the next four years, $t(19) = -1.02$, ns, $d = 0.23$.

To compare the pattern of findings at the explicit and implicit levels, effect sizes (Cohen's d) for the comparative statements and the IAT as a function of participants' motherhood status are reported in Figure 1. A positive or negative sign was assigned to each effect size to reflect, respectively, that identification with college education was stronger or weaker than identification with motherhood. For students with no children, the pattern of findings replicated the results of Study 1. Explicitly, these participants identified more with college education than with motherhood. At the implicit level, they identified more with motherhood than with college education. Responses provided by students with children revealed greater consistencies between their explicit and implicit self-concepts. At both levels of responding, they identified more with motherhood than with college education. Women who planned to have children within four years showed an intermediate pattern.

As predicted, students with children were more cognizant of or willing to report motherhood as an important aspect of their self-concept than were students with no children. The saliency and accessibility of their maternal role fostered an explicit alignment with motherhood. A reliable difference between students with and without children also emerged on the implicit measure. This finding is consistent with existing evidence that implicit associations stem from repeated experiences in a given social or cultural context (Banaji, 2001; Devos & Banaji, 2003; Greenwald & Banaji, 1995; Rudman, 2004). Raising a child ensured a repetition of experiences strengthening the extent to which the concept "motherhood" is linked to the self. In sum, daily

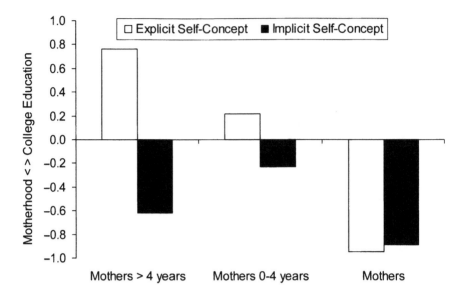

FIGURE 1 Study 2: Explicit and implicit self-concepts (Cohen's *d*) as a function of participants' motherhood status. Bar colors differentiate explicit and implicit responses. A positive effect size indicates a stronger identification with the concept "college education," whereas a negative effect size reflects a stronger identification with the concept "motherhood."

experiences influenced the extent to which the self-concept of college women was aligned with motherhood at both levels of responding.

Once again, these findings are based on a comparison of the direction of effects obtained on implicit and explicit measures. We focus on the extent to which the relative importance of college education and motherhood differs whether it is assessed at the explicit or implicit level. Bivariate correlations indicated that the IAT was positively correlated with the ratings of the stimuli ($r = +.31$, $p < .02$), but not with the comparative statements ($r = +.11$, *ns*). Correlations did not reach the traditional significance level ($p < .05$) when they were examined for each group. This is not very surprising given the small sample size. A replication of this study with a larger sample would allow us to determine whether the greater consistency between the explicit and implicit self-concept of college students who had children is also apparent in terms of a stronger positive correlation between these two levels.

Despite the differences between student populations at a large urban university and its satellite campus in a rural, largely Mexican American community, the results of this study replicated the findings in Study 1 with regard to university women who do not have children. Societal support within the community for identification with motherhood did not appear to determine self-reports; college education was chosen as the stronger component of their self-concept. At the implicit level, however, these undergraduates identified strongly with motherhood.

Study 3: Interrelations between Identification, Attitude, and Self-esteem

The first two studies focused on the extent to which college education and motherhood were incorporated into the self-concept of college women. In Study 3, we extended the scope of our investigations to examine the implicit affective connotations of these two concepts. In other words, our goal was to determine whether college women held a more positive implicit attitude toward motherhood than toward college education. As was the case for Study 2, the present study afforded us the opportunity to compare patterns of responses displayed by students who were mothers and students who had no children. More important, we examined the interrelations between self-esteem, identification with, and attitude toward college education and motherhood. Recently, Greenwald et al. (2002) proposed a unified theory that accounts for patterns of interrelations between self-esteem, self-concept, and attitude. Their approach draws its inspiration from theories of affective-cognitive consistency that dominated social psychology in the 1960s (Abelson et al., 1968). A core principle of the theory is that attitudes toward self and concepts closely associated with self (i.e., components of self-concept) tend to be of similar valence. This balance–congruity principle can be tested by examining the extent to which one of these constructs (self-esteem, identification, or attitude) can be predicted as a function of the other two. The theory posits that each construct should be a multiplicative function of the other two. For example, in the present context, college women's self-esteem should be a multiplicative function of the extent to which they identify with and value motherhood relative to college education. More precisely, for college women who strongly identify with motherhood, their liking for the concept "motherhood" should be positively correlated with their self-esteem. This could be stated as, "If motherhood is an important aspect of my self-concept and motherhood is good, then I can feel good about myself." Given the correlational nature of the data, this statement does not imply a specific causal flow between the constructs. According to the unified theory, similar results should emerge when the other constructs serve as dependent variables as well (Greenwald et al., 2002; Rudman & Goodwin, 2004). In Study 3, we tested the balance–congruity principle by examining the interrelations between identification with college education and motherhood, attitude toward these concepts, and self-esteem. These predictions were tested using only the IAT because previous research showed no systematic evidence of cognitive balance based on self-reports (Greenwald et al., 2002).

Method

Participants

Participants were 60 female college undergraduates at San Diego State University attending school on a satellite campus located in Brawley (approximately 120 miles east of San Diego). Participants received partial course credit for their participation. The sample included 52 Latinas, 4 Caucasians, 1 Filipina, 1 individual of multiethnic background, and 2 individuals who declined to report their ethnicity. Participants' age ranged from 18 to 41 years old; the median age was 22 years old. Twenty participants were mothers and 17 participants were married. Participants who had no children were asked to indicate in how many years they planned on having children. Estimates ranged from 1 to 9 years, with a median value of 4 years. For the purpose of analysis, participants were compared as a function of whether they were mothers ($n = 20$), planned on having children within 4 years or less ($n = 17$), or more than 4 years ($n = 23$).

Procedure

Participants completed a series of three IATs. The technical parameters of these tasks were identical to those described for Studies 1 and 2. The order of the IATs and the order of the combined blocks were counterbalanced across participants.

Implicit identification. Participants completed the IAT from Studies 1 and 2 assessing implicit identification with college education vs. motherhood.

Implicit attitude. To assess implicit attitude toward the concepts "college education" vs. "motherhood," we adapted a version of the IAT widely used in research on implicit attitudes (Nosek et al., in press). The evaluative dimension was operationalized using the labels "pleasant" and "unpleasant." The stimuli were ten pleasant words (rainbow, lucky, peace, joy, sunrise, pleasure, happiness, freedom, cheer, and laughter) and ten unpleasant words (agony, death, poison, grief, disaster, pain, tragedy, sorrow, hatred, and rotten) selected from published norms (Bellezza, Greenwald, & Banaji, 1986). The sixteen pictures described in Study 1 were used to represent the concepts "college education" and "motherhood." In one block of trials, participants were asked to categorize, as quickly as possible, "pleasant" and "college education" stimuli with one key and "unpleasant" and "motherhood" stimuli with another key. In another block of trials, the two pairs of concepts were combined in the opposite way: Participants were asked to categorize "pleasant" and "motherhood" stimuli with one key and "unpleasant" and "college education" stimuli with the other key.

Implicit self-esteem. Implicit self-esteem was assessed by asking participants on an IAT to categorize, as quickly as possible, "me" vs. "not-me" words and "pleasant" vs. "unpleasant" words (Bosson et al., 2000; Greenwald & Farnham, 2000). The stimuli were identical to those used in the tasks described above. In one block of trials, participants sorted, as fast as possible, "me" and "pleasant" stimuli on one side and "not-me" and "unpleasant" stimuli on the other side. In another block of trials, the opposite pairing was presented: "me" and "unpleasant" stimuli were combined and contrasted to "not-me" and "pleasant" stimuli.[7]

Results and Discussion

Data were aggregated and analyzed following the steps described for Study 2. Participants' age was introduced as a covariate in ANOVAs given that students with children were older than students who had no children, $F(2, 57) = 27.22$, $p < .001$, $\eta^2 = .49$. For each IAT, means and standard deviations as a function of participants' motherhood status are presented in Table 2.

Implicit Identification

On the identification IAT, we found once again that, overall, participants identified more strongly with motherhood than with college education, $M = -0.33$, $SD = 0.37$, $t(59) = -6.91$, $p < .001$, $d = 0.89$. This IAT D effect varied as function of participants' motherhood status, $F(2, 56) = 3.91$, $p < .03$, $\eta^2 = .12$ (see Identification in Table 2). Identification with motherhood was weaker among female college students who planned on having children in more than four years, $t(22) = -2.97$, $p < .008$, $d = 0.63$, than among female college students who already had children, $t(19) = -4.85$, $p < .001$, $d = 1.11$, or were planning on becoming mothers within the next four years, $t(16) = -4.38$, $p < .001$, $d = 1.09$.

Implicit Attitude

A significant IAT D effect was also found on the measure of implicit attitude, $M = -0.31$, $SD = 0.42$, $t(59) = -5.60$, $p < .001$, $d = 0.72$. This effect indicated that it

TABLE 2   Means and Standard Deviations for Implicit Measures, Study 3

| | Participants' motherhood status | | | | | |
| | Mothers > 4 years ($n = 23$) | | Mothers 0–4 years ($n = 17$) | | Mothers ($n = 20$) | |
Measure	M	SD	M	SD	M	SD
Identification	−0.19$_a$	0.31	−0.41	0.38	−0.41$_b$	0.38
Attitude	−0.34	0.40	−0.22	0.47	−0.34	0.42
Self-esteem	0.59	0.35	0.85	0.30	0.67	0.38

Note: For each measure, means in the same row with different subscripts are reliably different ($p < .05$) using the Bonferroni adjustment procedure.

was easier for participants to pair "pleasant" words with "motherhood" pictures and "unpleasant" words with "college education" pictures than to do the opposite. This effect was not moderated by participants' motherhood status, $F < 0.6$ (see Attitude in Table 2).

Implicit Self-esteem

Finally, performances on the IAT assessing implicit self-esteem revealed that participants held a relatively positive attitude toward the self, $M = 0.69$, $SD = 0.35$, $t(59) = 15.37$, $p < .001$, $d = 1.98$. This IAT D effect is evidence for a much stronger connection between the concepts "me" and "pleasant" than the concepts "me" and "unpleasant." Although a marginal effect of participants' motherhood status was found on this measure, $F(2, 56) = 2.67$, $p < .08$, $\eta^2 = .09$, pairwise comparisons did not reveal reliable differences between the three groups of participants (see Self-esteem in Table 2).

Balanced Identity Regression Analyses

Bivariate correlations suggested that the three IATs were tapping distinct constructs. The correlation between implicit identification and implicit attitude measures was marginal ($r = +.22$, $p < .09$) and these two tasks were not reliably correlated with the implicit self-esteem measure (respectively, $r = -.05$, *ns*, and $r = -.13$, *ns*). Following the steps described by Greenwald et al. (2002; see also Rudman & Goodwin, 2004), a series of three regression analyses was conducted to test the balance–congruity principle: self-esteem was regressed on identification, attitude, and their interaction (Model 1), attitude was regressed on identification, self-esteem, and their interaction (Model 2), and, finally, identification was regressed on attitude, self-esteem, and their interaction (Model 3). In each case, the predictors were centered and the interaction term was computed following standard practice (Aiken & West, 1991). The unified theory posits that only the interaction term should account significantly for the criterion variable. To test this proposition, the interaction term is always entered in Step 1 and the main effects are entered in Step 2. According to the theory, the interaction and the change in proportion of variance explained should be significant at Step 1. The proportion of variance explained should not increase significantly when the two main effects are entered at Step 2. Results for these analyses are presented in Table 3. As can be seen, these findings are consistent with the balance–congruity principle. For each model, the three following

TABLE 3 Regression Analyses Testing the Interrelations between Self-esteem, Identification, and Attitude, Study 3

Model	Step	β	t	ΔR^2	p
Model 1 (Self-esteem)					
Identification × Attitude	1	.32	2.56*	.10	.01
Identification × Attitude	2	.33	2.65*		
Identification	2	−.02	0.14		
Attitude	2	−.15	1.18	.02	.46
Model 2 (Attitude)					
Identification × Self-esteem	1	.32	2.81**	.12	.01
Identification × Self-esteem	2	.31	2.41*		
Identification	2	.18	1.46		
Self-esteem	2	−.02	0.18	.03	.35
Model 3 (Identification)					
Attitude × Self-esteem	1	.28	2.20*	.08	.03
Attitude × Self-esteem	2	.24	1.82		
Attitude	2	.16	1.19		
Self-esteem	2	−.04	0.34	.03	.44

Note: The criterion variable for each model is in parentheses. *$p < .05$; **$p < .01$.

predictions were supported: (1) The proportion of variance explained was significant when the interaction was entered in the model; (2) The interaction was significant; and (3) Adding the two main effects did not significantly increase the proportion of variance explained. Figure 2 illustrates the interaction between identification and attitude when self-esteem is the criterion variable. Simple slopes were examined for values reflecting a strong identification with or preference for motherhood (2 *SD* below the means) and for values corresponding to a strong identification with or preference for college education (2 *SD* above the means). The pattern suggested that, to the extent that participants identified with motherhood, a more favorable attitude toward motherhood accounted for higher self-esteem. In addition, to the extent that participants identified with college education, a more favorable attitude toward college education accounted for higher self-esteem.[8]

Once again, we found that, overall, college women implicitly identified more strongly with motherhood than with college education. In line with the findings of Study 2, this effect was moderated by motherhood status. Not surprisingly, students who had children displayed a stronger automatic association between self and motherhood (relative to college education) than students for whom motherhood was a more distant prospect. Assessments of implicit attitudes revealed that motherhood elicited more positive affects than college education. The implicit appeal of motherhood was as strong among students who were not mothers as it was among students who were currently raising children. This suggests that the IAT is tapping a positive affective reaction to a social role that is probably learned early on by young women rather than an automatic attitude grounded in current daily experiences. In other words, the automatic positivity of motherhood (relative to college education) is a reflection of what is socially constructed as a desirable role for women.

Finally, the findings indicated that the extent to which a concept was linked to the self and elicited a positive attitude accounts for students' self-esteem. As predicted, the more students valued and identified with motherhood, the higher their

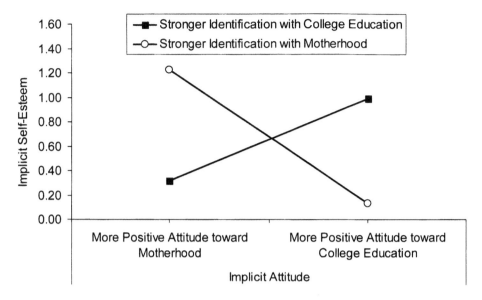

FIGURE 2   Study 3: Implicit self-esteem as a function of implicit identification and implicit attitude.

self-esteem. Once again, causal links between identification, attitude, and self-esteem should not be implied based on these correlational data. It is likely that causal relationships between these constructs are multidirectional. The important finding is that the pattern of interrelations indicates that college women possess a balanced identity. It is also important to stress that the extent to which motherhood and college education are linked to the self cannot be reduced to an attitudinal response to these concepts. Identification and attitude are distinct constructs, and their confluence accounts for implicit self-esteem. This not only supports a well-established psychological principle of affective-cognitive consistency, it also provides preliminary evidence for the predictive validity of the IATs developed specifically for the present research.

General Discussion

Taken together, the results of these three studies show that undergraduate women do not express a strong attachment to motherhood when asked about their self-concept. Leaving aside the students who were mothers for a moment, undergraduate women report stronger identification with college education than with motherhood on introspective assessments. Self-reports suggest that traditional gender roles are now less pervasive in accordance with the emphasis on educational and career opportunities for women. On the other hand, implicit assessments indicate that motherhood remains a more important component of self-concept than college education. Thus, implicit measures reveal the subtle, yet pervasive influence of traditional gender roles on the self-concept of college women. On responses reflecting deliberative processes, college women do not stress the importance of motherhood; they defined themselves in line with their current academic goals and with contemporary expectations of women. However, assessments of thoughts that cannot be consciously manipulated indicate that family aspirations are an important component of college women's self-concepts.

Multiple factors contribute to this dissociation between self-views based on introspection and self-definitions produced when conscious control is relatively unavailable. The present research was not intended to disentangle various explanatory principles. The aim of the present research was, first and foremost, to document such striking discrepancies. As predicted, stronger evidence for gender stereotypic self-definitions emerges from less consciously controllable responses than from more deliberative responses. At the explicit level, college women define themselves in line with contemporary expectations of women. Currently pursuing a college degree, they stress their academic and professional ambitions rather than their aspirations to become mothers. The fact that the studies were conducted in the college setting (i.e., participants completed the measures on campus) may have contributed to make college education a central aspect of their working self-concept. Academic goals are relatively more salient than aspirations to start a family in this context. Thus, it is particularly remarkable that, in this setting, college women automatically link the concept of self to a greater extent to motherhood than to college education. As we pointed out earlier, there is no doubt that motherhood is not a gender neutral concept; it is linked to women more so than to men. However, this observation is insufficient to account for the discrepancy between explicit and implicit self-definitions. The motherhood – women associative link should have driven the explicit and implicit measures in the same direction but identification with motherhood was revealed only on the implicit measure. The data show that thoughts operating outside of conscious control are more likely to reflect self-definitions consistent with traditional gender roles than self-report would suggest. Future studies comparing men and women and measuring the extent to which concepts such as "college education" and "parenthood" are implicitly and explicitly linked to gender categories would provide a more direct test of this account.

As expected, motherhood is the stronger component of the implicit and explicit self-concepts of students who have children. Mothers are, by definition, more likely to have considered motherhood as part of their self-concept. Moreover, the dramatic differences in social context and responsibilities between mothers and non-mothers would dictate different levels of contact with motherhood in their daily lives. As a result, students with children are more cognizant of or willing to express their attachment to the role of mother. In contrast to the discrepancies documented for students who do not have children, the explicit and implicit responses are more consistent for students who have children. These results may not be very surprising, but the stark contrast between the explicit self-concept of students who have children and students who do not have children stresses that for the latter group motherhood is not defined explicitly as a current aspiration.

The present findings may have important implications for women pursuing a higher education. The data indicate that implicit academic identification among college women might be hindered when college education and motherhood are framed as competing self-definitions. Interferences between important identities or roles have been shown to negatively impact performance and well-being (Settles, 2004; Settles, Sellers, & Damas, 2002). The relative difficulty in linking the self to the academic domain might not be the only consequence of dual aspirations. Study 3 suggests that, in comparison to college education, motherhood automatically elicits more positive affective reactions than college education. More important, the more college women link the self to motherhood, the more attitudes toward the self and toward motherhood tend to be of similar valence. Although we did not test this hypothesis at the explicit level, previous research suggests that patterns of affective – cognitive consistencies emerge more systematically from implicit rather than explicit data (Greenwald et al., 2002). Based on current research on self-esteem (Crocker & Wolfe, 2001), one would expect that staking one's self-esteem on family or academic aspirations has important cognitive, affective, and behavioral consequences.

Further research is needed to grasp the downstream effects of discrepancies between explicit and implicit self-definitions. An interesting avenue for future work on this topic could be derived from research suggesting that discrepancies between explicit and implicit self-esteem are particularly potent in determining behavior when people become aware of their ambivalent self-views (Jordan, Spencer, & Zanna, 2005; Jordan, Spencer, Zanna, Hoshino-Browne, & Correll, 2003; Spencer, Jordan, Logel, & Zanna, 2005). According to this perspective, implicit self-esteem might often operate at an automatic or unconscious level, but at times implicit views may seep into consciousness. Under these circumstances, discrepancies between implicit and explicit self-esteem may motivate people to reduce this ambivalence and have powerful effects on self-image maintenance. The present data set does not tackle these issues, but, following a similar reasoning, future studies could explore when and how college women respond to situations bringing to mind a discrepancy between their explicit and implicit self-definitions. It is likely that, in some situations, college women have a phenomenological experience of this discrepancy and that this experience has motivational implications.

The present research provides firm evidence, for the first time, that the strong connection between self and motherhood may not be accessible through introspection or be willingly acknowledged among women pursuing a college education. These data clearly document a discrepancy between explicit and implicit self-knowledge. As such, the findings contribute to a growing body of research challenging common assumptions about the role of reflexive consciousness and deliberate decisions in self-related processes (Devos & Banaji, 2003). It is a matter for future research to elucidate more systematically factors that exacerbate or reduce discrepancies between explicit and implicit identification with these domains, as well as their cognitive, affective, and behavioral ramifications.

Notes

1. Four participants who had children were not included in the analyses because Study 2 revealed reliable variations as a function of whether participants had children or not.
2. Participants also completed two IATs assessing identification with "college education" and "motherhood" relative to a more neutral concept. Findings based on these IATs are not reported here because further investigations are needed to validate these tasks.
3. Data from this participant were also discarded for analyses conducted on the explicit measures.
4. For the multi-items scales and the ratings of the stimuli, difference scores were computed to parallel the format of the IAT.
5. In this paper, multiple pairwise comparisons were always performed using the Bonferroni adjustment procedure.
6. Because many items on the scale measuring identification with motherhood assumed that students were not yet mothers or took on a different meaning whether participants had children or not, analyses performed on the multi-item scales are not reported.
7. Participants also completed the set of explicit measures used in Studies 1 and 2. For the sake of brevity and because the findings were consistent with those reported for Study 2, analyses conducted on the explicit measures are not reported.
8. The small sample size prevented us from examining whether or not these patterns were moderated by participants' motherhood status.

References

Abelson, R. P., Aronson, E., McGuire, W. J., Newcomb, T. M., Rosenberg, M. J., & Tannenbaum, P. (Eds.). (1968). *Theories of cognitive consistency: A sourcebook*. Chicago: Rand-McNally.

Aiken, L. S., & West, S. G. (1991). *Multiple regression: Testing and interpreting interactions*. Thousand Oaks, CA: Sage.

Baber, K. M., & Monaghan, P. (1988). College women's career and motherhood expectations: New options, old dilemmas. *Sex Roles, 19*, 189–203.

Banaji, M. R. (2001). Implicit attitudes can be measured. In H. L. Roediger, III, J. S. Nairne, I. Neath, & A. Surprenant (Eds.), *The nature of remembering: Essays in honor of Robert G. Crowder* (pp. 117–150). Washington, DC: American Psychological Association.

Banaji, M. R., & Hardin, C. D. (1996). Automatic stereotyping. *Psychological Science, 7*, 136–141.

Bargh, J. A. (1982). Attention and automaticity in the processing of self-relevant information. *Journal of Personality and Social Psychology, 43*, 425–436.

Bargh, J. A., & Tota, M. E. (1988). Context-dependent automatic processing in depression: Accessibility of negative constructs with regard to self but not others. *Journal of Personality and Social Psychology, 54*, 925–939.

Battle, A., & Wigfield, A. (2003). College women's value orientations toward family, career, and graduate school. *Journal of Vocational Behavior, 62*, 56–75.

Bellezza, F. S., Greenwald, A. G., & Banaji, M. R. (1986). Words high and low in pleasantness as rated by male and female college students. *Behavior Research Methods, Instruments, and Computers, 18*, 299–303.

Blair, I. V., & Banaji, M. R. (1996). Automatic and controlled processes in stereotype priming. *Journal of Personality and Social Psychology, 70*, 1142–1163.

Blair, I. V., Ma, J. E., & Lenton, A. P. (2001). Imagining stereotypes away: The moderation of implicit stereotypes through mental imagery. *Journal of Personality and Social Psychology, 81*, 828–841.

Blanton, H., & Jaccard, J. (2006a). Arbitrary metrics in psychology. *American Psychologist, 61*, 27–41.

Blanton, H., & Jaccard, J. (2006b). Tests of multiplicative models in psychology: A case study using the unified theory of implicit attitudes, stereotypes, self-esteem, and self-concept. *Psychological Review, 113*, 155–165.

Bosson, J. K., Swann, W. B., & Pennebaker, J. W. (2000). Stalking the perfect measure of implicit self-esteem: The blind men and the elephant revisited. *Journal of Personality and Social Psychology, 79*, 631–643.

Crocker, J., & Wolfe, C. T. (2001). Contingencies of self-worth. *Psychological Review, 108*, 593–623.

Cunningham, W. A., Preacher, K. J., & Banaji, M. R. (2001). Implicit attitude measures: Consistency, stability, and convergent validity. *Psychological Science, 12*, 163–170.

Devos, T., & Banaji, M. R. (2003). Implicit self and identity. In M. R. Leary & J. P. Tangney (Eds.), *Handbook of self and identity* (pp. 153–175). New York: Guilford Press.

Devos, T., & Banaji, M. R. (2005). American = White? *Journal of Personality and Social Psychology, 88*, 447–466.

Diekman, A. B., & Eagly, A. H. (2000). Stereotypes as dynamic constructs: Women and men of the past, present, and future. *Personality and Social Psychology Bulletin, 26*, 1171–1188.

Diekman, A. B., Eagly, A. H., Mladinic, A., & Ferreira, M. C. (2005). Dynamic stereotypes about women and men in Latin America and the United States. *Journal of Cross Cultural Psychology, 36*, 209–226.

Draine, S. C. (1998). *Inquisit* [Computer Software]. Seattle, WA: Millisecond Software.

Fazio, R. H., & Olson, M. A. (2003). Implicit measures in social cognition research: Their meaning and uses. *Annual Review of Psychology, 54*, 297–327.

Gawronski, B., Hofmann, W., & Wilbur, C. J. (2006). Are "implicit" attitudes unconscious? *Consciousness and Cognition, 15*, 485–499.

Gorman, K. A., & Fritzsche, B. A. (2002). The good-mother stereotype: Stay at home (or wish that you did!). *Journal of Applied Social Psychology, 32*, 2190–2201.

Greenwald, A. G., & Banaji, M. R. (1995). Implicit social cognition: Attitudes, self-esteem, and stereotypes. *Psychological Review, 102*, 4–27.

Greenwald, A. G., Banaji, M. R., Rudman, L. A., Farnham, S. D., Nosek, B. A., & Mellot, D. S. (2002). A unified theory of implicit attitudes, stereotypes, self-esteem, and self-concept. *Psychological Review, 109*, 3–25.

Greenwald, A. G., & Farnham, S. D. (2000). Using the Implicit Association Test to measure self-esteem and self-concept. *Journal of Personality and Social Psychology, 79*, 1022–1038.

Greenwald, A. G., McGhee, D. E., & Schwartz, J. L. K. (1998). Measuring individual differences in implicit cognition: The implicit association test. *Journal of Personality and Social Psychology, 74*, 1464–1480.

Greenwald, A. G., & Nosek, B. A. (2001). Health of the Implicit Association Test at age 3. *Zeitschrift Fuer Experimentelle Psychologie, 48*, 85–93.

Greenwald, A. G., Nosek, B. A., & Banaji, M. R. (2003). Understanding and using the Implicit Association Test: 1. An improved scoring algorithm. *Journal of Personality and Social Psychology, 85*, 197–216.

Greenwald, A. G., Nosek, B. A., & Sriram, N. (2006a). Consequential validity of the Implicit Association Test: Comment on Blanton and Jaccard (2006). *American Psychologist, 61*, 56–61.

Greenwald, A. G., Rudman, L. A., Nosek, B. A., & Zayas, V. (2006b). Why so little faith? A reply to Blanton and Jaccard's (2006) skeptical view of testing pure multiplicative theories. *Psychological Review, 113*, 170–180.

Hare-Mustin, R. T., Bennett, S. K., & Broderick, P. C. (1983). Attitude toward motherhood: Gender, generational, and religious comparisons. *Sex Roles, 9*, 643–661.

Harris, R. J., & Firestone, J. M. (1998). Changes in predictors of gender role ideologies among women: A multivariate analysis. *Sex Roles, 38*, 239–252.

Herrera, R. S., & DelCampo, R. L. (1995). Beyond the superwoman syndrome: Work satisfaction and family functioning among working-class, Mexican American women. *Hispanic Journal of Behavioral Sciences, 17*, 49–60.

Higgins, E. T., Van Hook, E., & Dorfman, D. (1988). Do self-attributes form a cognitive structure? *Social Cognition, 6*, 177–206.

Hoffnung, M. (2004). Wanting it all: Career, marriage, and motherhood during college-educated women's 20s. *Sex Roles, 50*, 711–723.

Hofmann, W., Gawronski, B., Gschwendner, T., Le, H., & Schmitt, M. (2005). A meta-analysis on the correlation between the Implicit Association Test and explicit self-report measures. *Personality and Social Psychology Bulletin, 31*, 1369–1385.

Jordan, C. H., Spencer, S. J., & Zanna, M. P. (2005). Types of high self-esteem and prejudice: How implicit self-esteem relates to ethnic discrimination among high explicit self-esteem individuals. *Personality and Social Psychology Bulletin, 31*, 693–702.

Jordan, C. H., Spencer, S. J., Zanna, M. P., Hoshino-Browne, E., & Correll, J. (2003). Secure and defensive high self-esteem. *Journal of Personality and Social Psychology, 85*, 969–978.

Jost, J. T., Banaji, M. R., & Nosek, B. A. (2004). A decade of system justification theory: Accumulated evidence of conscious and unconscious bolstering of the status quo. *Political Psychology, 25*, 881–920.

Jost, J. T., Pelham, B. W., & Carvallo, M. R. (2002). Non-conscious forms of system justification: Implicit and behavioral preferences for higher status groups. *Journal of Experimental Social Psychology, 38*, 586–602.

Kamerman, S. B., & Gatenio, S. (2003). Overview of the current policy context. In D. Cryer & R. M. Clifford (Eds.), *Early childhood education and care in the USA* (pp. 1–30). Baltimore: Paul H. Brookes.

Kihlstrom, J. F., & Cantor, N. (1984). Mental representation of the self. In L. Berkowitz (Ed.), *Advances in experimental social psychology* (Vol. 17, pp. 1–47). Orlando, FL: Academic Press.

Kihlstrom, J. F., & Klein, S. B. (1994). The self as a knowledge structure. In R. S. Wyer, Jr., & T. K. Srull (Eds.), *Handbook of social cognition* (Vol. 1, pp. 153–208). Hillsdale, NJ: Lawrence Erlbaum Associates, Inc.

Knaub, P. K., Eversoll, D. B., & Voss, J. H. (1983). Is parenthood a desirable adult role? An assessment of attitudes held by contemporary women. *Sex Roles, 9,* 355–362.

Markus, H. (1977). Self-schemata and processing information about the self. *Journal of Personality and Social Psychology, 35,* 63–78.

Niemann, Y. F., Romero, A., & Arbona, C. (2000). Effects of cultural orientation on the perception of conflict between relationship and education goals for Mexican American college students. *Hispanic Journal of Behavioral Sciences, 22,* 46–63.

Nosek, B. A., Banaji, M. R., & Greenwald, A. G. (2002a). Harvesting implicit group attitudes and beliefs from a demonstration website. *Group Dynamics, 6,* 101–115.

Nosek, B. A., Banaji, M. R., & Greenwald, A. G. (2002b). Math = male, me = female, therefore math ≠ me. *Journal of Personality and Social Psychology, 83,* 44–59.

Nosek, B. A., Greenwald, A. G., & Banaji, M. R. (2005). Understanding and using the Implicit Association Test: II. Method variables and construct validity. *Personality and Social Psychology Bulletin, 31,* 166–180.

Nosek, B. A., Greenwald, A. G., & Banaji, M. R. (in press). The Implicit Association Test at age 7: A methodological and conceptual review. In J. A. Bargh (Ed.), *Automatic processes in social thinking and behavior.* Philadelphia: Psychology Press.

Rogers, T. B., Kuiper, N. A., & Kirker, W. S. (1977). Self-reference and the encoding of personal information. *Journal of Personality and Social Psychology, 35,* 677–688.

Rudman, L. A. (2004). Sources of implicit attitudes. *Current Directions in Psychological Science, 13,* 79–82.

Rudman, L. A., Feinberg, J., & Fairchild, K. (2002). Minority members' implicit attitudes: Automatic in-group bias as a function of group status. *Social Cognition, 20,* 294–320.

Rudman, L. A., & Goodwin, S. A. (2004). Gender differences in automatic in-group bias: Why do women like women more than men like men? *Journal of Personality and Social Psychology, 87,* 494–509.

Rudman, L. A., Greenwald, A. G., & McGhee, D. E. (2001). Implicit self-concept and evaluative implicit gender stereotypes: Self and in-group share desirable traits. *Personality and Social Psychology Bulletin, 27,* 1164–1178.

Rudman, L. A., & Kilianski, S. E. (2000). Implicit and explicit attitudes toward female authority. *Personality and Social Psychology Bulletin, 26,* 1315–1328.

Settles, I. H. (2004). When multiple identities interfere: The role of identity centrality. *Personality and Social Psychology Bulletin, 30,* 487–500.

Settles, I. H., Sellers, R. M., & Damas, A., Jr. (2002). One role or two? The function of psychological separation in role conflict. *Journal of Applied Psychology, 87,* 574–582.

Spade, J. Z., & Reese, C. A. (1991). We've come a long way, maybe: College students' plans for work and family. *Sex Roles, 24,* 309–321.

Spence, J. T., & Hahn, E. D. (1997). The Attitudes Toward Women scale and attitude change in college students. *Psychology of Women Quarterly, 21,* 17–34.

Spencer, S. J., Jordan, C. H., Logel, C. E. R., & Zanna, M. P. (2005). Nagging doubts and a glimmer of hope: The role of implicit self-esteem in self-image maintenance. In A. Tesser, J. V. Wood, & D. A. Stapel (Eds.), *On building, defending and regulating the self: A psychological perspective* (pp. 153–170). New York: Psychology Press.

Strauman, T. J., & Higgins, E. T. (1987). Automatic activation of self-discrepancies and emotional syndromes: When cognitive structures influence affect. *Journal of Personality and Social Psychology, 53,* 1004–1014.

Twenge, J. M. (1997a). Attitudes toward women, 1970–1995: A meta-analysis. *Psychology of Women Quarterly, 21,* 35–51.

Twenge, J. M. (1997b). Changes in masculine and feminine traits over time: A meta-analysis. *Sex Roles, 36,* 305 – 325.

US Department of Education, National Center for Education Statistics. (2005). *The condition of education 2005, NCES 2005 – 094.* Washington, DC: US Government Printing Office.

Vasquez, M. J. (1982). Confronting barriers to the participation of Mexican American women in higher education. *Hispanic Journal of Behavioral Sciences, 4,* 147 – 165.

Self and Identity, 6: 278 – 280, 2007
http://www.psypress.com/sai
ISSN: 1529-8868 print/1529-8876 online

Subject Index

Action Control Scale (ACS90) 124 – 125
  demand-related subscale (AOD) 124 – 125,
  127 – 128, 130
  threat-related subscale (AOT) 125, 127 – 128,
  130
Action orientation 121 – 122, 124 – 125, 130 – 133
Affect regulation
  and implicit self 118 – 136
  intuitive 120 – 122, 131 – 132
Affective priming task 118 – 136
African Americans 99, 239, 242 – 243, 245 – 251,
  259
Alcohol 233
Apologies 98
  failure of 209 – 222
Asian Americans 259
Associative models 119
Attitude, and self-esteem 266 – 271
Autonomy 189 – 208
Avoidance *see* unforgiveness

Balance – congruity principle 267, 269
Balanced identity analyses 249 – 251,
  269 – 271
Beck Depression Inventory (BDI-II) 104 – 111,
  113
Behavior, habitual 119
Benevolence *see* forgiveness

Causal certainty 214, 216 – 219
Children
  and adaptive pathways 252
  implicit associations in 99
  and social groups 238 – 255
Cognitive Style Questionnaire (CSQ) 104 – 105,
  107
Cognitive Vulnerability to Depression (CVD)
  Project 103 – 105, 113
Compensatory cognition 174 – 176
Conflict
  intergroup 157
  interpersonal 209
Confluence model 132
Consensus, exaggerated estimates of 229 – 230
Control motivation 189 – 208

Coping strategies 167 – 169
  and minorities 98 – 99

Defensive zeal *see* zeal
Defensiveness 193, 211
Depression 109 – 110
  cognitive models of 103 – 105
  and negative events 111 – 112
  predictors of 101 – 102
  risk of 98
  and self-esteem 148
  vulnerability – stress models of 99,
  101 – 117
Diagnostic and Statistical Manual (DSM) of
  Mental Disorders 103 – 104
Discrepant self-esteem 138 – 141, 144 – 149
Discrimination 139, 191
Dysfunctional Attitudes Scale (DAS) 104 – 105,
  107

Education 99
  and self-concept 256 – 277
Ego threat 209 – 211, 218 – 220
Emotion
  regulation of 98
  and self 118, 133
Empathy 212, 214, 216, 218 – 219
Ethnicity 107
European Americans 259, 263, 267
Explicit Identification Questionnaire 161
Explicit self-esteem 98, 110 – 111, 193, 195 – 196,
  199
  defined 138
  and depression 148
  moderating apology and forgiveness
  209 – 222
  and perfectionism 137 – 153
Extended self model 99
Extremism 99
  defensive 223 – 237

Favoritism, in-group 238, 240, 247
Feedback, negative 140
Filipina Americans 259, 263, 267
Forgiveness 209 – 222

Gating variables 233
Gender 107, 194
  and balance 252
  bias 175
  malleability of self-concept 173–188
  norms 173
  relations 257
  roles 256–277
  situational salience of 176–177, 179, 185
  stereotypes 173, 184–185
General Causality Orientations Questionnaire (GCOS) 198–199
Glimmer of hope hypothesis 98, 140, 146
Go/No Go Association Task (GNAT) 99, 158, 160–162, 167–168
Group membership 98
Groups
  attitude to 245–247, 251
  common identity model 156–157, 169
  high-status 176
  identity 247–251
  mixed status 154–172
  social 238–255
  stigmatized minority 154
  superordinate 155, 162–163, 168, 170

Hispanic Americans 99, 238–255
Hopelessness theory 103–105

Identification, and self-esteem 266–271
Identification measures, explicit 166
Identity, collective–self 119
Implicit Association Test (IAT) 99, 138, 192, 202, 210, 225, 228
  child-friendly version 241–244
  and education 258, 260–262, 265–271
  and motherhood 258, 260–262, 265–271
  and self-concept malleability 179–183
  self–other 102–114
  stimuli 188, 255
Implicit attitude 268–269
Implicit consistency 238–255
Implicit identification 268
Implicit self 97–100
  and affect regulation 118–136
  clinical consequences of 99
  models 119–120
  research findings 119–120
Implicit self-assessment 99
Implicit self-constructs 99
Implicit self-esteem 119, 213, 269
  and apology/forgiveness 209–222
  aspects of 101–117
  and autonomy/control 191, 193, 195–196, 199
  and defensive extremism 223–237
  and depression 102, 104

moderating role of 137–153
  and perfectionism 138, 142–143
  and threat 223–237
Implicit self-esteem measure 195
Implicit Self-Evaluation Survey 138
Impression management 97, 191
In-group identity model 155
Indirect assessment techniques 97
Initials-Preference task (IPT) 103–108, 110–112, 114, 138, 142–143
Intergroup relations 167–169

Latina Americans 99, 241, 259, 263, 267
Leadership 98, 173–188
Life Events Scale (LES) 105–107
Life stress 111–112

Mexican Americans 263–266
Minorities 98–99, 239
Mixed status groups, multiple contrasting identities in 154–172
Motherhood 99
  and self-concept 256–277
Motivation primes 192–194, 198, 208
Multidimensional Perfectionism Scale (MPS) 143
Multiple contrasting identities in, mixed status groups 154–172

Name letter effect (NLE) 99, 142, 191, 210
Name Letter Test (NLT) 213
Narcissism 211, 220
Neuropsychology 234

Optimal distinctiveness model 155
Optimism, unrealistic 140

Parent–child interactions 147–148
Perfectionism 141, 143
  adaptive 143, 145–146
  maladaptive 143–145
  and self-esteem 137–153
Perseverance 140
Personality systems interactions (PSI) theory 99, 120
Prejudice 158
Priming, and motivation orientation 192–193
Profile of Mood Scales (POMS) 128
Psychological dysfunction 98

Race
  attitudes 240
  bias 175
Reporting bias 113
Research Diagnostic Criteria (RDC) 104
Revenge *see* unforgiveness

Rosenburg Self-Esteem Scale (RSES) 102, 128, 138, 142, 213
  and depression 104 – 108, 110 – 111, 114

Self
  attitudes toward 102
  automatic beliefs about 179
  controlled beliefs about 180
  and emotion 118, 133
  experience of 97
  priming 118 – 136
  role of 118
Self-assessment, implicit 99
Self-awareness 177
Self-belief, automatic and controlled 182 – 183
Self-concept
  automatic 180 – 181
  controlled 181 – 182
  and education 256 – 277
  explicit – implicit discrepancies in 259 – 263
  gender related 173 – 188
  and motherhood 256 – 277
  and status 180 – 182
  and threat 176, 183 – 185
  working 174 – 176
Self-constructs, implicit 99
Self-deception 97, 138, 191 – 192
Self-defense 120
Self-determination theory (SDT) 99, 189 – 190, 192, 201
Self-discrepancy theory 112
Self-enhancement 209, 211 – 212
Self-esteem
  and attitude 266 – 271
  and autonomy 189 – 208
  in children 244 – 245
  contingent 138
  and control motivation 189 – 208
  defensive 98, 191, 193 – 194, 196, 200, 210 – 213, 218 – 220
  and depression 148
  discrepant 138 – 141, 144 – 149
  explicit *see* explicit self-esteem
  fragile 98, 137 – 138
  and gender 144
  and identification 266 – 271
  implicit *see* implicit self-esteem
  low 113
  maintenance 132
  negative outcomes of 137
  and parenting 147 – 148
  and perfectionism 142, 144, 146 – 147
  secure 137 – 138, 211 – 212, 218 – 220

  unstable 138
  vulnerable 101
Self-expansion model 157, 167, 169
Self – group overlap 163 – 166
Self – group Overlap Measure 158 – 160, 168
Self-perception 174
Self-presentation 113, 158
Self-promotion 233 – 234
Self-regard 191
Self-regulation 132
Self-related constructs, interrelations among 99
Self-reports 99, 113
Self-threat 224 – 226, 233
Self-worth 147, 190, 202, 209, 220, 225
Social desirability bias 111
Social identity theory (SIT) 154, 156, 251 – 252
Social status, manipulation of 178
Social stereotyping 119
Socioeconomic status 107
State orientation 121 – 122, 124 – 125, 130 – 133
State Self-Esteem Scale (SSES) 195, 199
  sex difference in 203
Status
  and self-concept 180 – 182
  threat to 176, 183 – 185
Stereotypes, gender 173, 184 – 185
Stimulus onset asynchrony (SOA) 122
Stroop task 175
Subliminal priming 99, 122, 127 – 130, 192
Subliminal priming measure 192, 195, 199, 202
Supraliminal priming 128, 130, 192

Threat 98, 120, 193, 223 – 237
  ego 209 – 211, 218 – 220
  manipulation 194 – 195, 199
  to social status 176, 183 – 185
Transgressions, interpersonal 209 – 212, 219 – 220
Transgressions-Related Interpersonal Motivations scale (TRIM-12) 214

Unforgiveness 213, 217
Unified theory 99

Vulnerability 233

White Americans 99, 239, 245 – 251, 259, 267
Women, self-concept 256 – 277
Working self-concept model 174

Zeal 99, 223 – 237
  as escapism 224